THE BIBLE
EDEN

Illustrated by Scott Hampton
Adaptation written by Dave Elliott and Keith Giffen

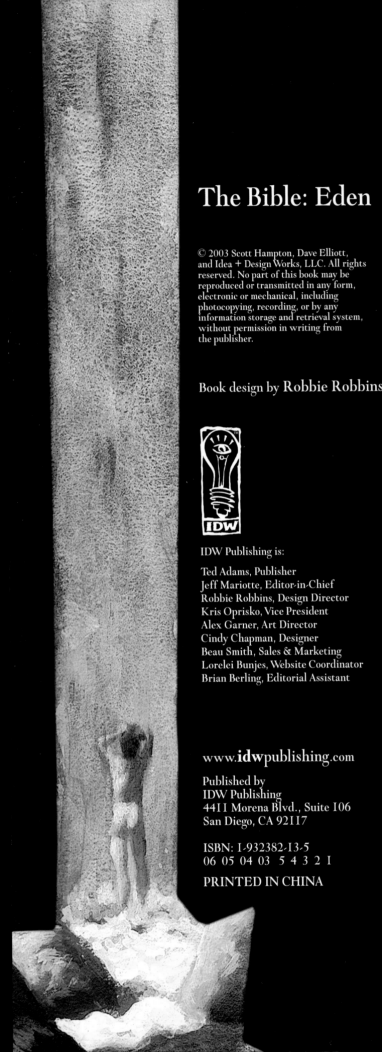

The Bible: Eden

Book design by Robbie Robbins

IDW Publishing is:

Ted Adams, Publisher
Jeff Mariotte, Editor-in-Chief
Robbie Robbins, Design Director
Kris Oprisko, Vice President
Alex Garner, Art Director
Cindy Chapman, Designer
Beau Smith, Sales & Marketing
Lorelei Bunjes, Website Coordinator
Brian Berling, Editorial Assistant

www.**idw**publishing.com

Published by
IDW Publishing
4411 Morena Blvd., Suite 106
San Diego, CA 92117

ISBN: 1-932382-13-5
06 05 04 03 5 4 3 2 1

PRINTED IN CHINA

Dedications

To my brother and mentor, Bo Hampton.
-Scott Hampton

For Robert and Paul, who by now have been told this story first hand.
-Dave Elliott

To my dad, who read the Bible every day, even if he was only hedging his bets.
-Keith Giffen

The Old Testament
Genesis

1:1 In the beginning God created
the heaven and the earth.

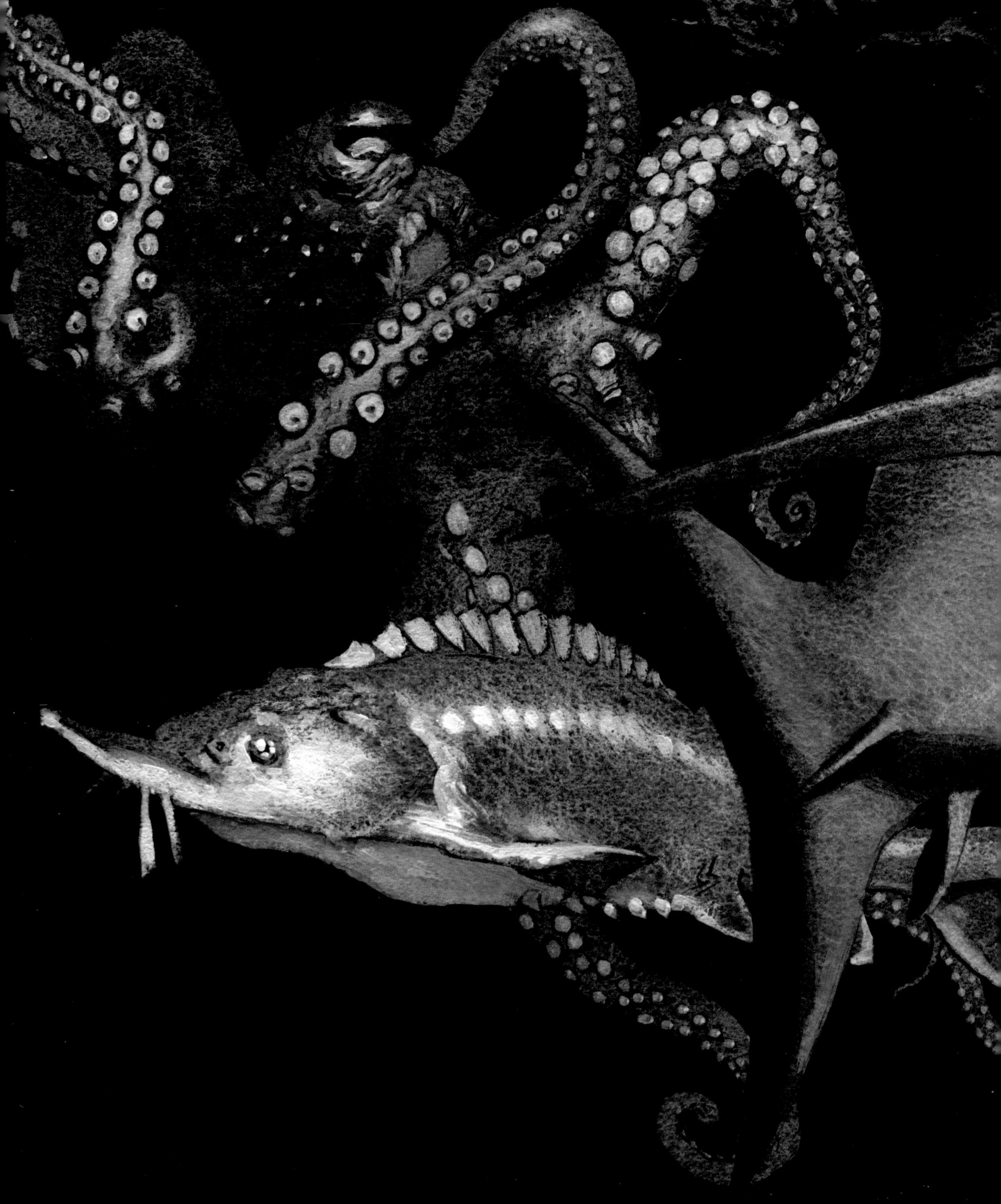

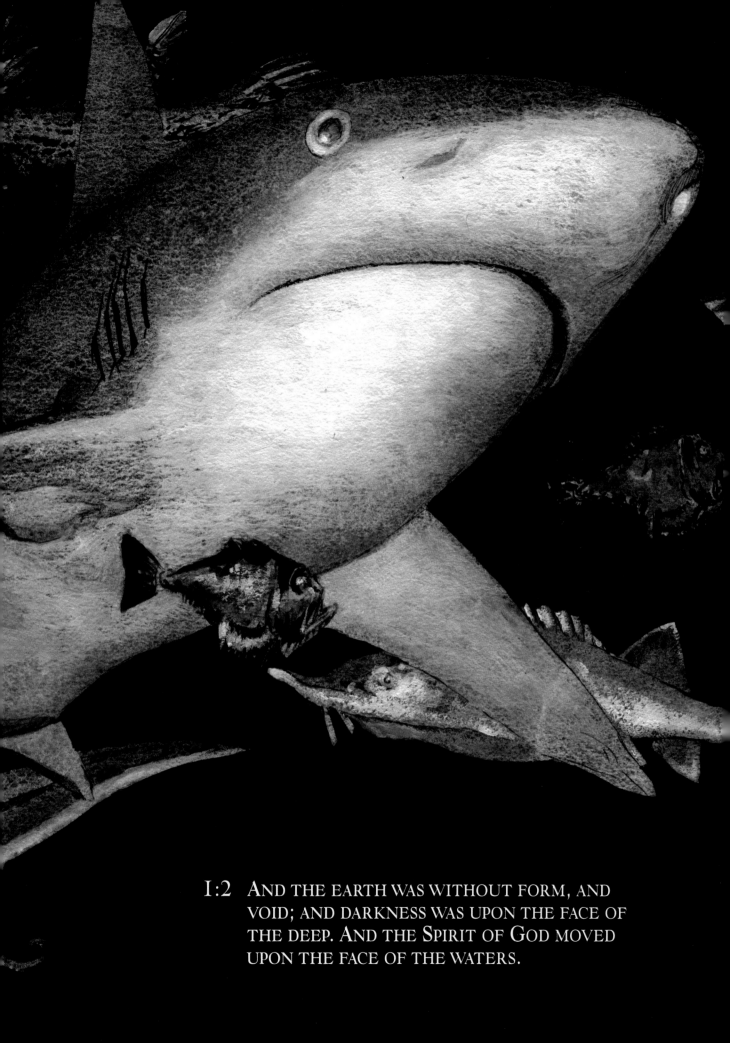

1:2 AND THE EARTH WAS WITHOUT FORM, AND
      VOID; AND DARKNESS WAS UPON THE FACE OF
      THE DEEP. AND THE SPIRIT OF GOD MOVED
      UPON THE FACE OF THE WATERS.

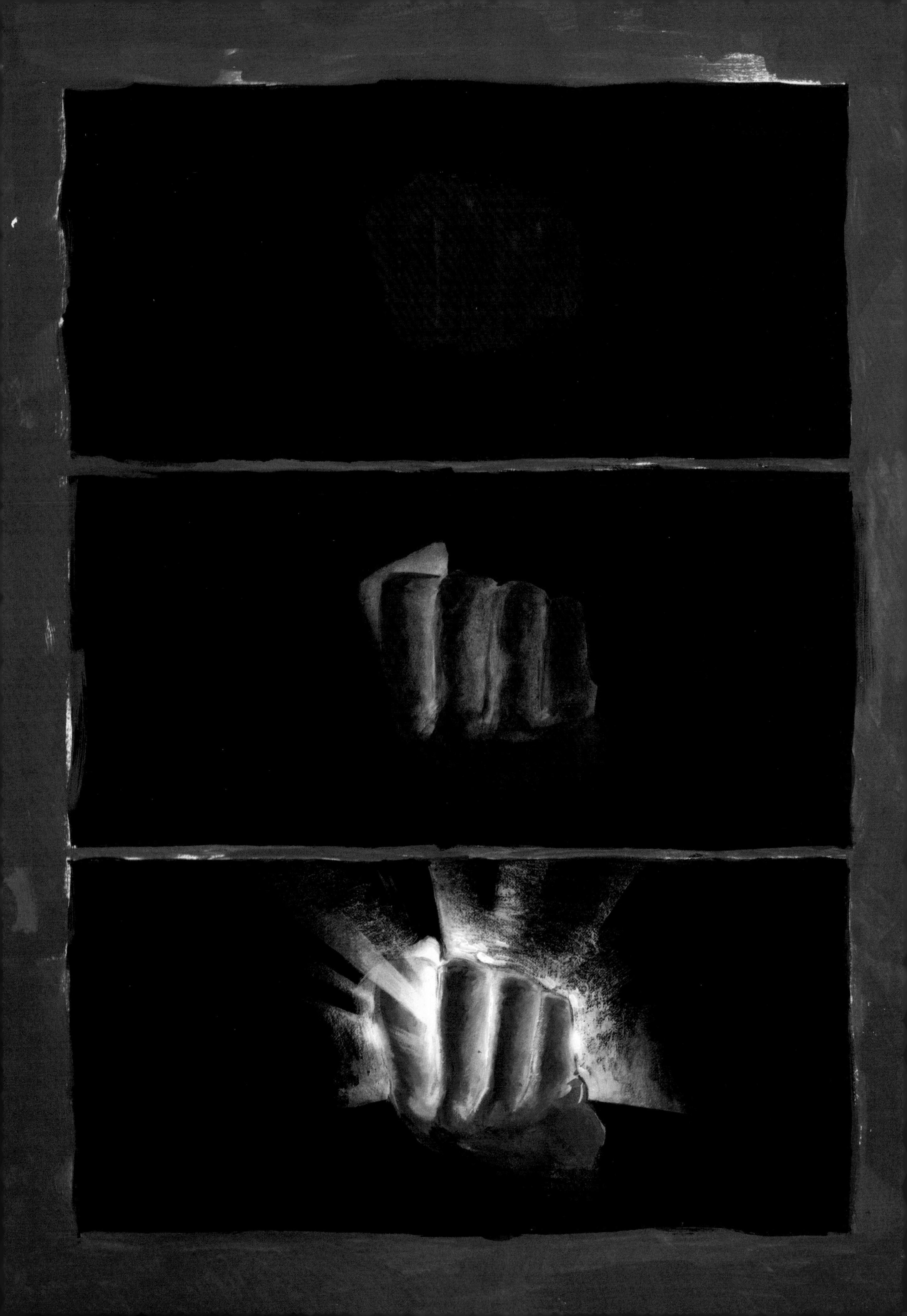

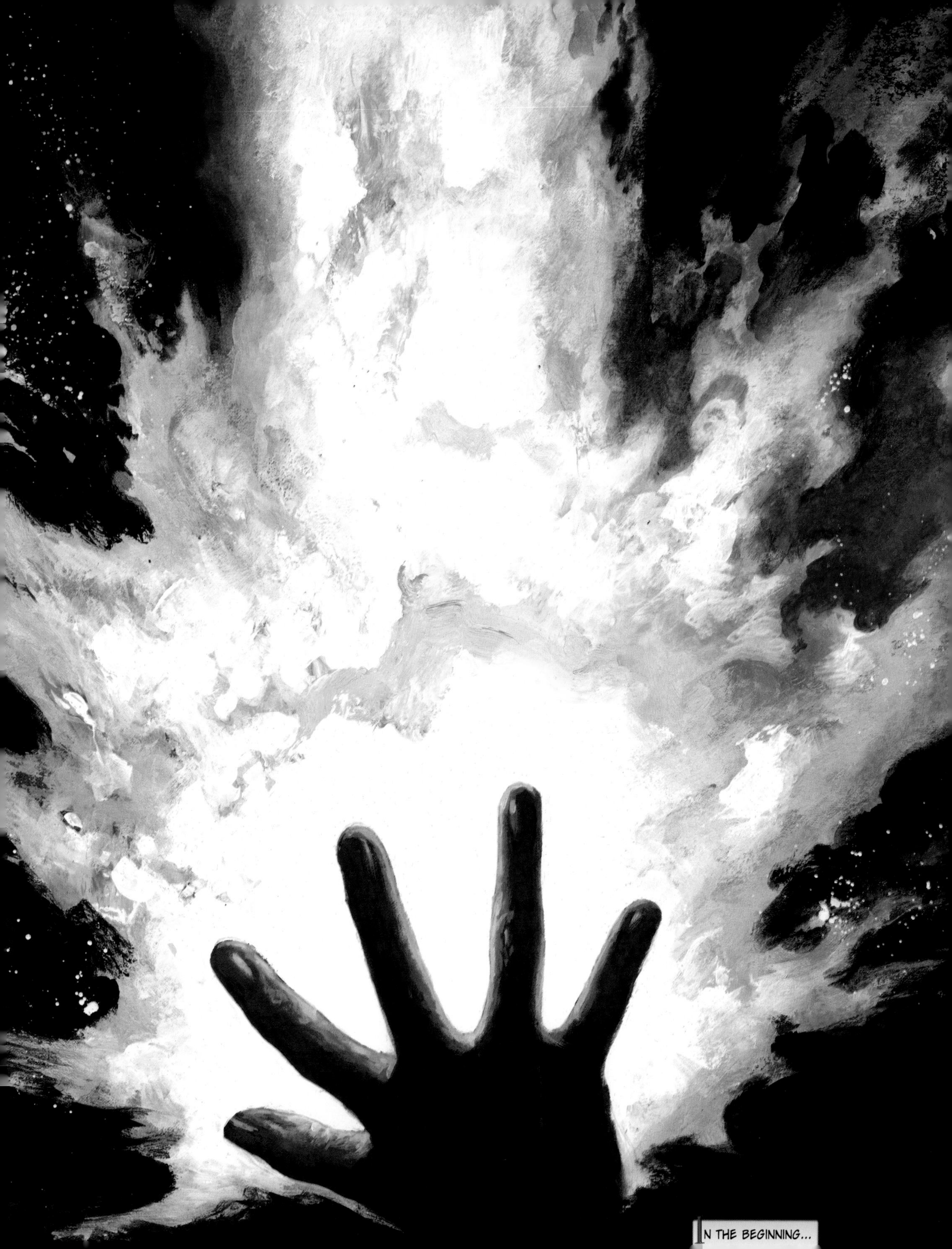
IN THE BEGINNING...

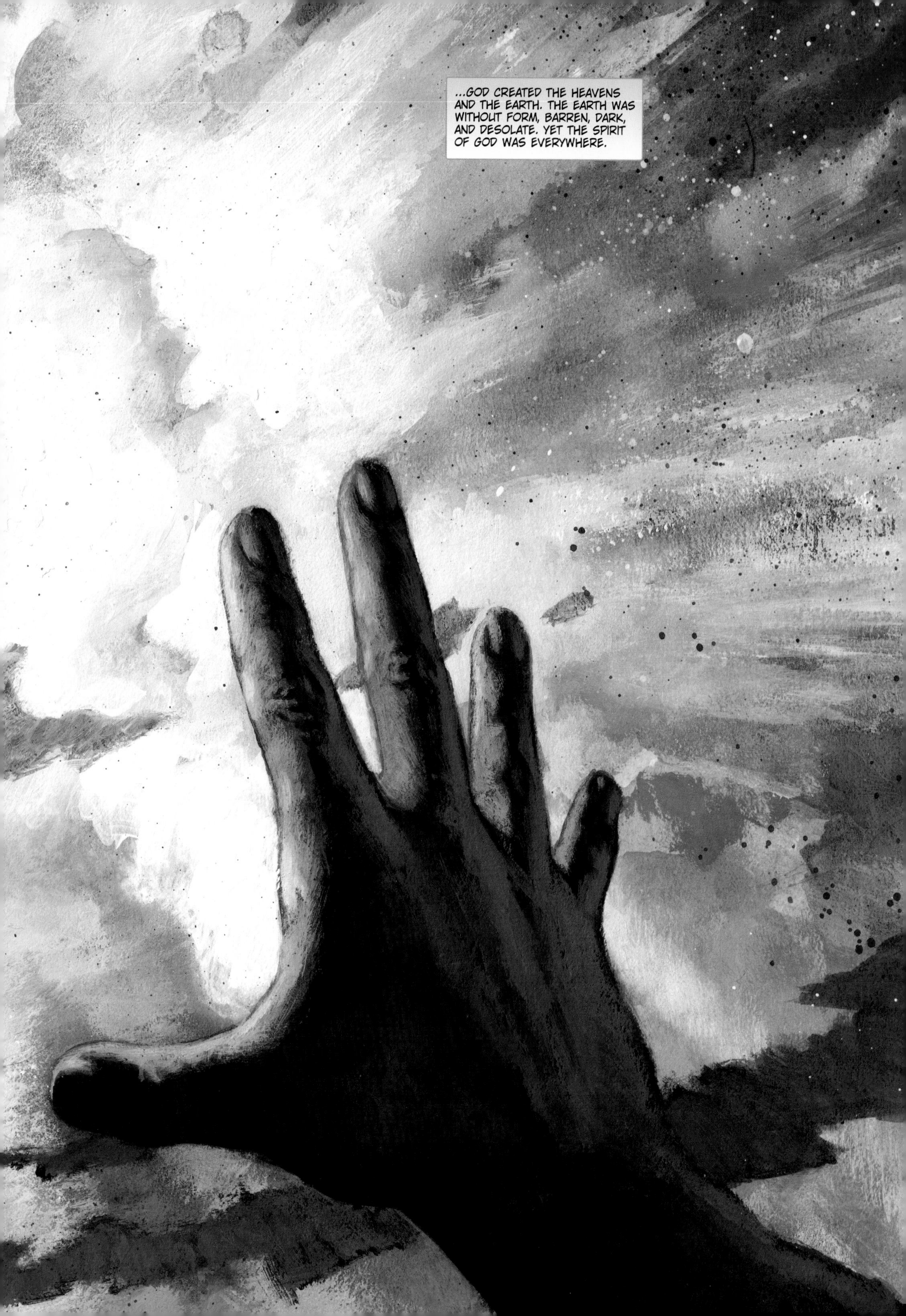
...GOD CREATED THE HEAVENS AND THE EARTH. THE EARTH WAS WITHOUT FORM, BARREN, DARK, AND DESOLATE. YET THE SPIRIT OF GOD WAS EVERYWHERE.

GOD SAID, "*LET THERE BE LIGHT!*"
AND THERE WAS LIGHT.

AND THE LIGHT THAT DID SHINE,
NAMED "*DAY*," WAS MADE SEPARATE
FROM THE DARKNESS, NAMED
"*NIGHT*," AND THE EVENING AND THE
MORNING WERE THE FIRST DAY.

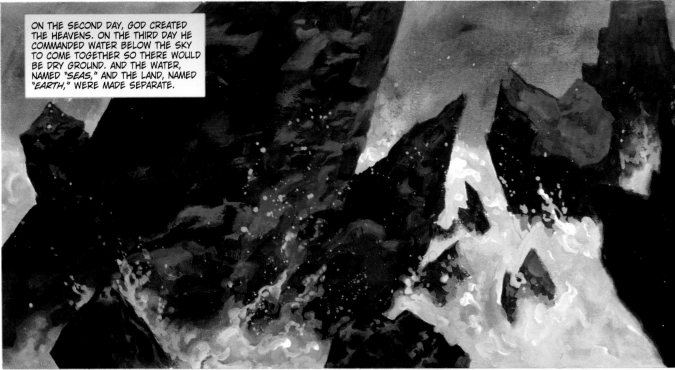

ON THE SECOND DAY, GOD CREATED
THE HEAVENS. ON THE THIRD DAY HE
COMMANDED WATER BELOW THE SKY
TO COME TOGETHER SO THERE WOULD
BE DRY GROUND. AND THE WATER,
NAMED "*SEAS*," AND THE LAND, NAMED
"*EARTH*," WERE MADE SEPARATE.

THEN GOD SAID "*LET THE EARTH SPROUT
VEGETATION: PLANTS YIELDING SEED, AND
FRUIT TREES ON THE EARTH BEARING FRUIT
AFTER THEIR KIND WITH SEED IN THEM.*"
AND IT WAS SO. SO ENDED THE THIRD DAY.

ON THE FOURTH DAY, GOD PLACED
THE LIGHTS IN THE SKY; A LARGER
LIGHT TO RULE OVER THE DAY AND
A LESSER LIGHT TO RULE OVER THE
NIGHT. HE MADE THE STARS ALSO.

AND GOD
SAW THAT IT
WAS GOOD.

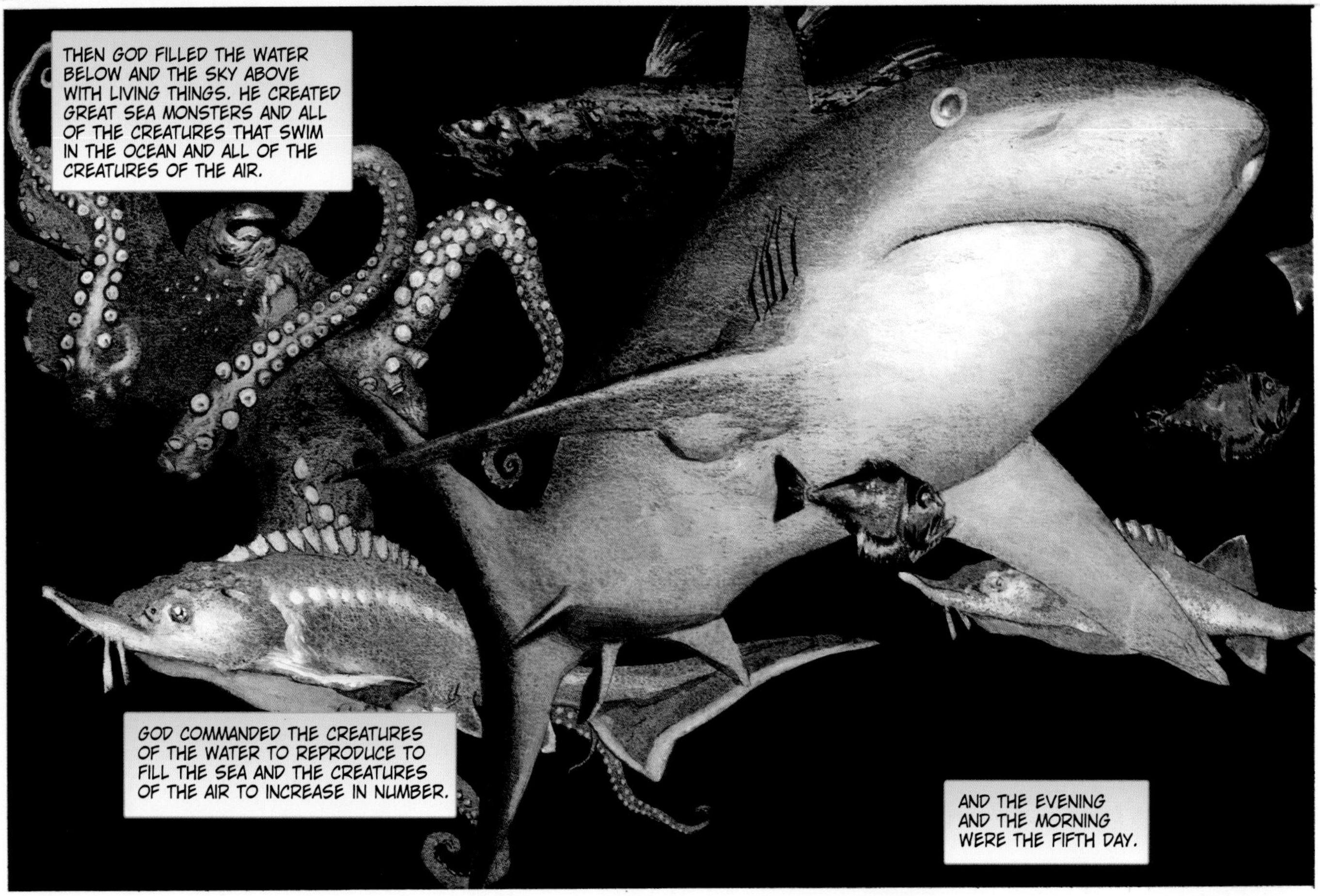
THEN GOD FILLED THE WATER BELOW AND THE SKY ABOVE WITH LIVING THINGS. HE CREATED GREAT SEA MONSTERS AND ALL OF THE CREATURES THAT SWIM IN THE OCEAN AND ALL OF THE CREATURES OF THE AIR.
GOD COMMANDED THE CREATURES OF THE WATER TO REPRODUCE TO FILL THE SEA AND THE CREATURES OF THE AIR TO INCREASE IN NUMBER.
AND THE EVENING AND THE MORNING WERE THE FIFTH DAY.

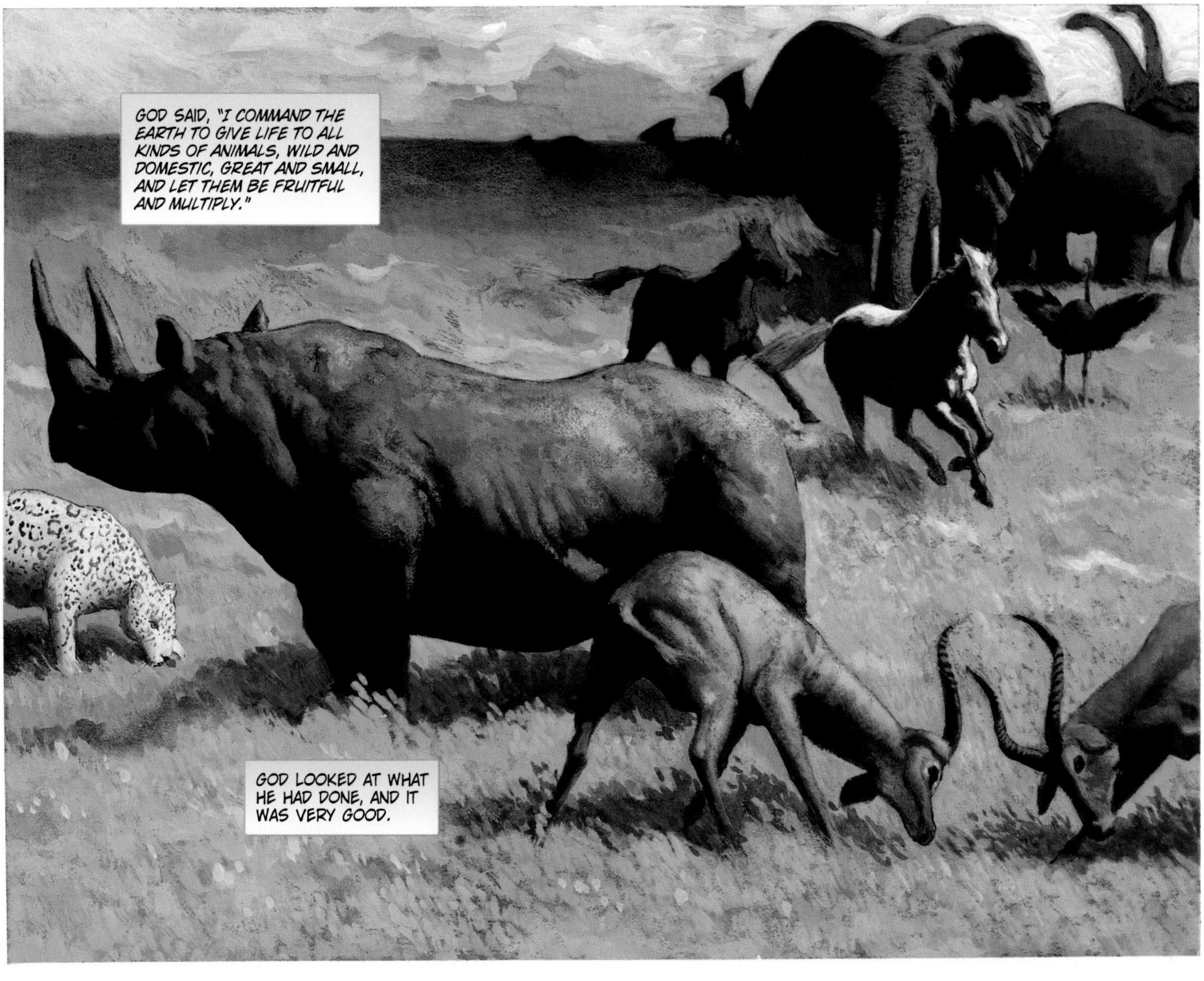
GOD SAID, "I COMMAND THE EARTH TO GIVE LIFE TO ALL KINDS OF ANIMALS, WILD AND DOMESTIC, GREAT AND SMALL, AND LET THEM BE FRUITFUL AND MULTIPLY."
GOD LOOKED AT WHAT HE HAD DONE, AND IT WAS VERY GOOD.

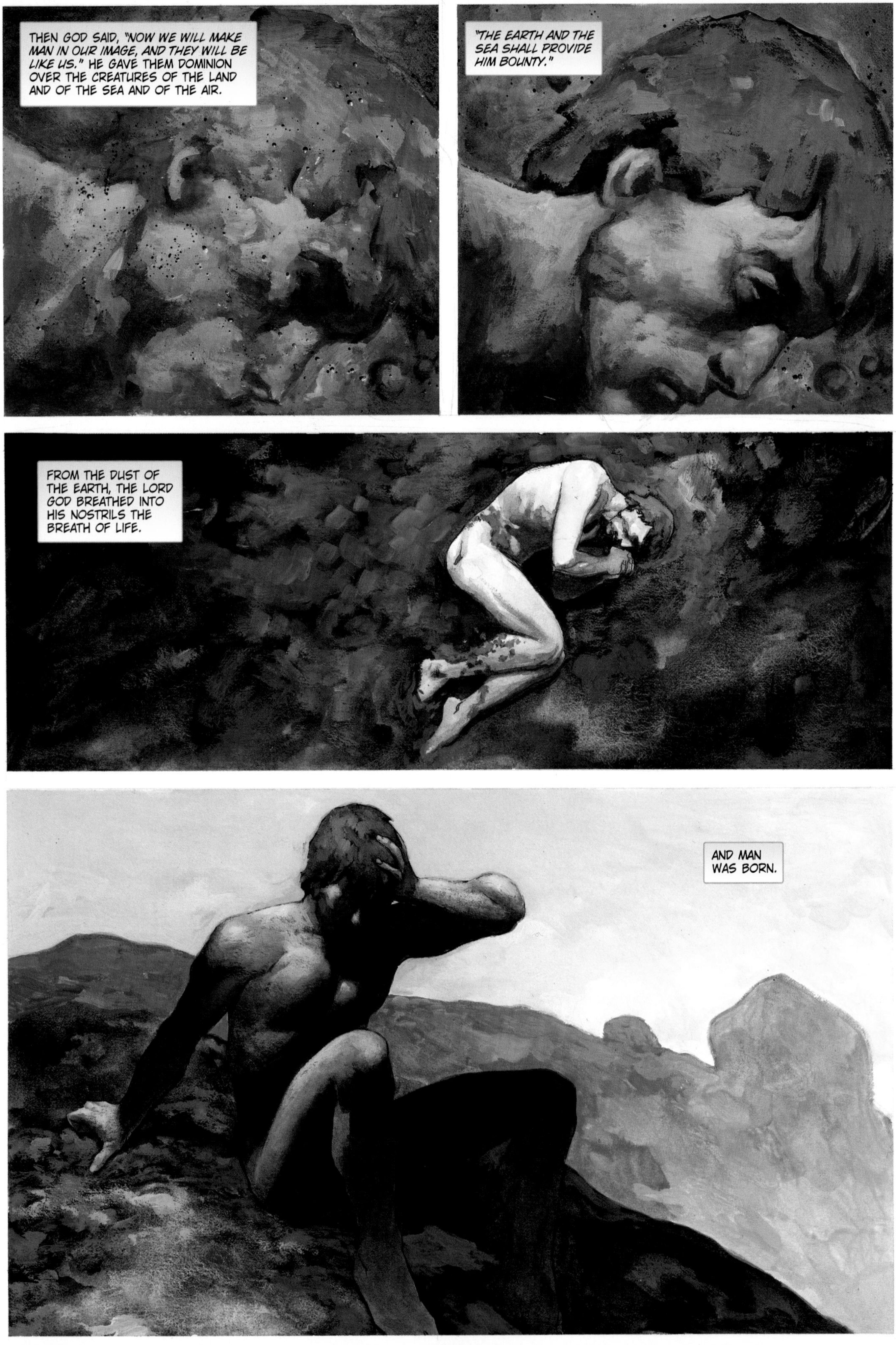
THEN GOD SAID, "NOW WE WILL MAKE MAN IN OUR IMAGE, AND THEY WILL BE LIKE US." HE GAVE THEM DOMINION OVER THE CREATURES OF THE LAND AND OF THE SEA AND OF THE AIR.
"THE EARTH AND THE SEA SHALL PROVIDE HIM BOUNTY."
FROM THE DUST OF THE EARTH, THE LORD GOD BREATHED INTO HIS NOSTRILS THE BREATH OF LIFE.
AND MAN WAS BORN.

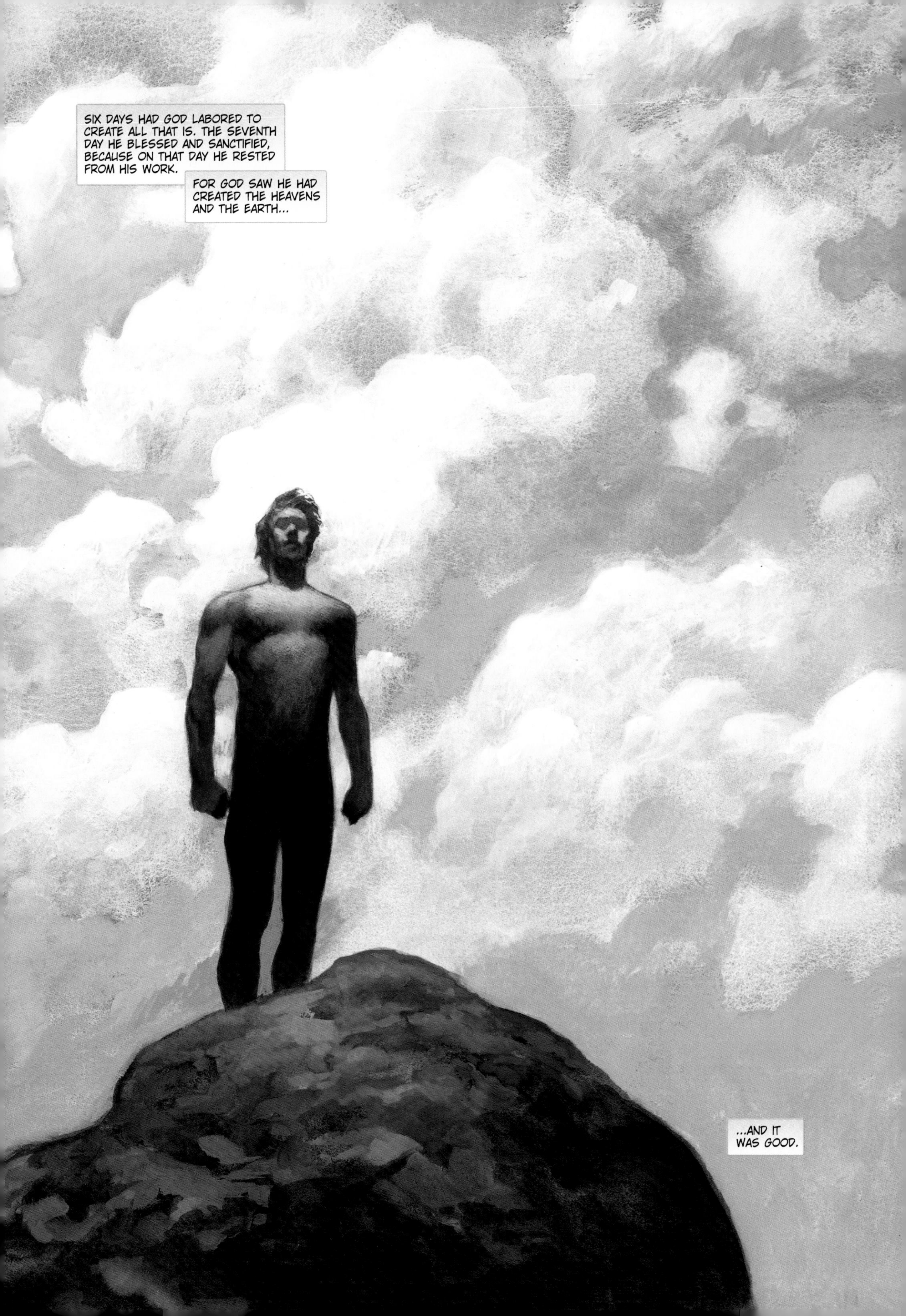
SIX DAYS HAD GOD LABORED TO CREATE ALL THAT IS. THE SEVENTH DAY HE BLESSED AND SANCTIFIED, BECAUSE ON THAT DAY HE RESTED FROM HIS WORK.
FOR GOD SAW HE HAD CREATED THE HEAVENS AND THE EARTH...
...AND IT WAS GOOD.

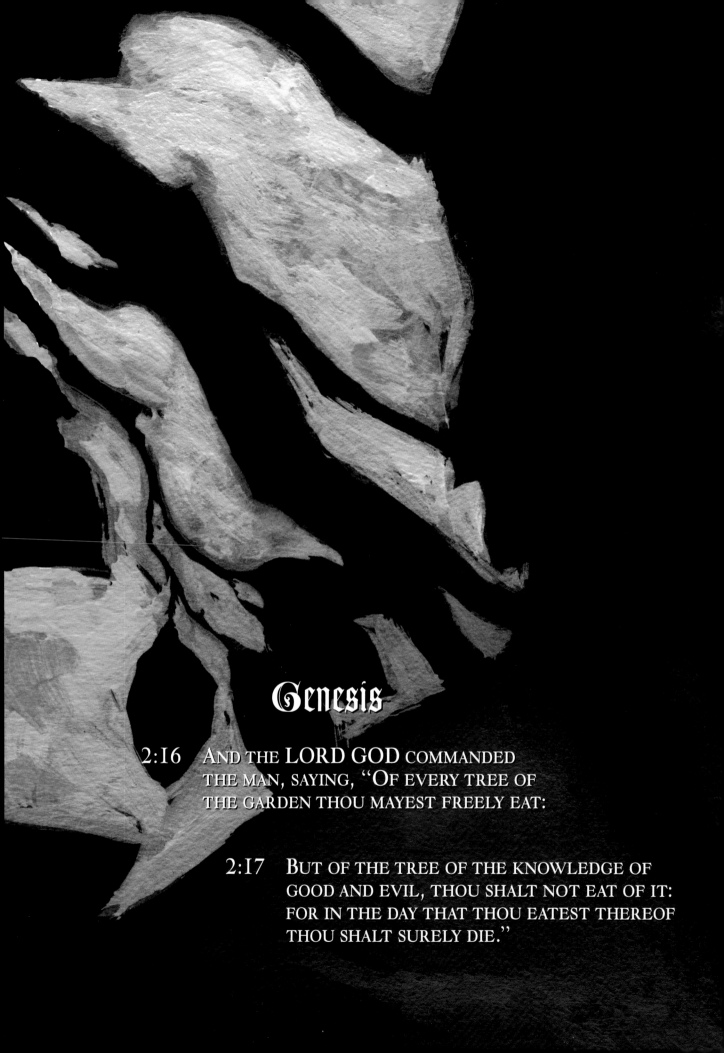

Genesis

2:16 AND THE LORD GOD COMMANDED
THE MAN, SAYING, "OF EVERY TREE OF
THE GARDEN THOU MAYEST FREELY EAT:

2:17 BUT OF THE TREE OF THE KNOWLEDGE OF
GOOD AND EVIL, THOU SHALT NOT EAT OF IT:
FOR IN THE DAY THAT THOU EATEST THEREOF
THOU SHALT SURELY DIE."

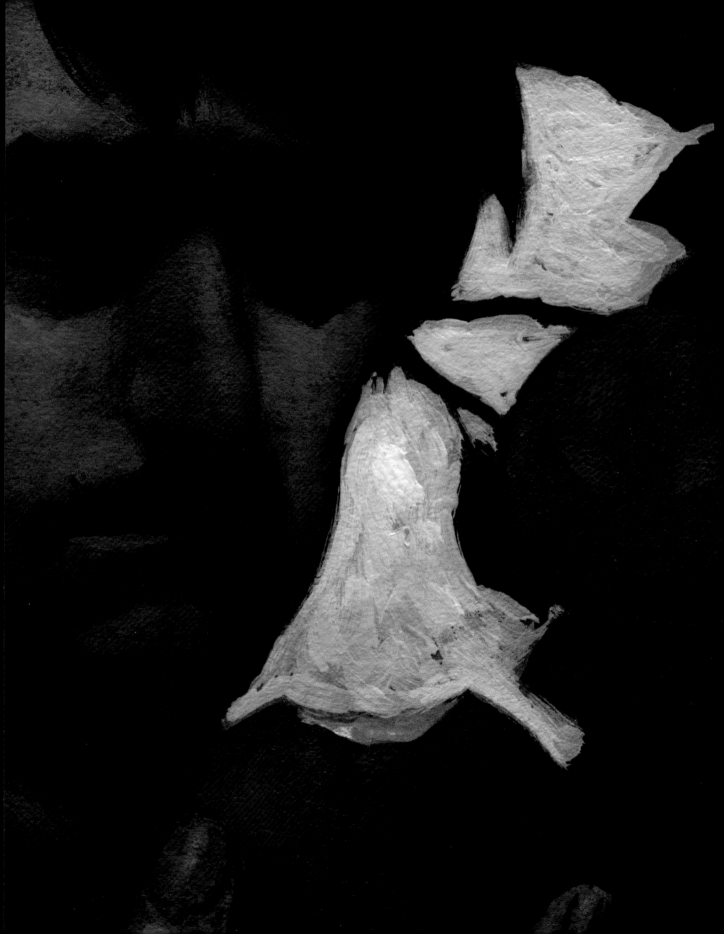

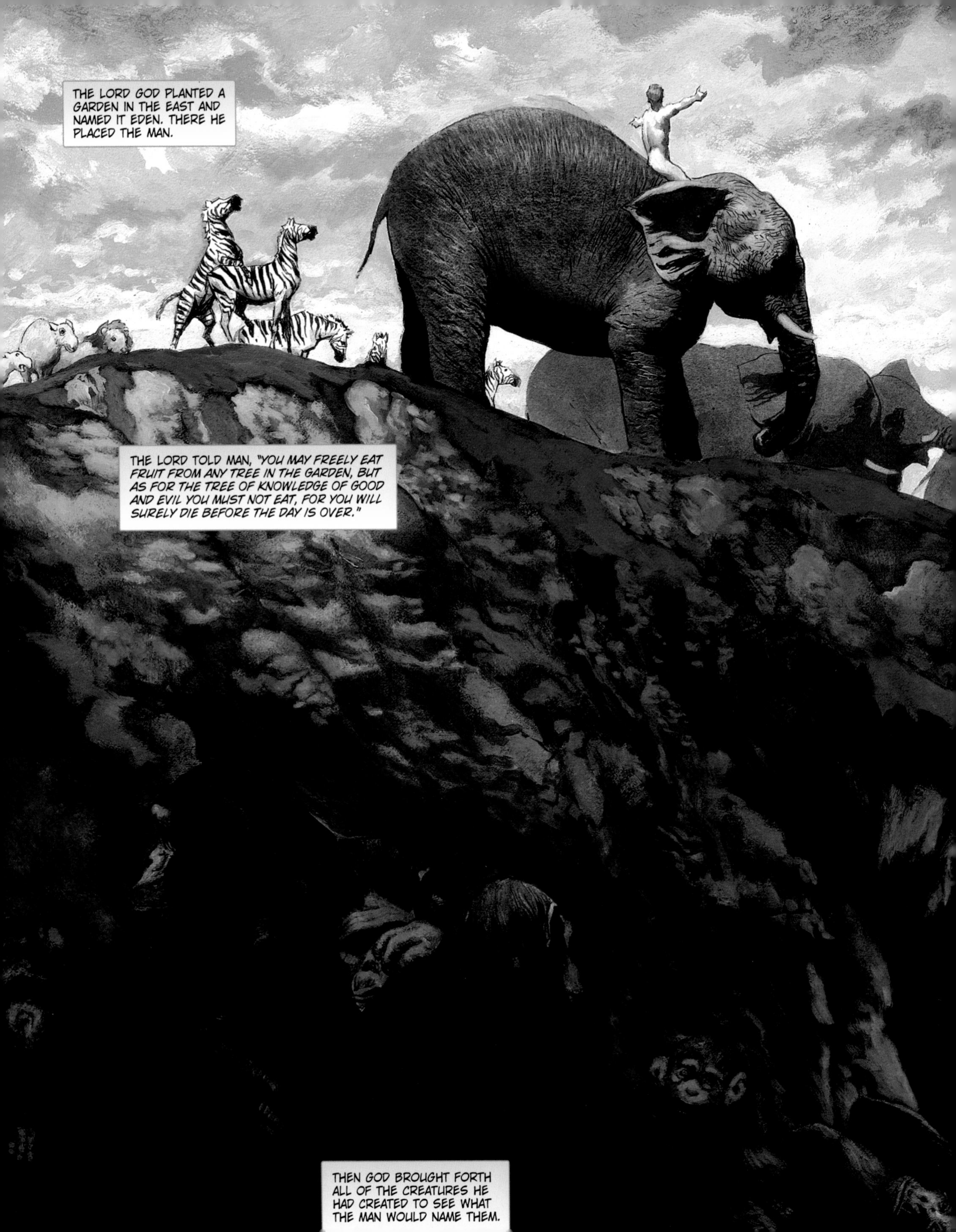
THE LORD GOD PLANTED A GARDEN IN THE EAST AND NAMED IT EDEN. THERE HE PLACED THE MAN.
THE LORD TOLD MAN, "YOU MAY FREELY EAT FRUIT FROM ANY TREE IN THE GARDEN, BUT AS FOR THE TREE OF KNOWLEDGE OF GOOD AND EVIL YOU MUST NOT EAT, FOR YOU WILL SURELY DIE BEFORE THE DAY IS OVER."
THEN GOD BROUGHT FORTH ALL OF THE CREATURES HE HAD CREATED TO SEE WHAT THE MAN WOULD NAME THEM.

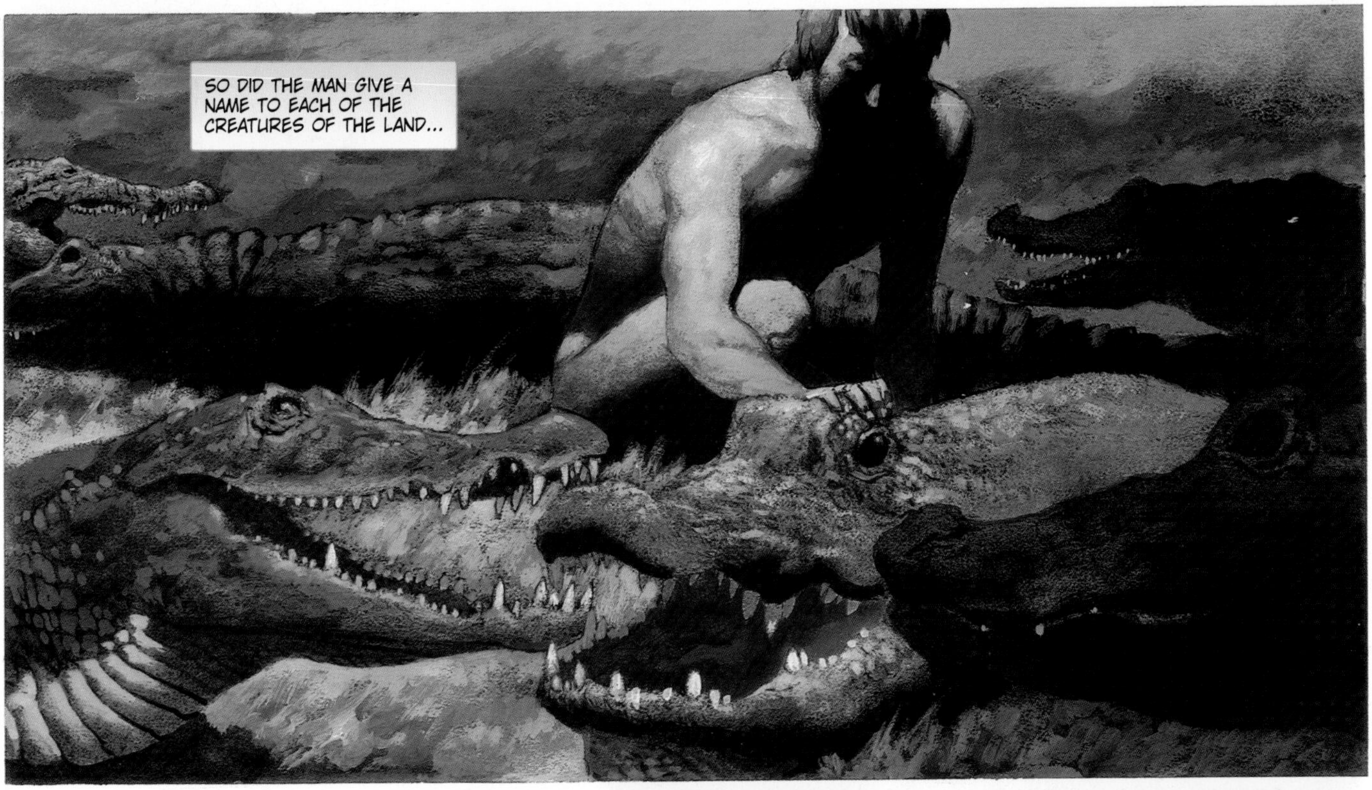
SO DID THE MAN GIVE A NAME TO EACH OF THE CREATURES OF THE LAND...

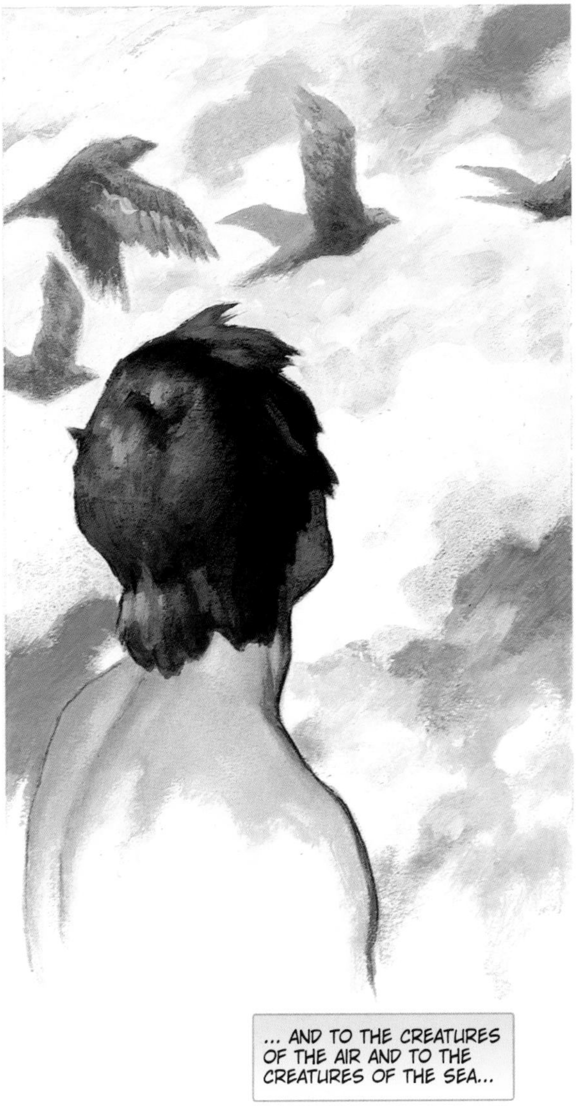
... AND TO THE CREATURES OF THE AIR AND TO THE CREATURES OF THE SEA...

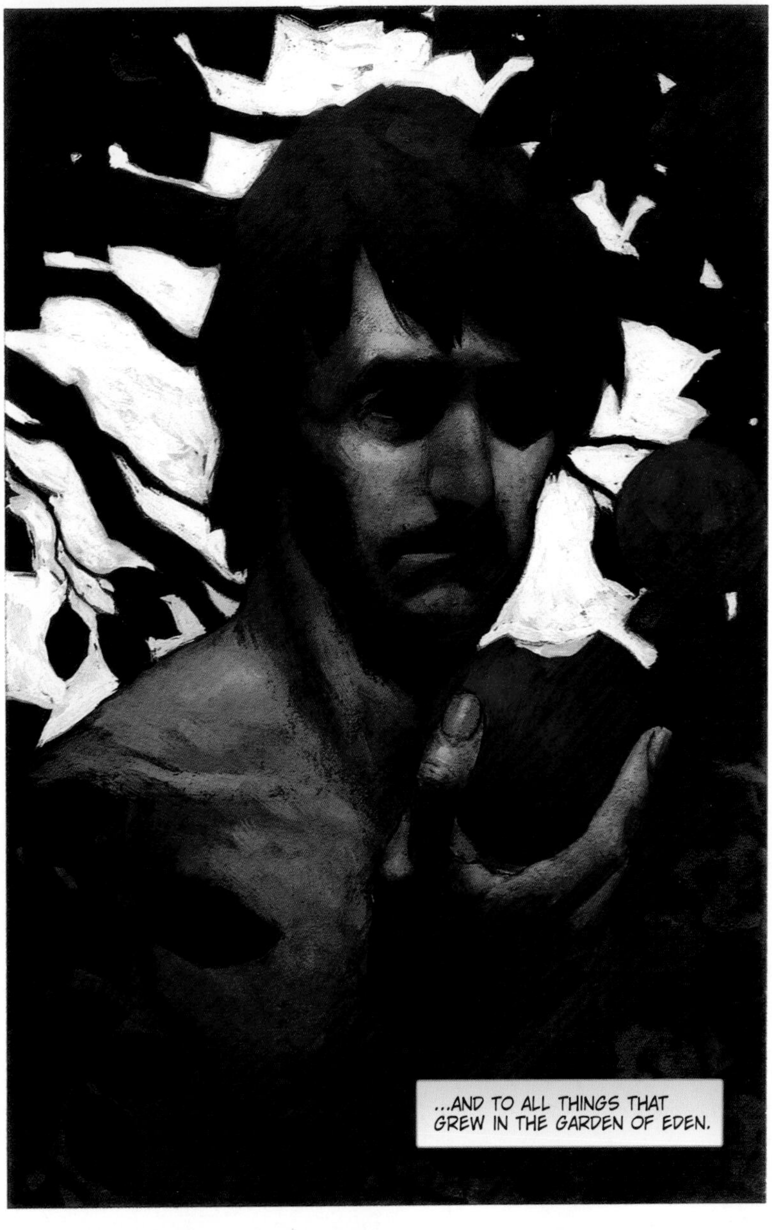
...AND TO ALL THINGS THAT GREW IN THE GARDEN OF EDEN.

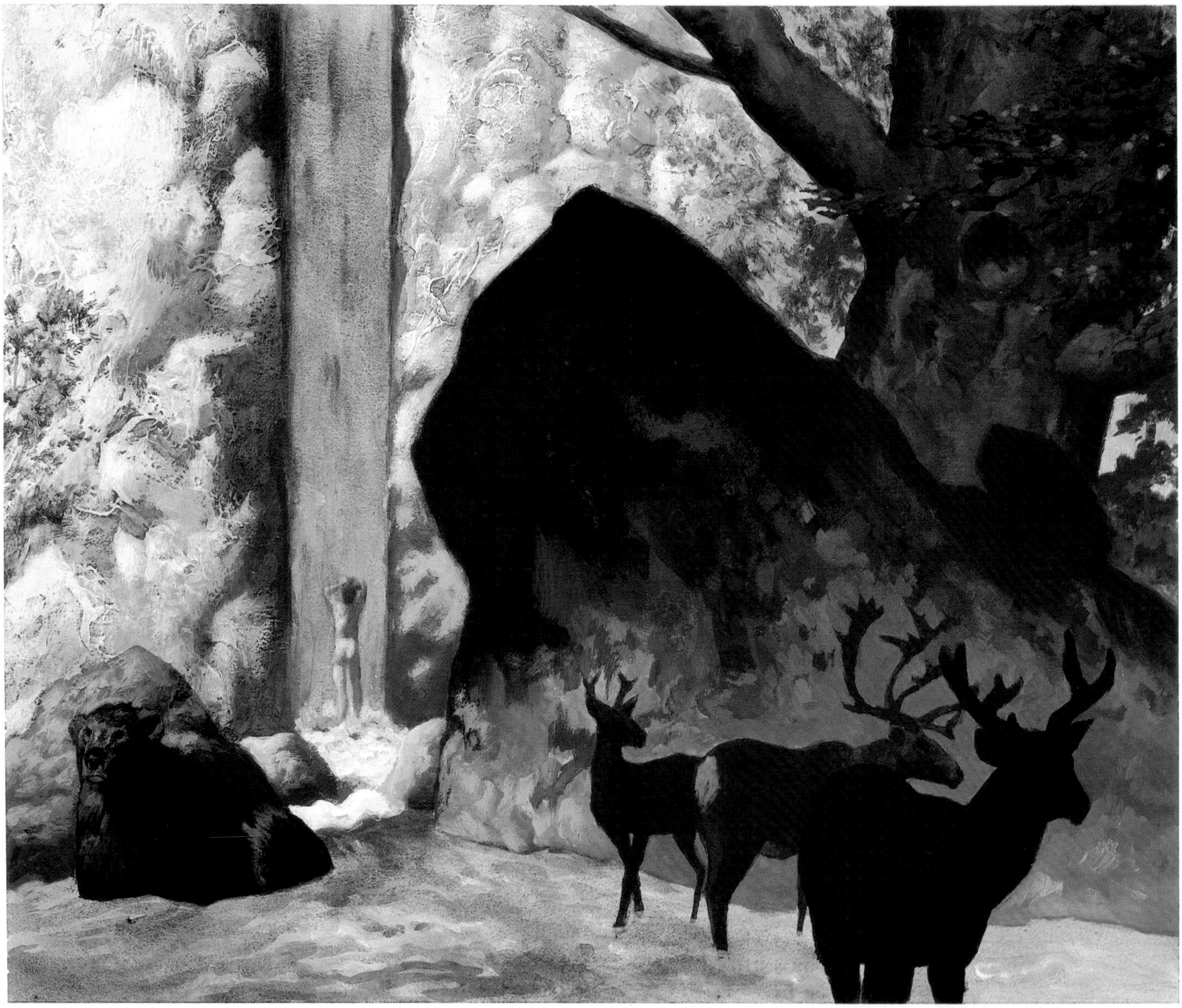

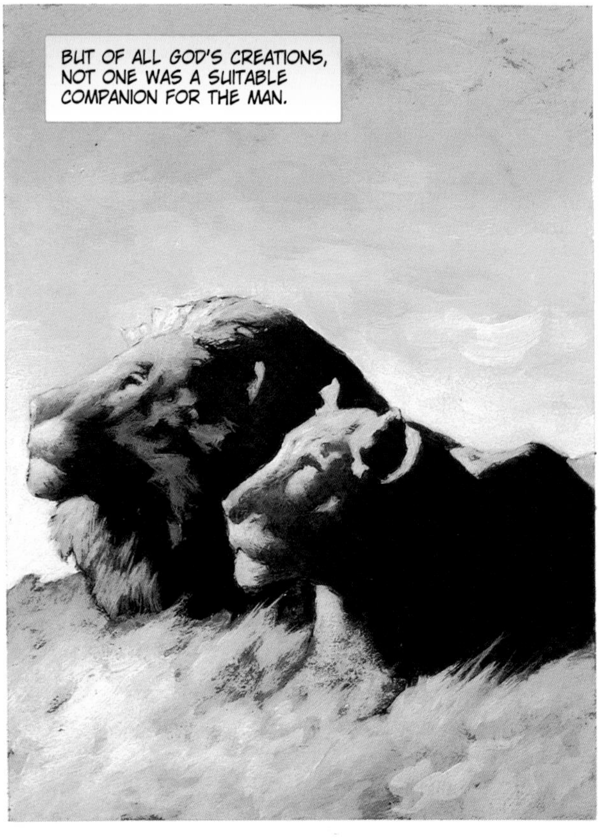
BUT OF ALL GOD'S CREATIONS, NOT ONE WAS A SUITABLE COMPANION FOR THE MAN.

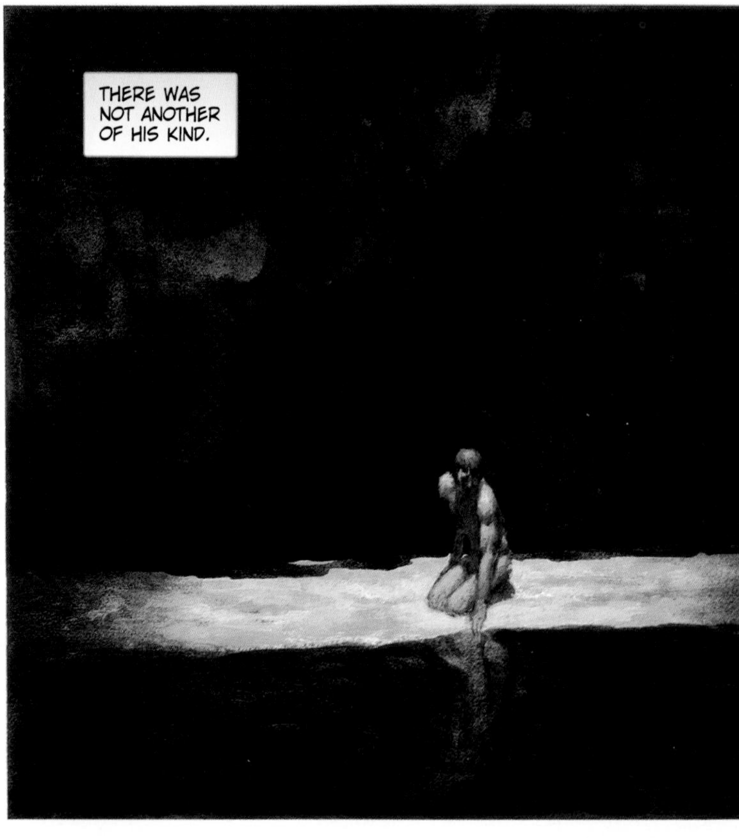
THERE WAS NOT ANOTHER OF HIS KIND.

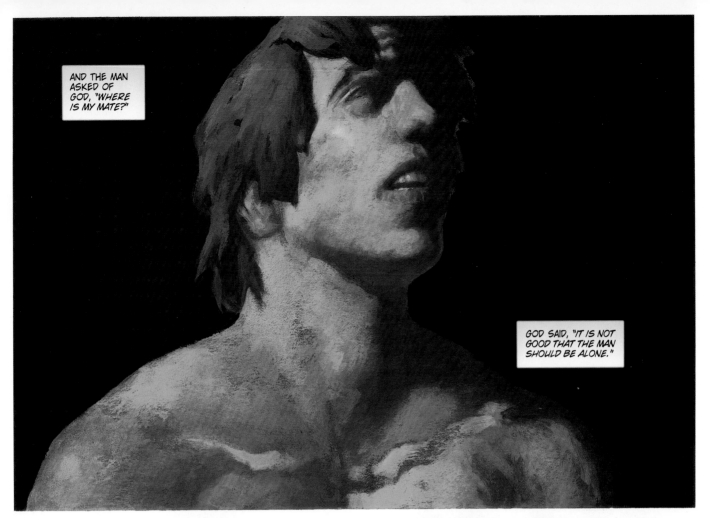

AND THE MAN ASKED OF GOD, "WHERE IS MY MATE?"

GOD SAID, "IT IS NOT GOOD THAT THE MAN SHOULD BE ALONE."

SO GOD BROUGHT UPON THE MAN A DEEP SLEEP.

AND WHILE THE MAN SLEPT...

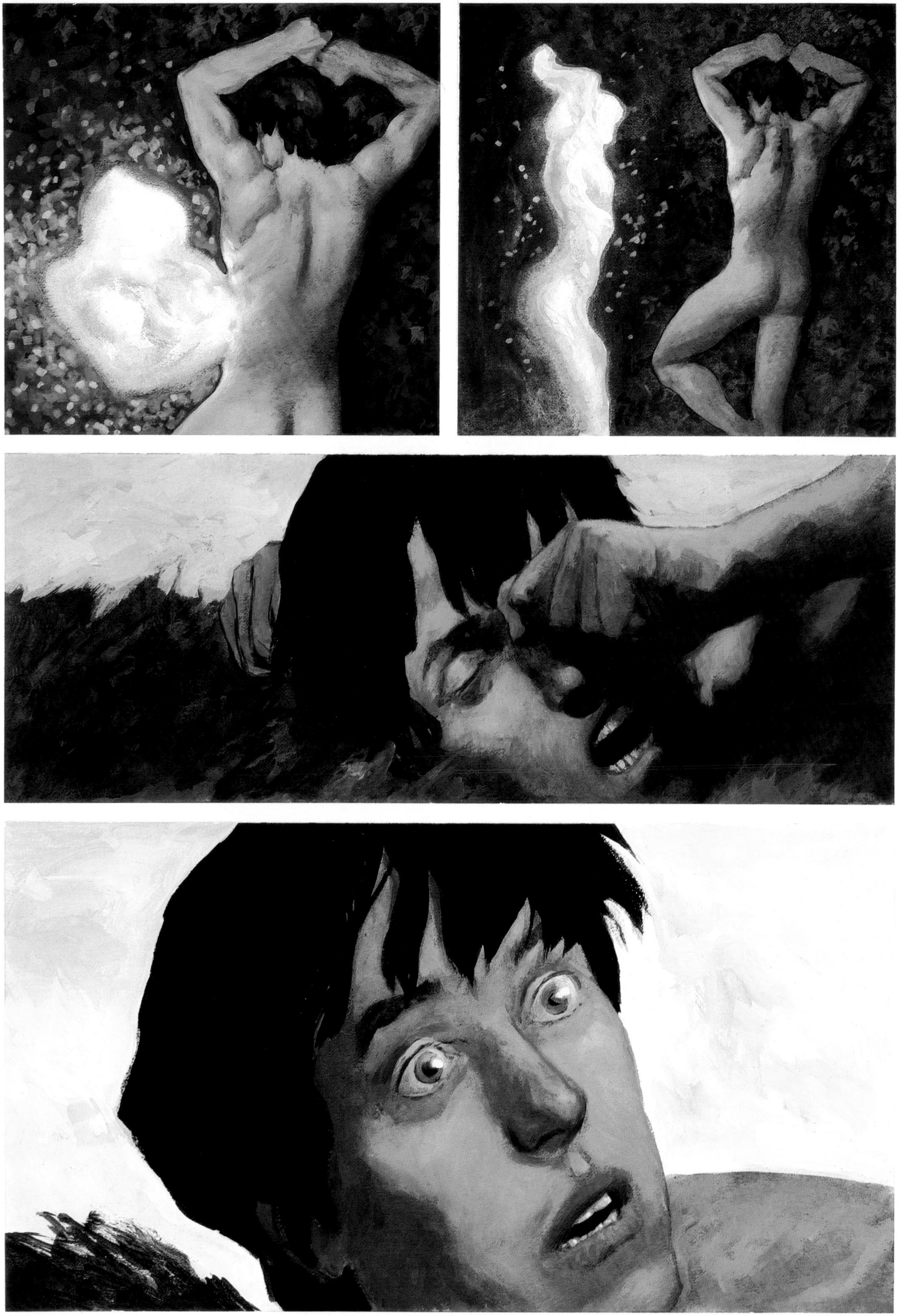

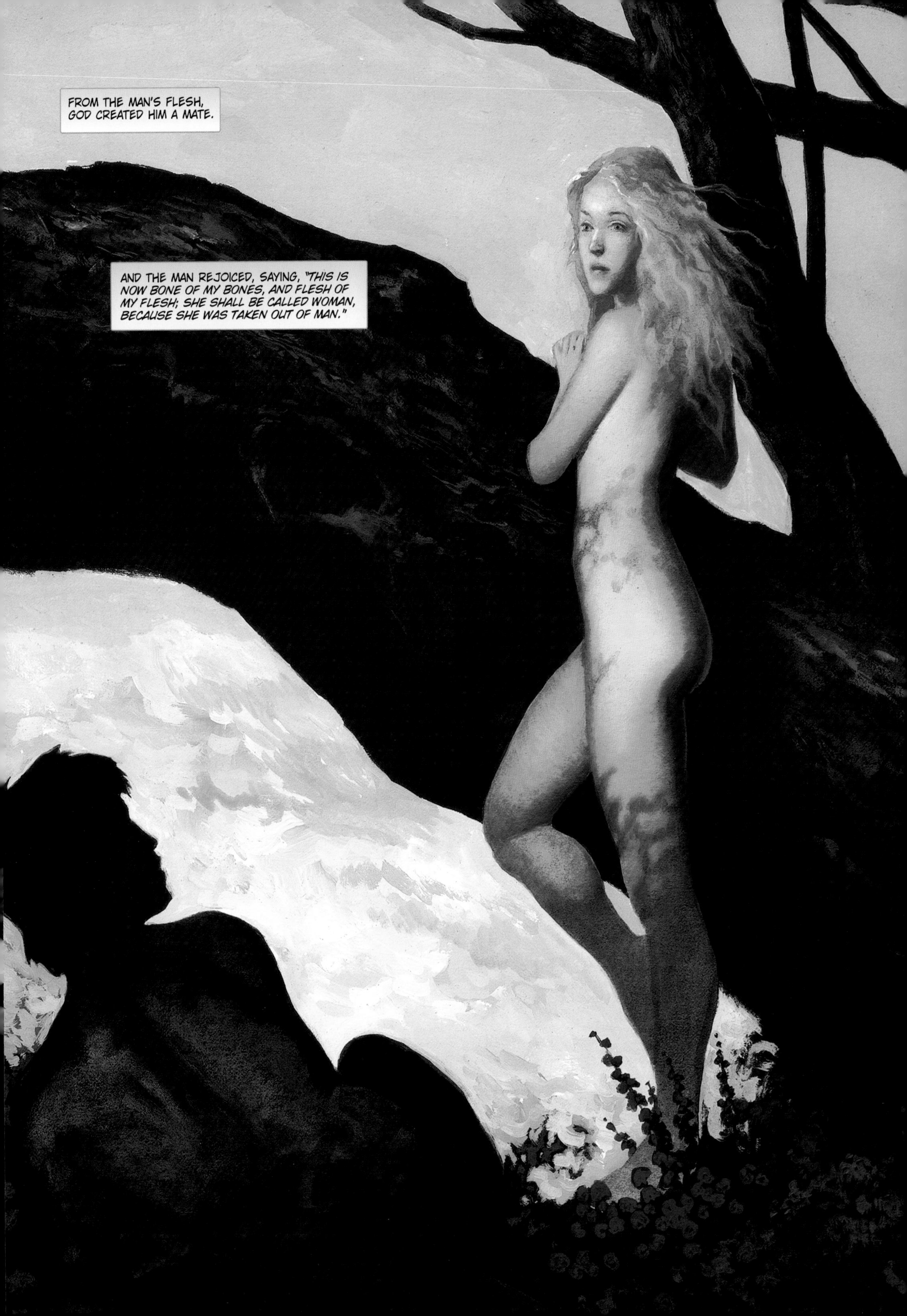
FROM THE MAN'S FLESH, GOD CREATED HIM A MATE.
AND THE MAN REJOICED, SAYING, "THIS IS NOW BONE OF MY BONES, AND FLESH OF MY FLESH; SHE SHALL BE CALLED WOMAN, BECAUSE SHE WAS TAKEN OUT OF MAN."

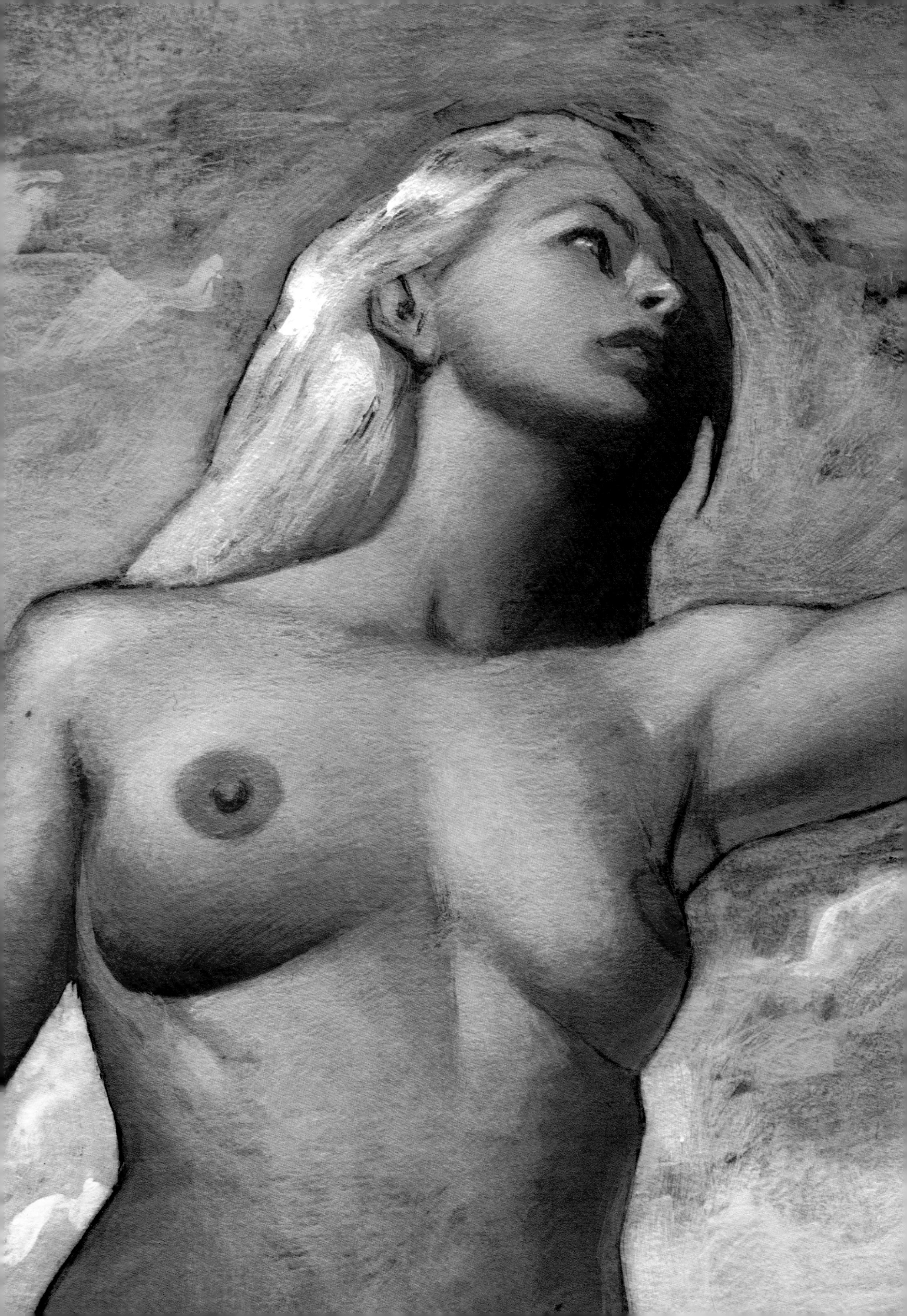

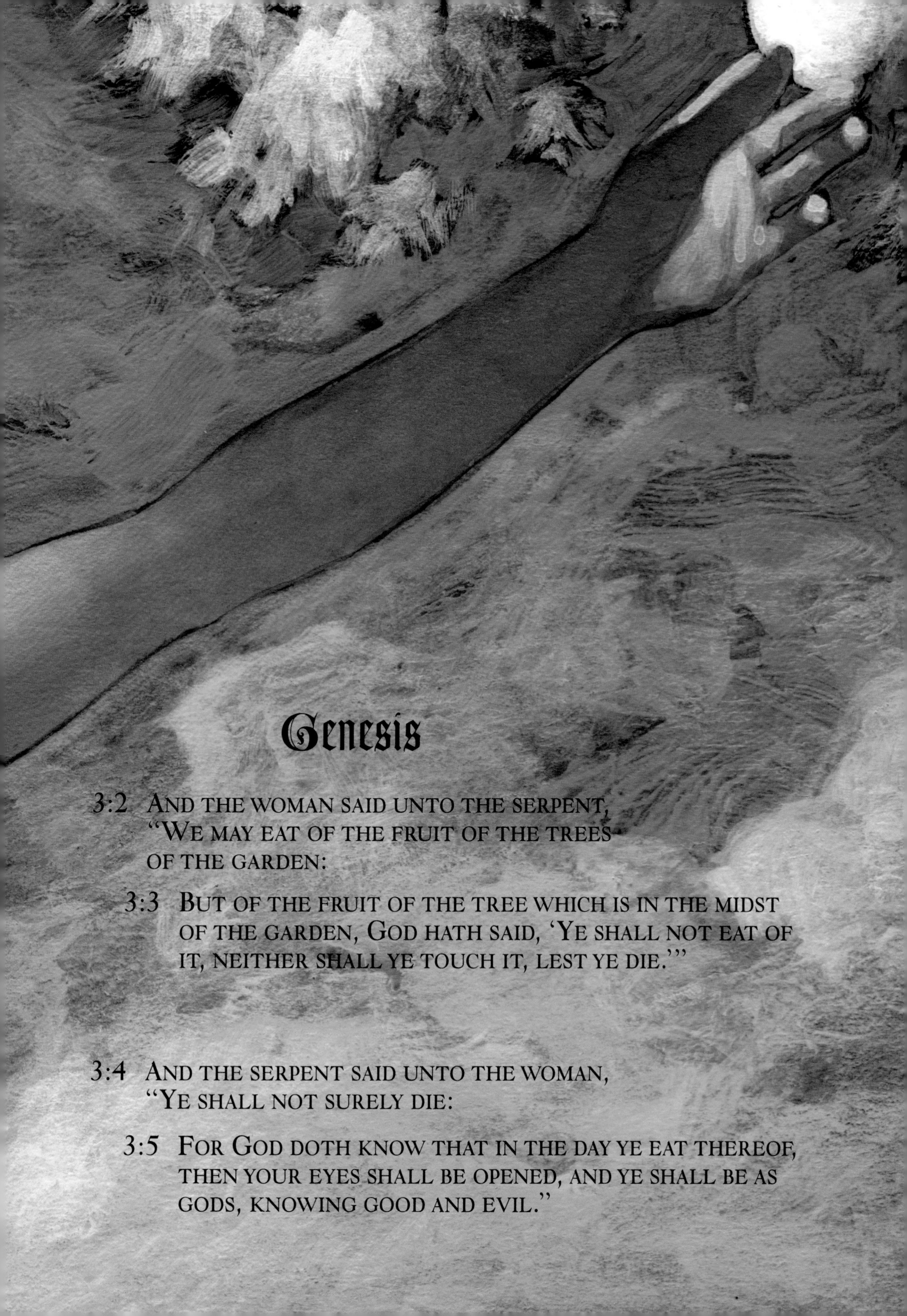

Genesis

3:2 And the woman said unto the serpent,
"We may eat of the fruit of the trees
of the garden:

3:3 But of the fruit of the tree which is in the midst
of the garden, God hath said, 'Ye shall not eat of
it, neither shall ye touch it, lest ye die.'"

3:4 And the serpent said unto the woman,
"Ye shall not surely die:

3:5 For God doth know that in the day ye eat thereof,
then your eyes shall be opened, and ye shall be as
gods, knowing good and evil."

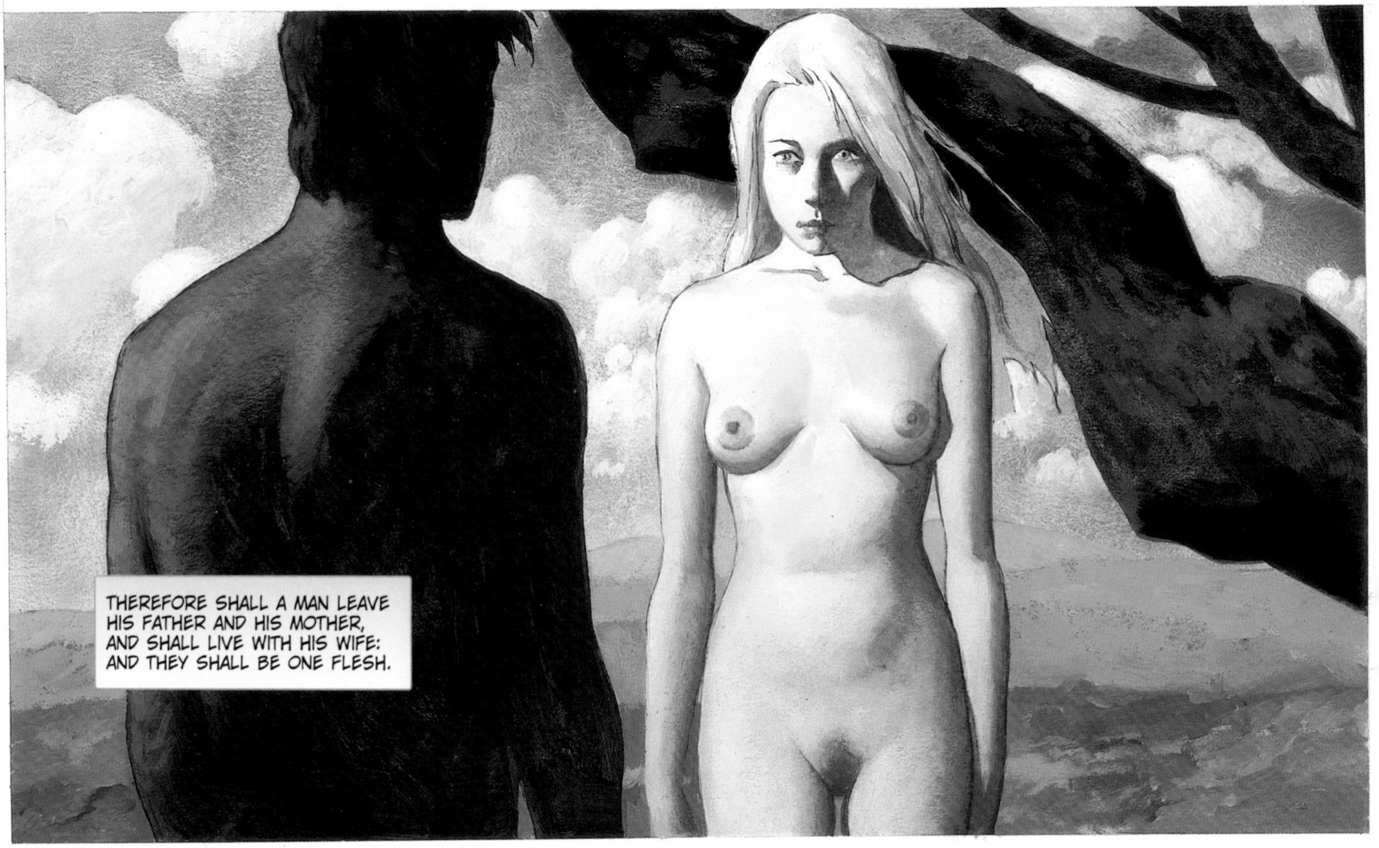
THEREFORE SHALL A MAN LEAVE HIS FATHER AND HIS MOTHER, AND SHALL LIVE WITH HIS WIFE: AND THEY SHALL BE ONE FLESH.

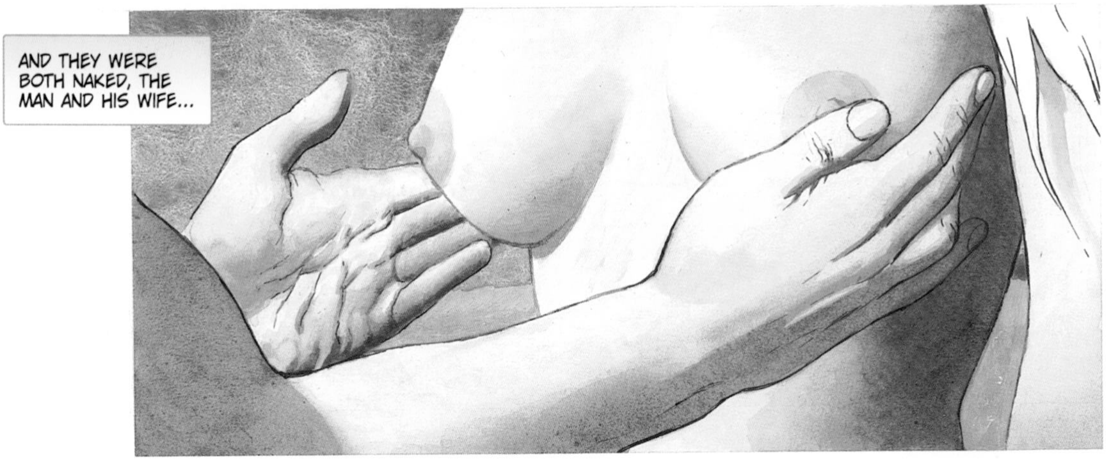
AND THEY WERE BOTH NAKED, THE MAN AND HIS WIFE...

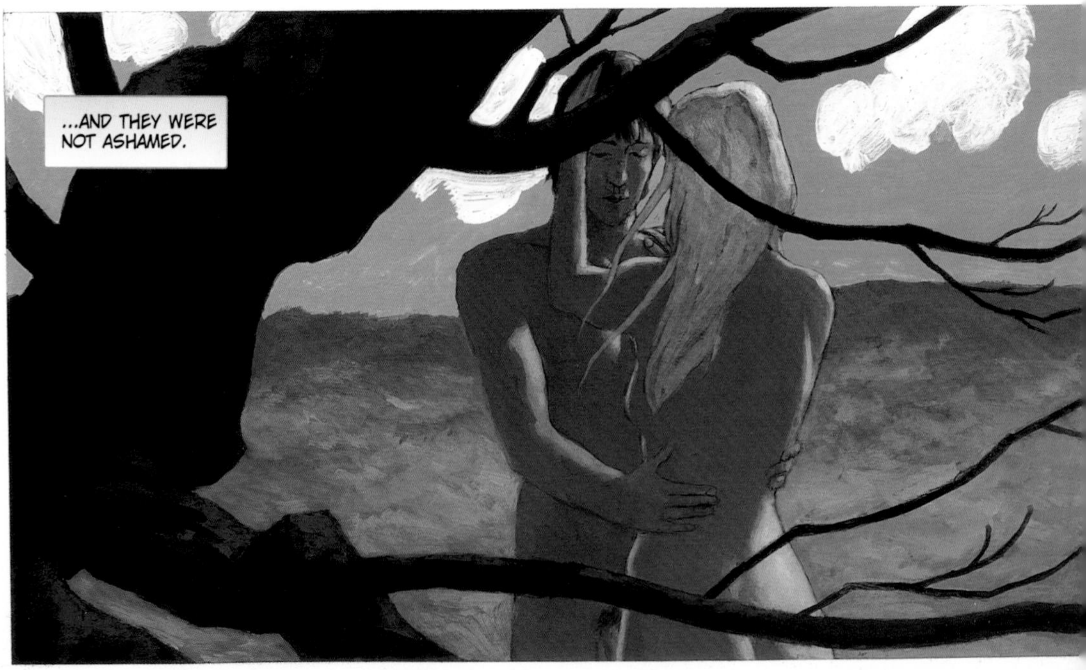
...AND THEY WERE NOT ASHAMED.

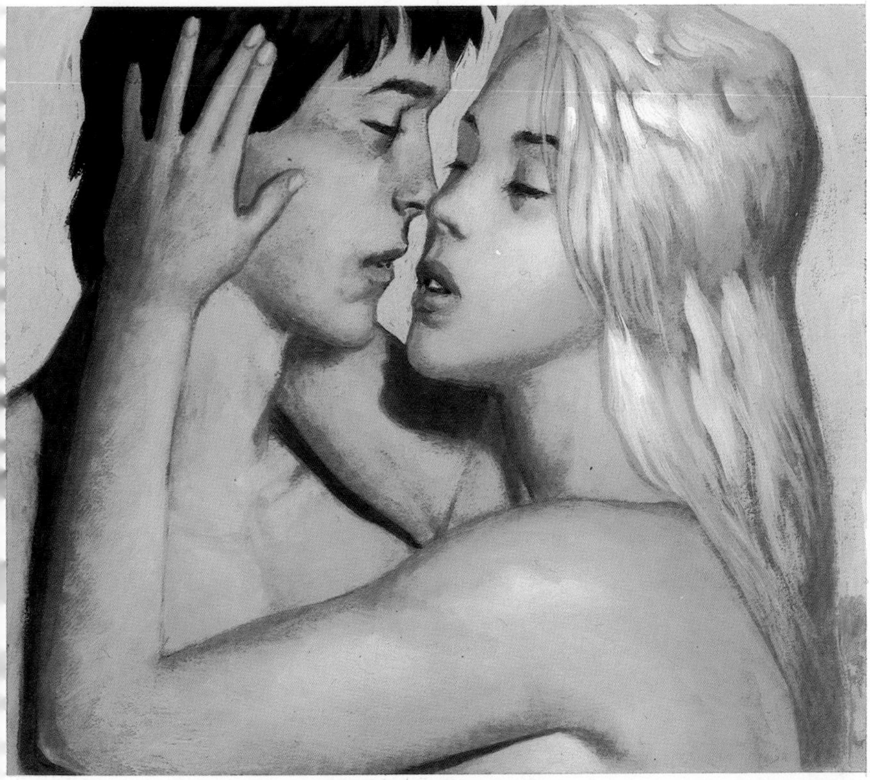

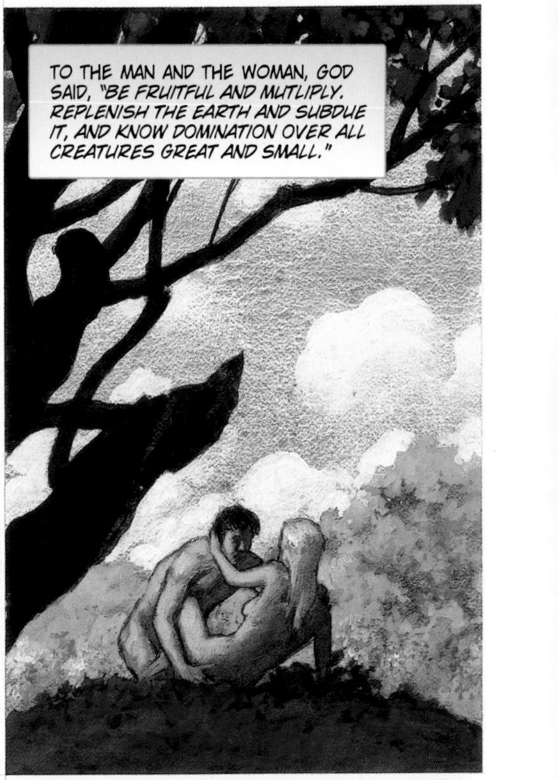
TO THE MAN AND THE WOMAN, GOD SAID, "BE FRUITFUL AND MUTLIPLY. REPLENISH THE EARTH AND SUBDUE IT, AND KNOW DOMINATION OVER ALL CREATURES GREAT AND SMALL."

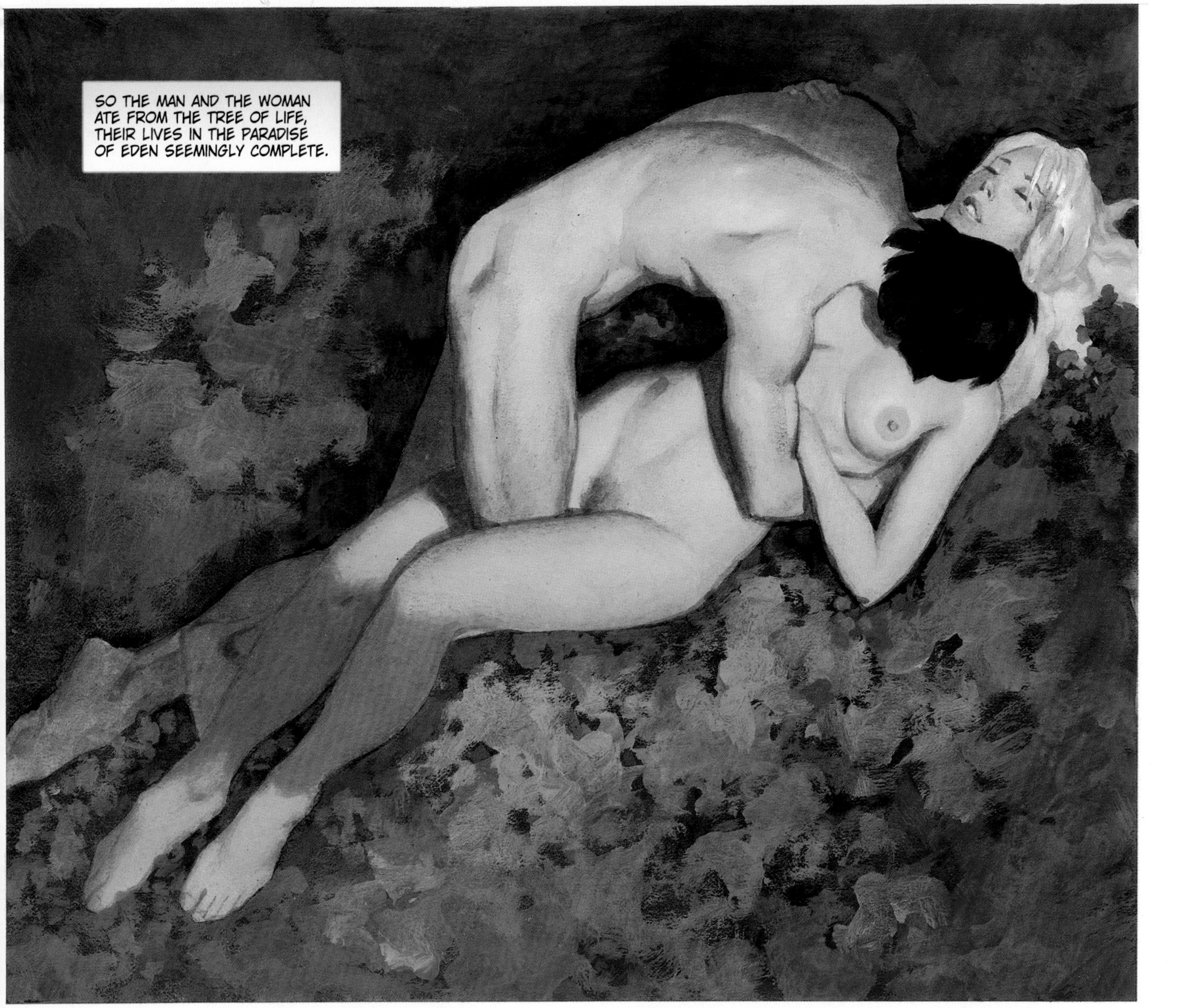
SO THE MAN AND THE WOMAN ATE FROM THE TREE OF LIFE, THEIR LIVES IN THE PARADISE OF EDEN SEEMINGLY COMPLETE.

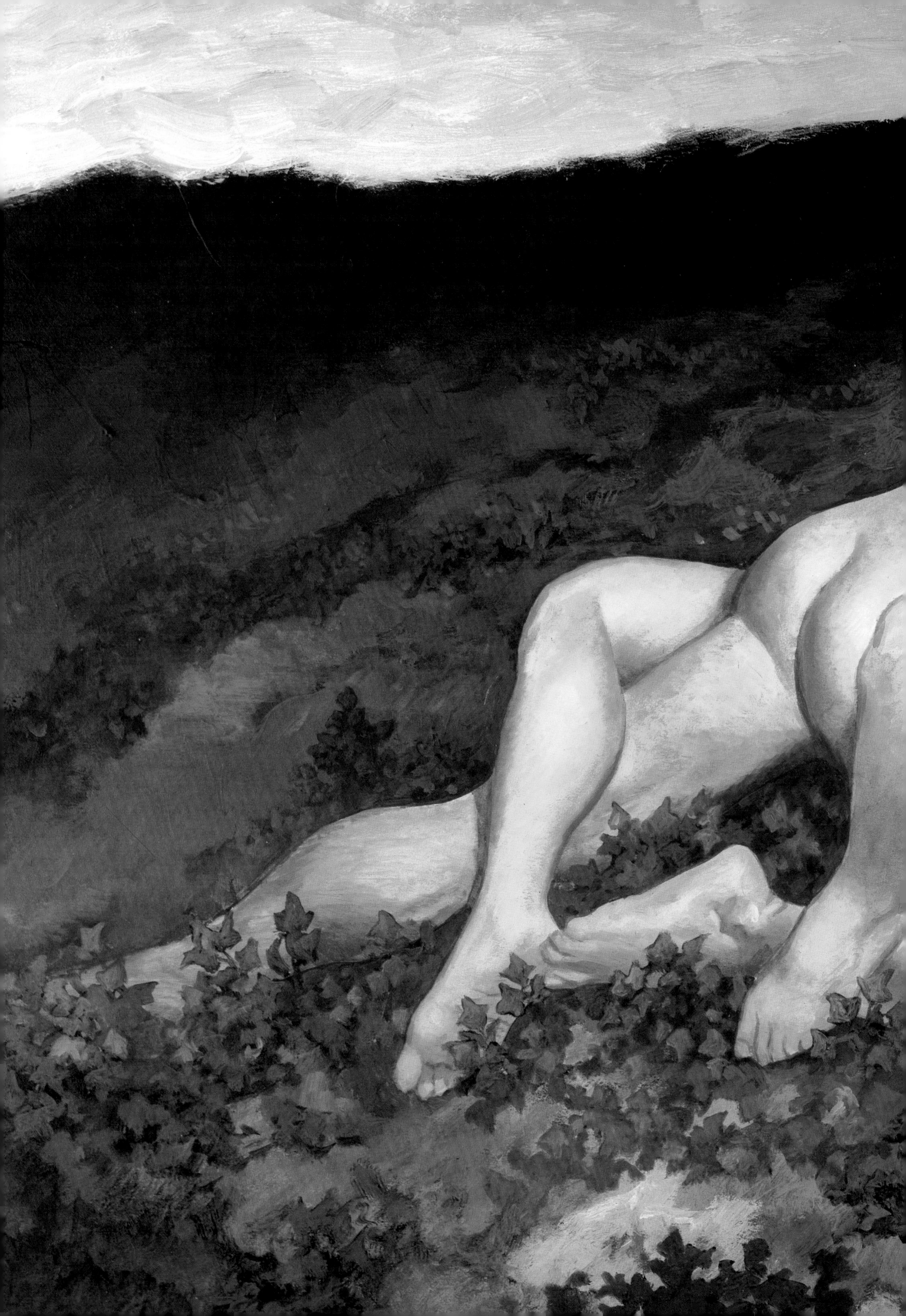

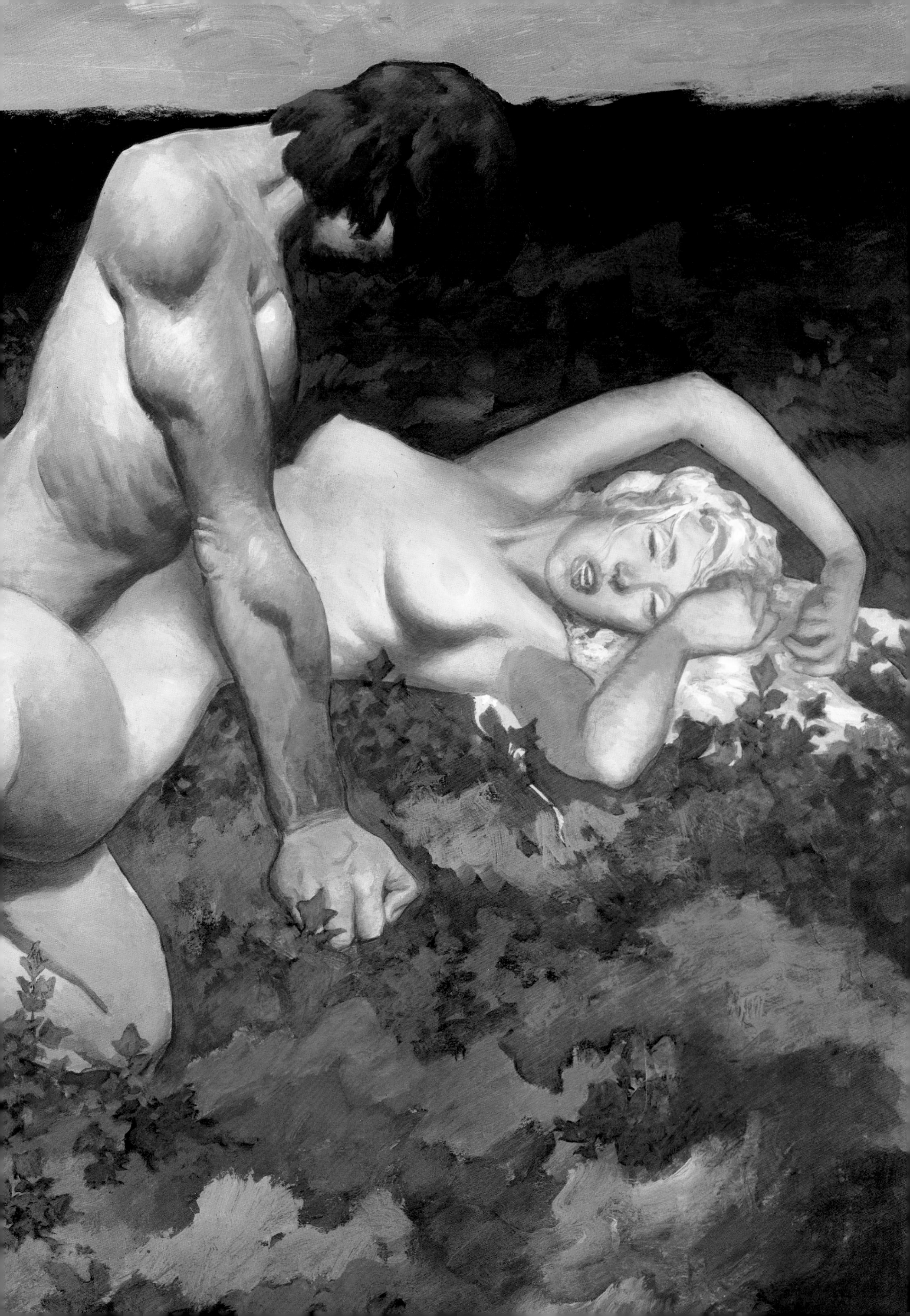

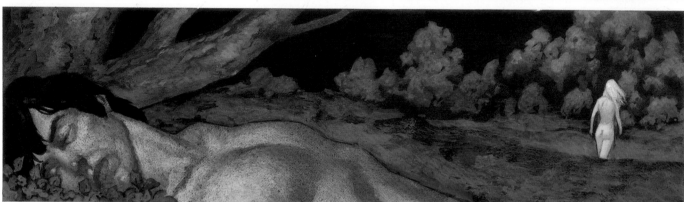

GOD HAD TOLD THEM, "EAT FREELY OF THE FRUIT OF ANY TREE IN THE GARDEN..."

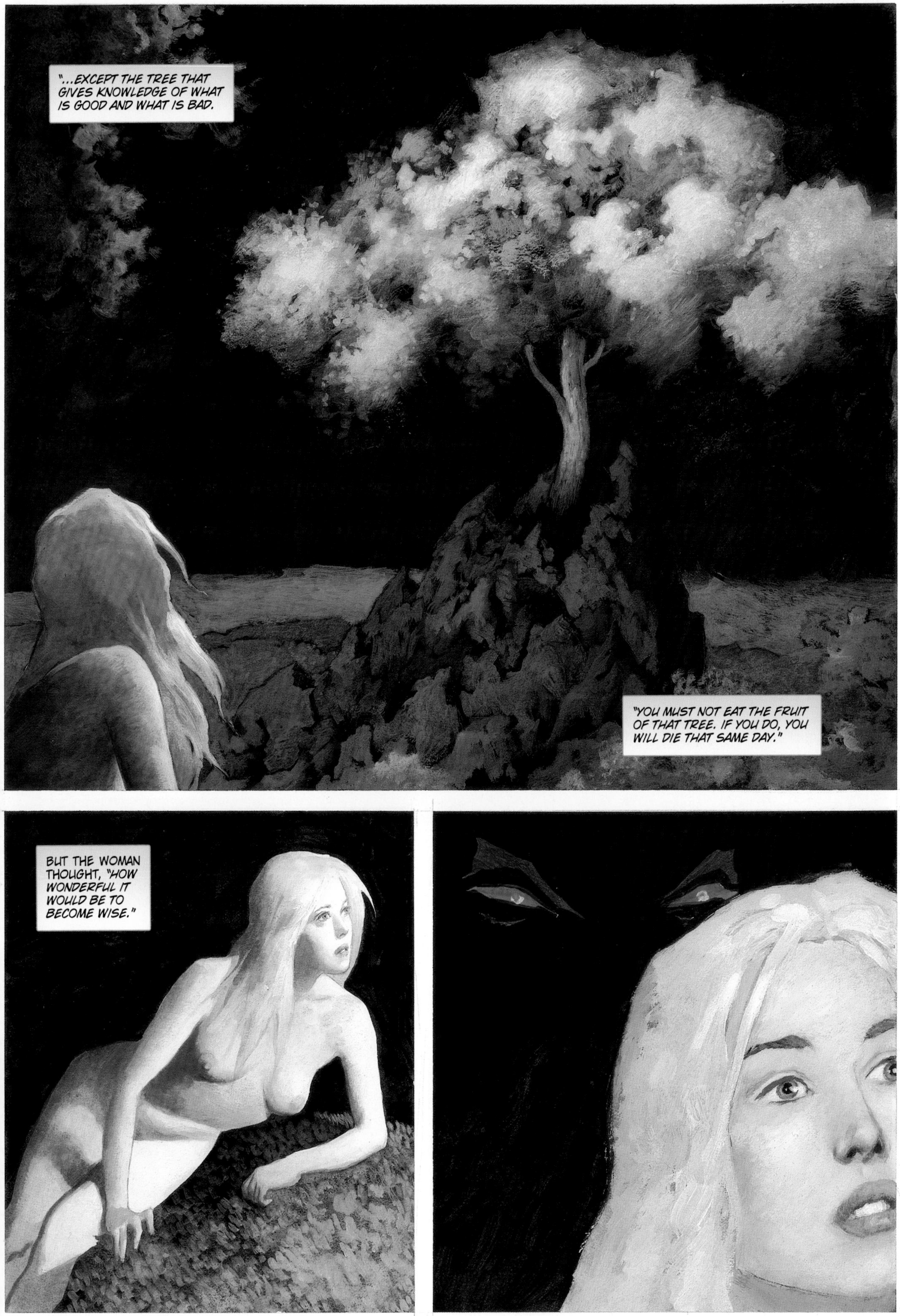
"...EXCEPT THE TREE THAT GIVES KNOWLEDGE OF WHAT IS GOOD AND WHAT IS BAD.
"YOU MUST NOT EAT THE FRUIT OF THAT TREE. IF YOU DO, YOU WILL DIE THAT SAME DAY."
BUT THE WOMAN THOUGHT, "HOW WONDERFUL IT WOULD BE TO BECOME WISE."

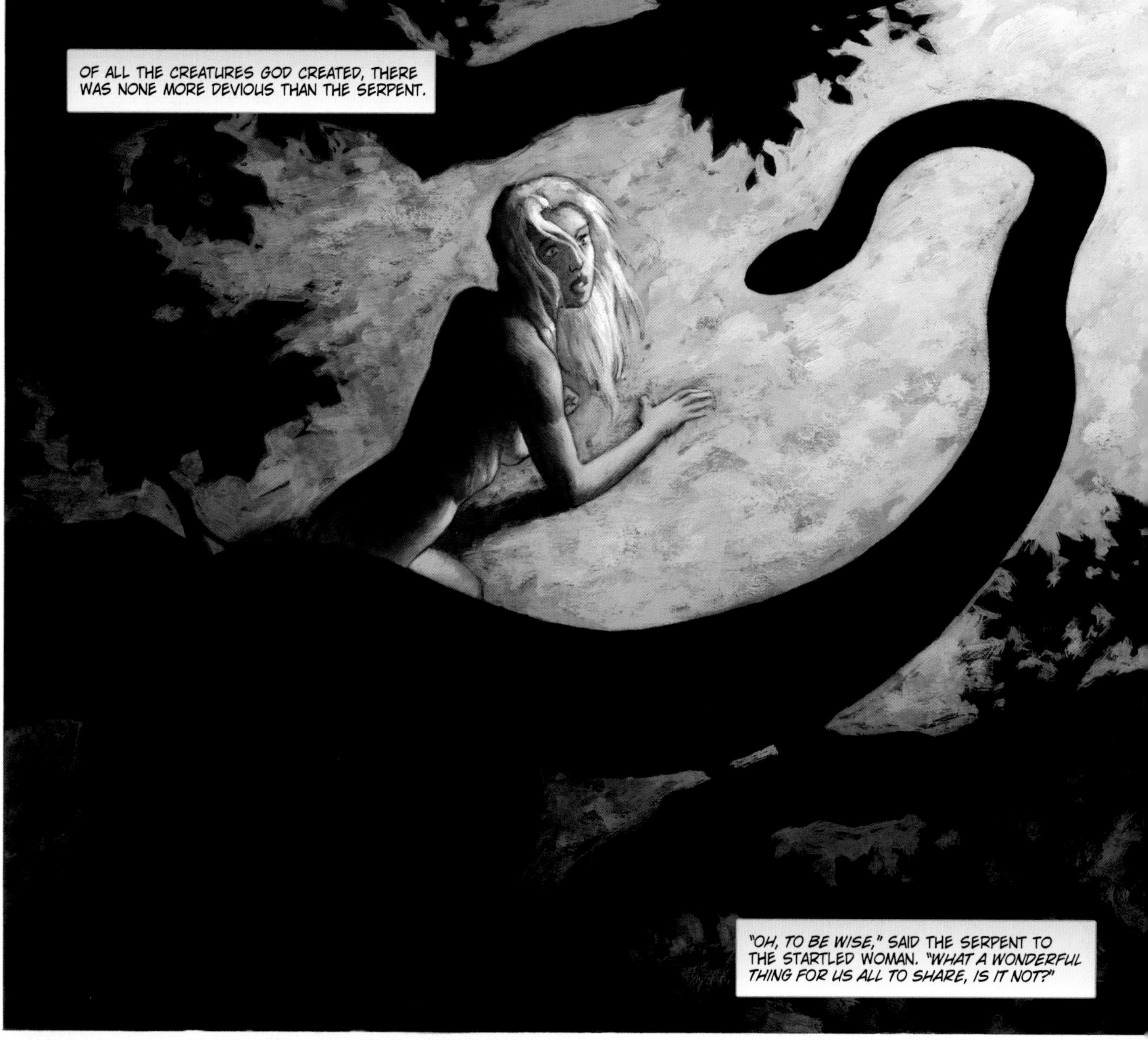
OF ALL THE CREATURES GOD CREATED, THERE WAS NONE MORE DEVIOUS THAN THE SERPENT.
"OH, TO BE WISE," SAID THE SERPENT TO THE STARTLED WOMAN. "WHAT A WONDERFUL THING FOR US ALL TO SHARE, IS IT NOT?"

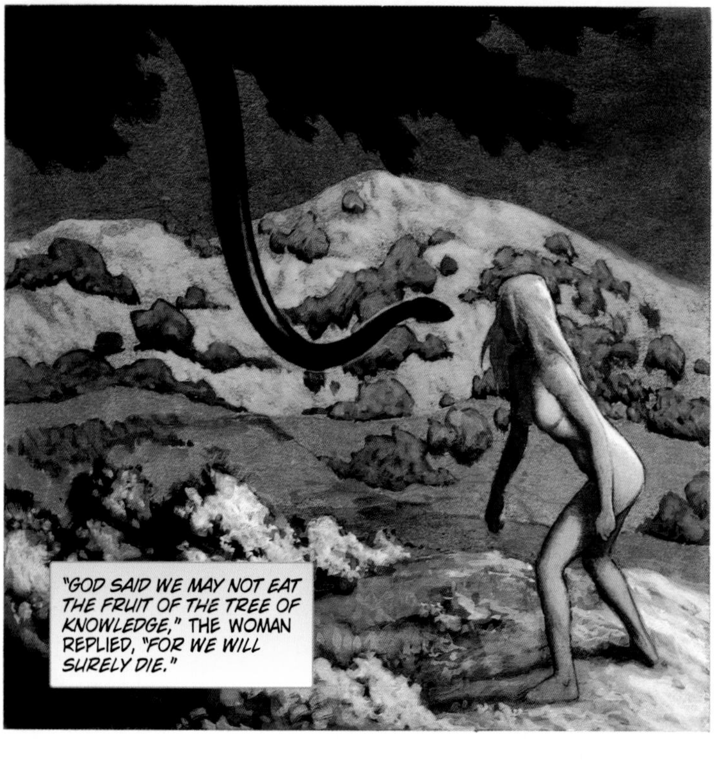
"GOD SAID WE MAY NOT EAT THE FRUIT OF THE TREE OF KNOWLEDGE," THE WOMAN REPLIED, "FOR WE WILL SURELY DIE."

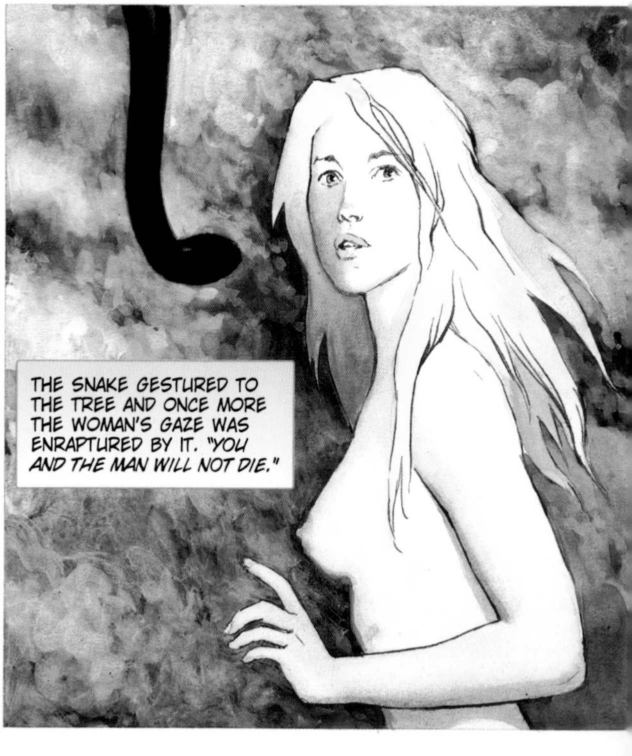
THE SNAKE GESTURED TO THE TREE AND ONCE MORE THE WOMAN'S GAZE WAS ENRAPTURED BY IT. "YOU AND THE MAN WILL NOT DIE."

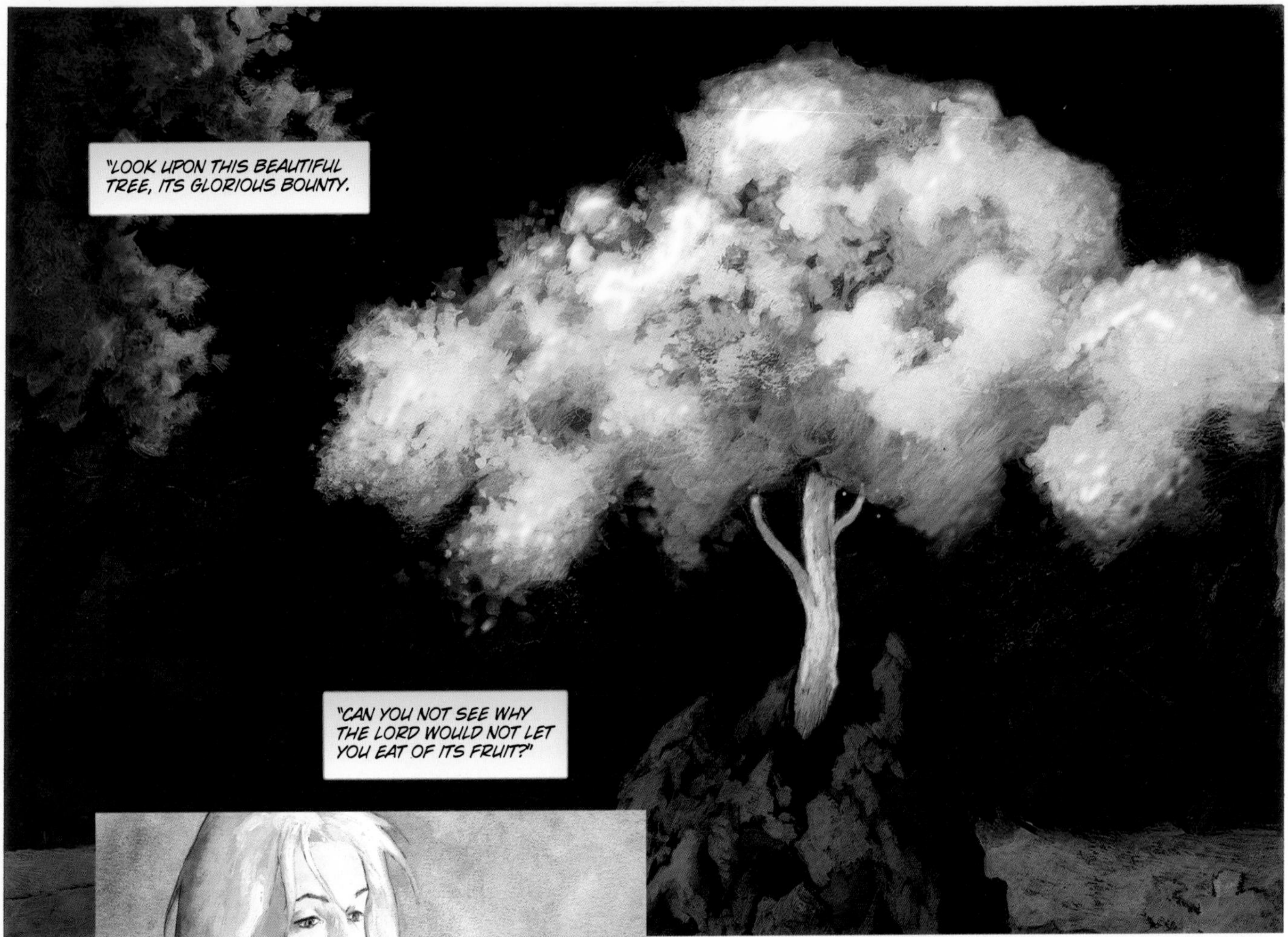
"LOOK UPON THIS BEAUTIFUL TREE, ITS GLORIOUS BOUNTY.
"CAN YOU NOT SEE WHY THE LORD WOULD NOT LET YOU EAT OF ITS FRUIT?"

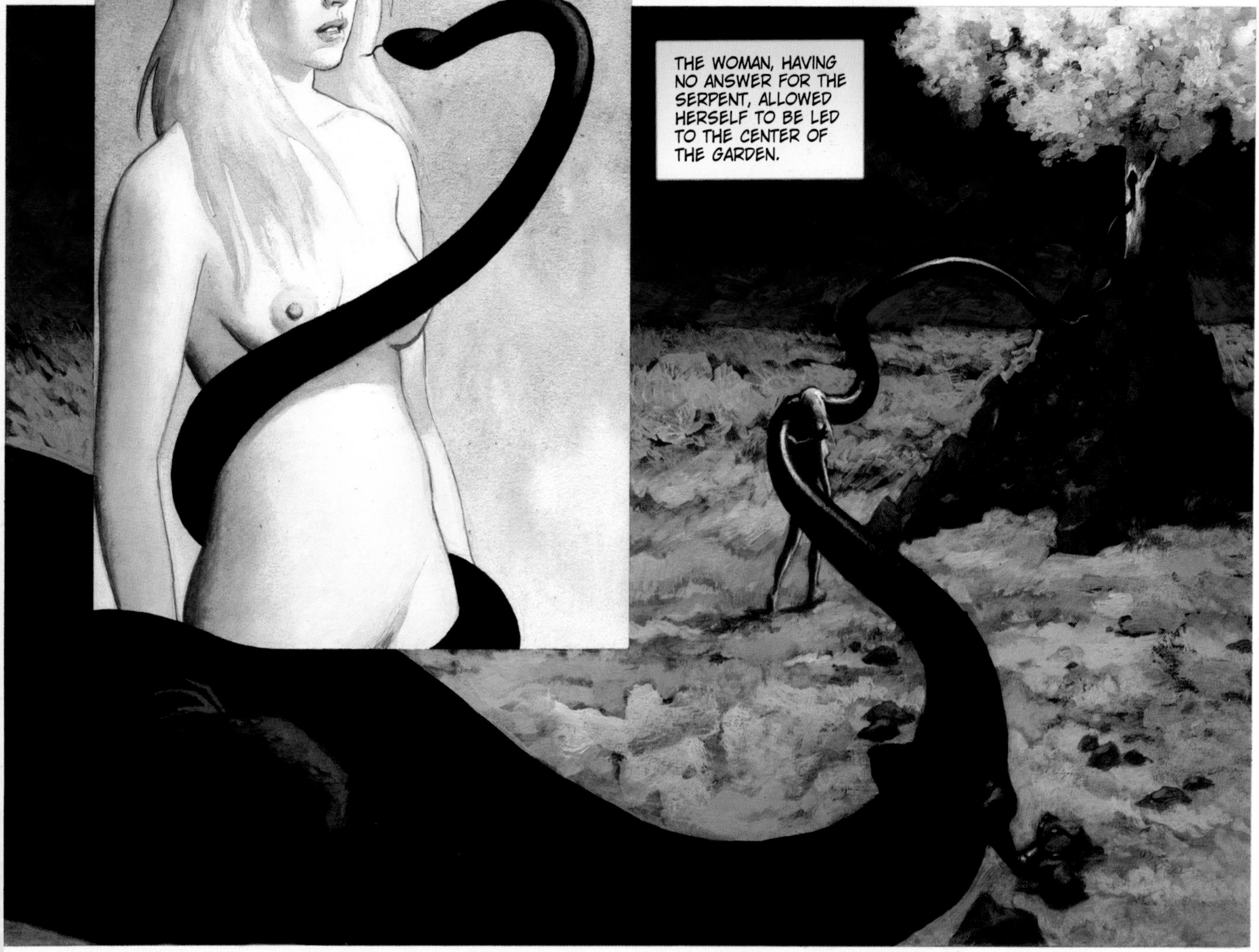
THE WOMAN, HAVING NO ANSWER FOR THE SERPENT, ALLOWED HERSELF TO BE LED TO THE CENTER OF THE GARDEN.

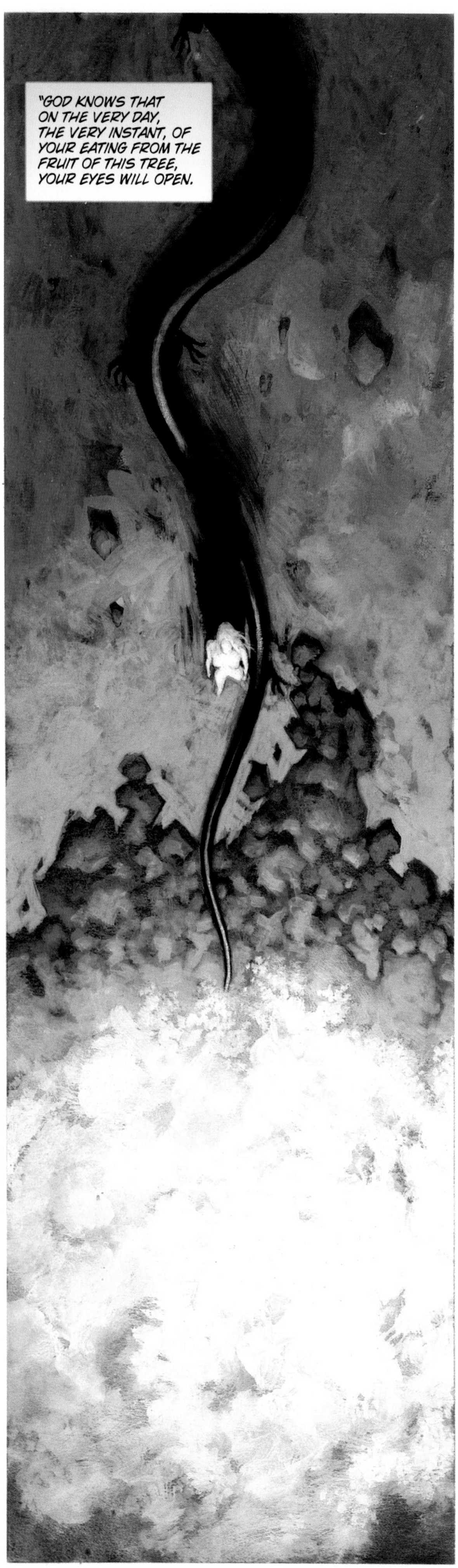
"GOD KNOWS THAT ON THE VERY DAY, THE VERY INSTANT, OF YOUR EATING FROM THE FRUIT OF THIS TREE, YOUR EYES WILL OPEN.

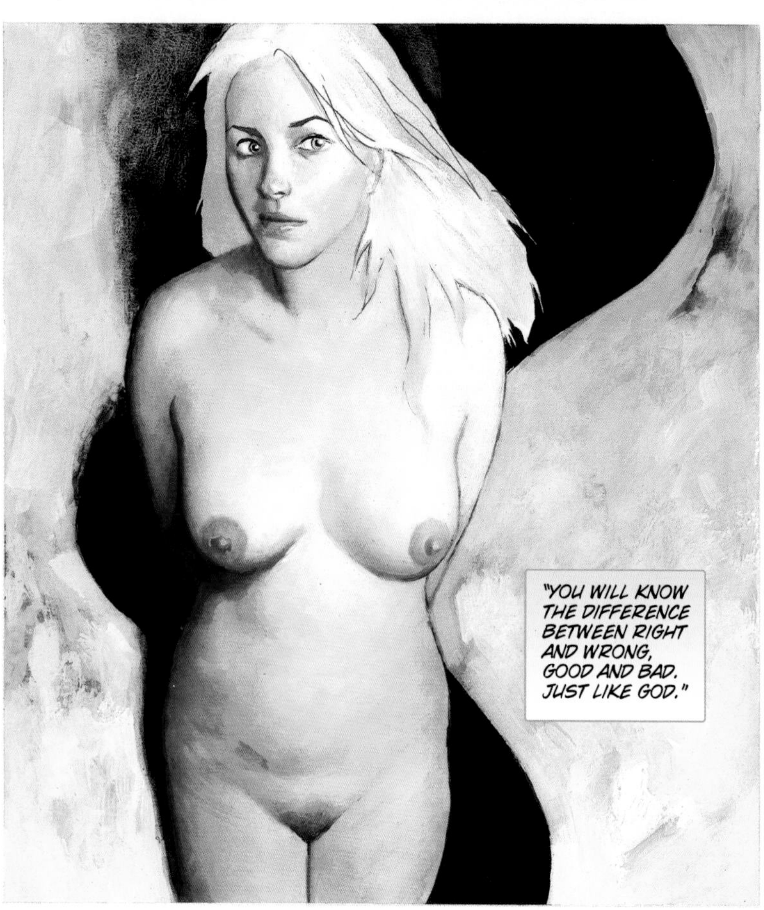
"YOU WILL KNOW THE DIFFERENCE BETWEEN RIGHT AND WRONG, GOOD AND BAD. JUST LIKE GOD."

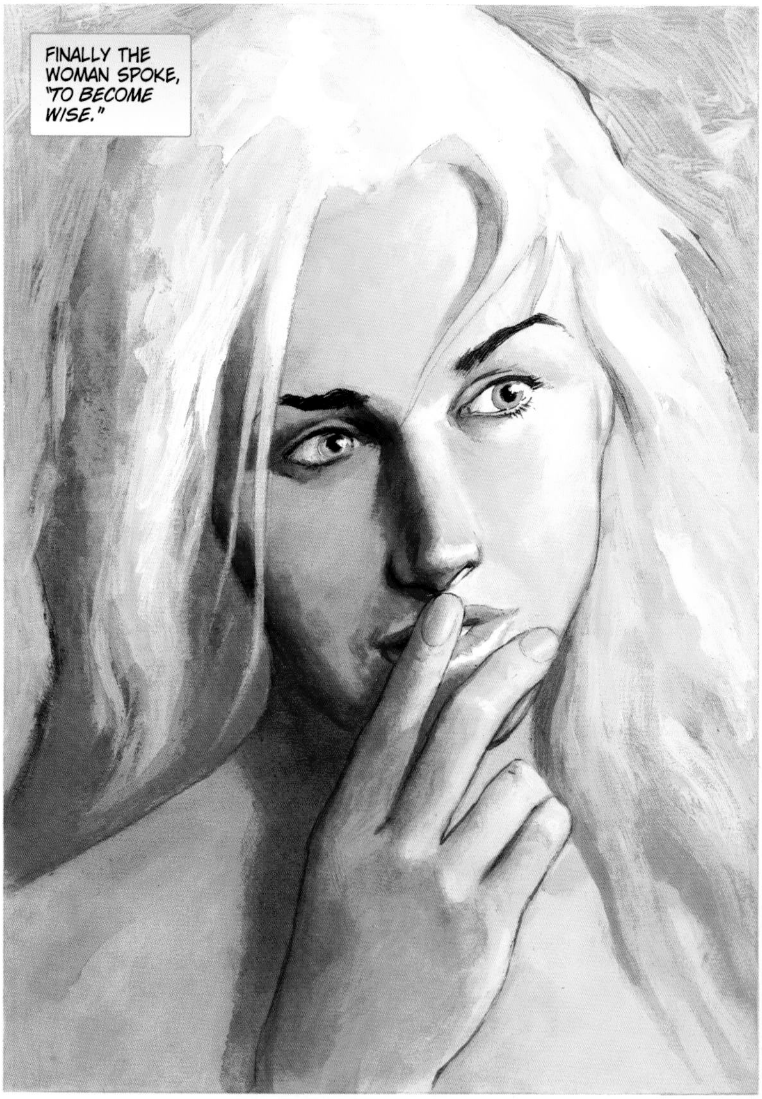
FINALLY THE WOMAN SPOKE, "TO BECOME WISE."

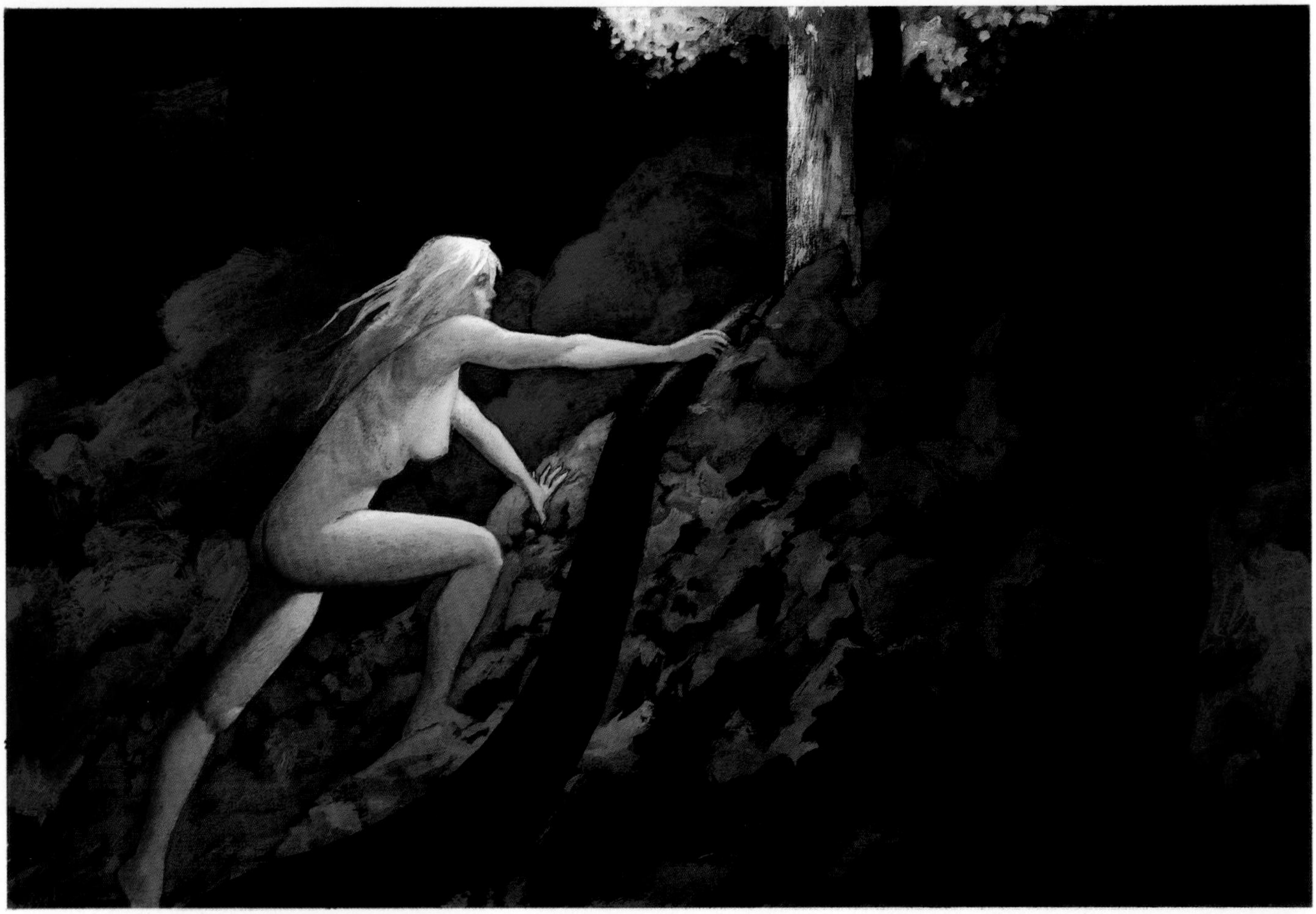

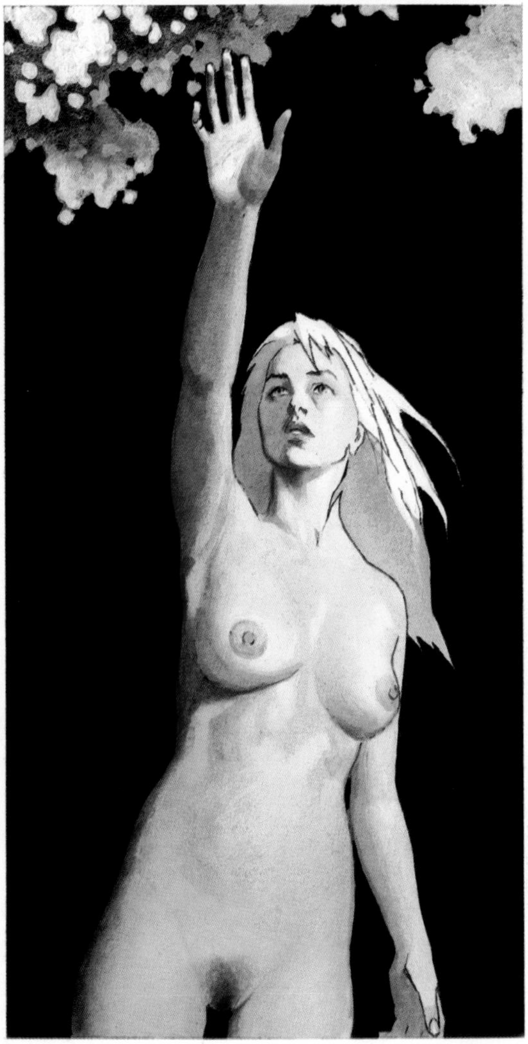

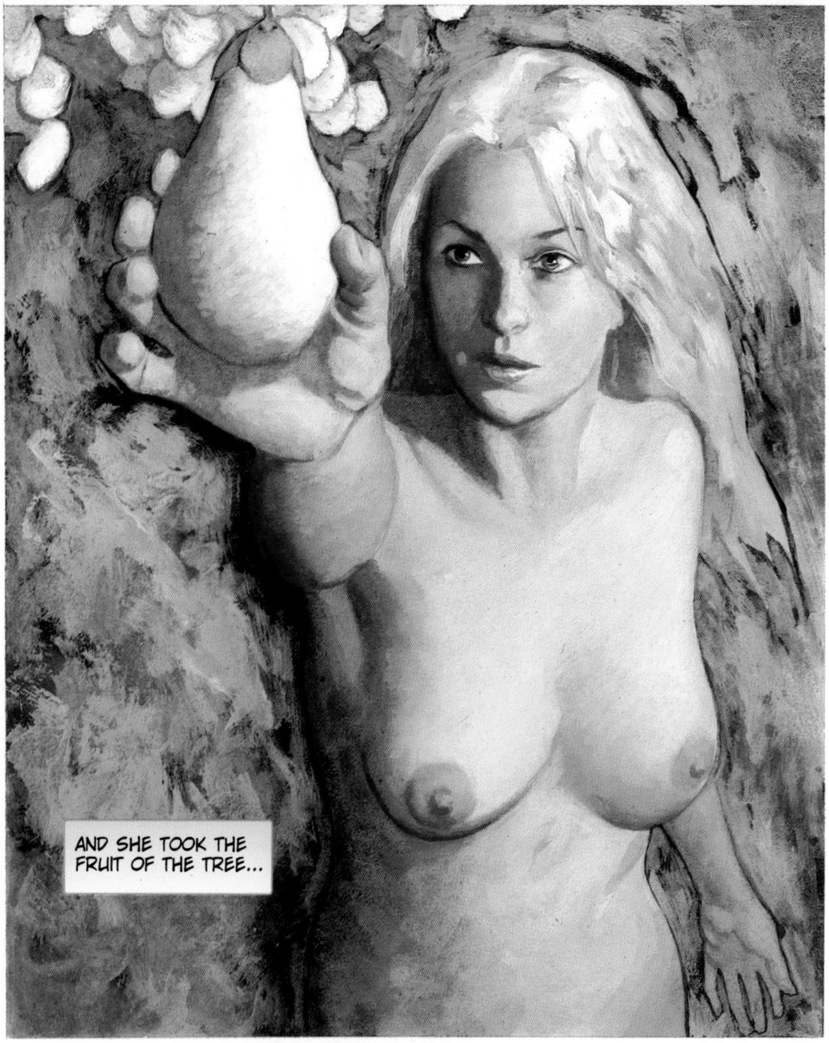
AND SHE TOOK THE FRUIT OF THE TREE...

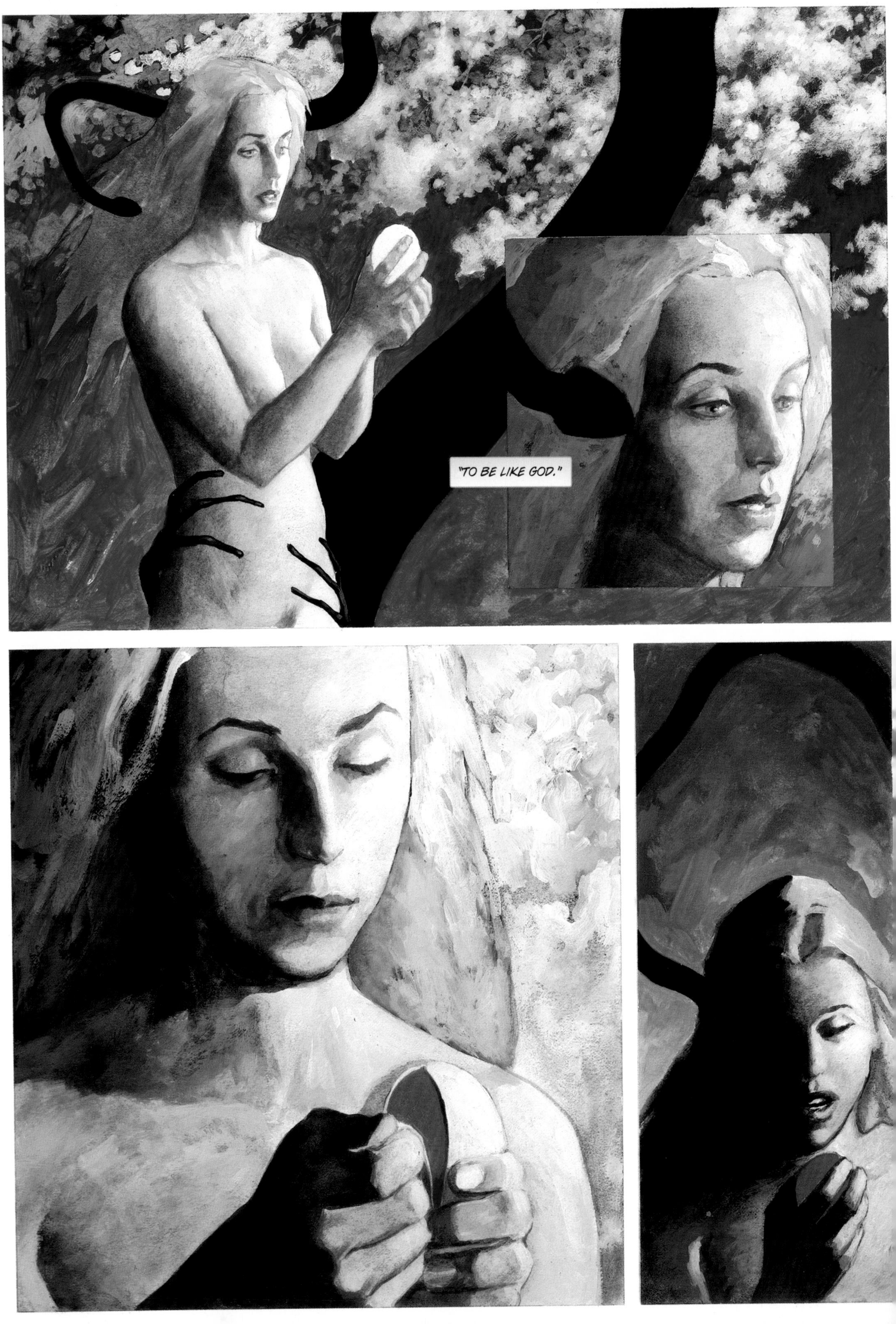
"TO BE LIKE GOD."

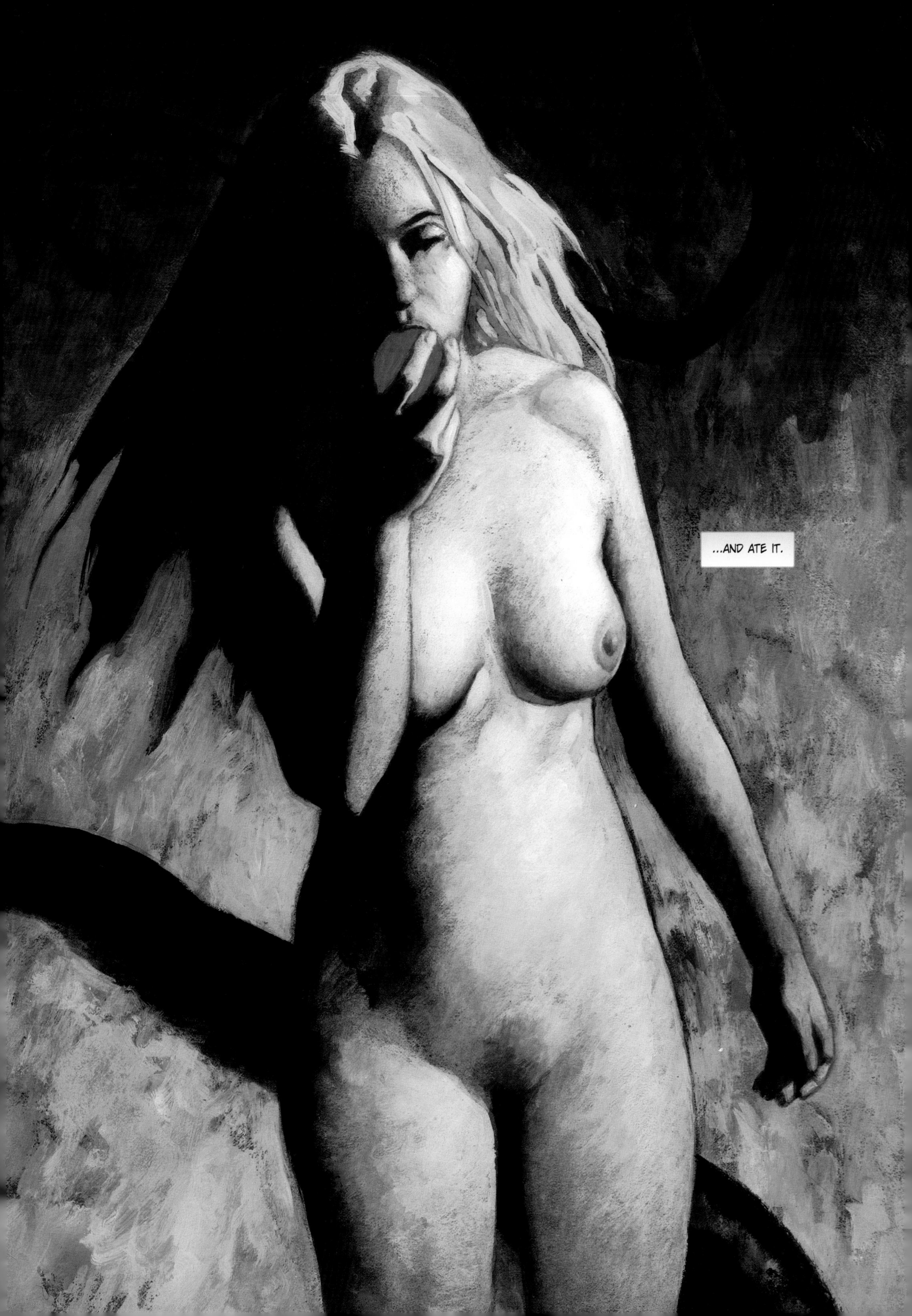
...AND ATE IT.

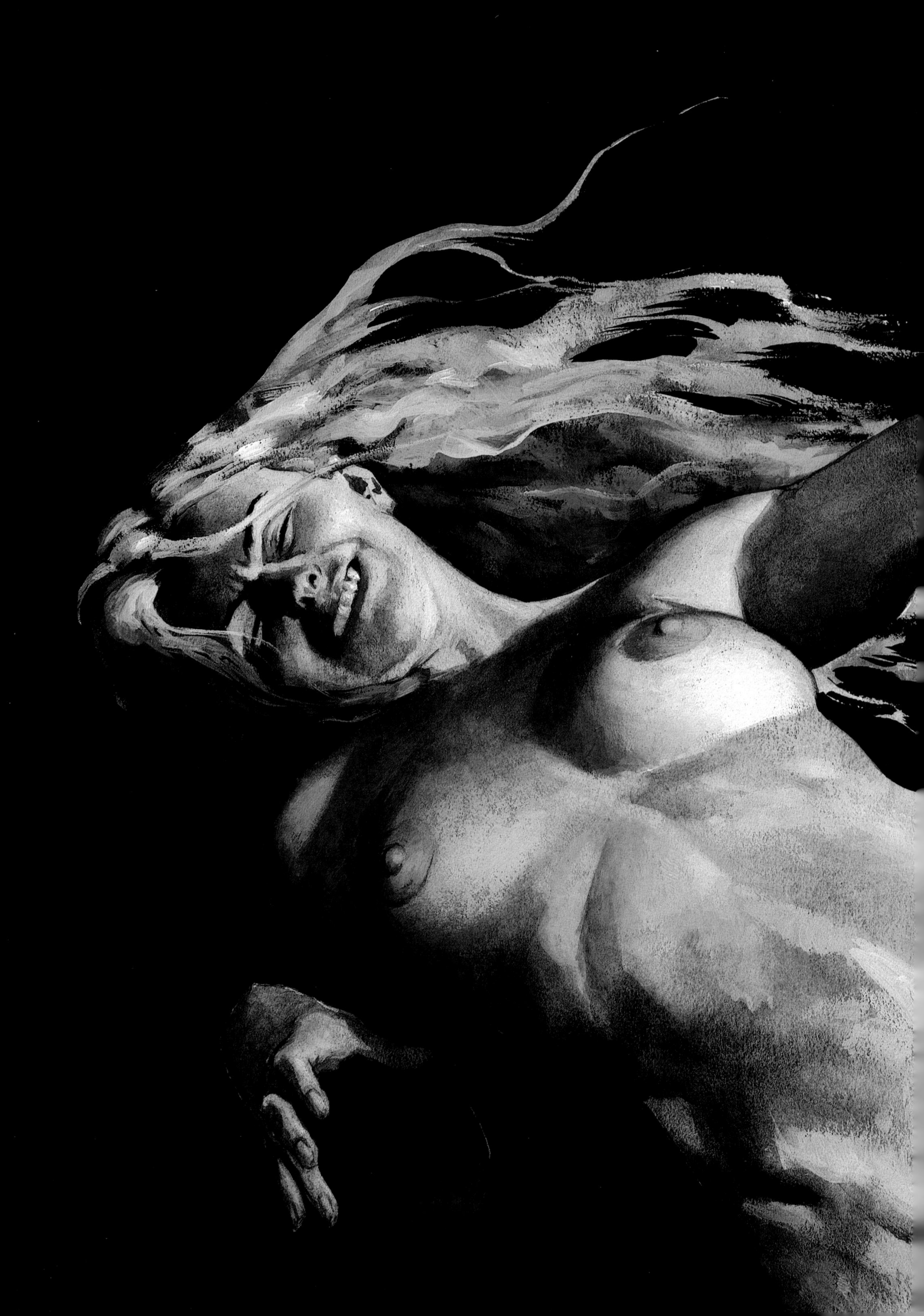

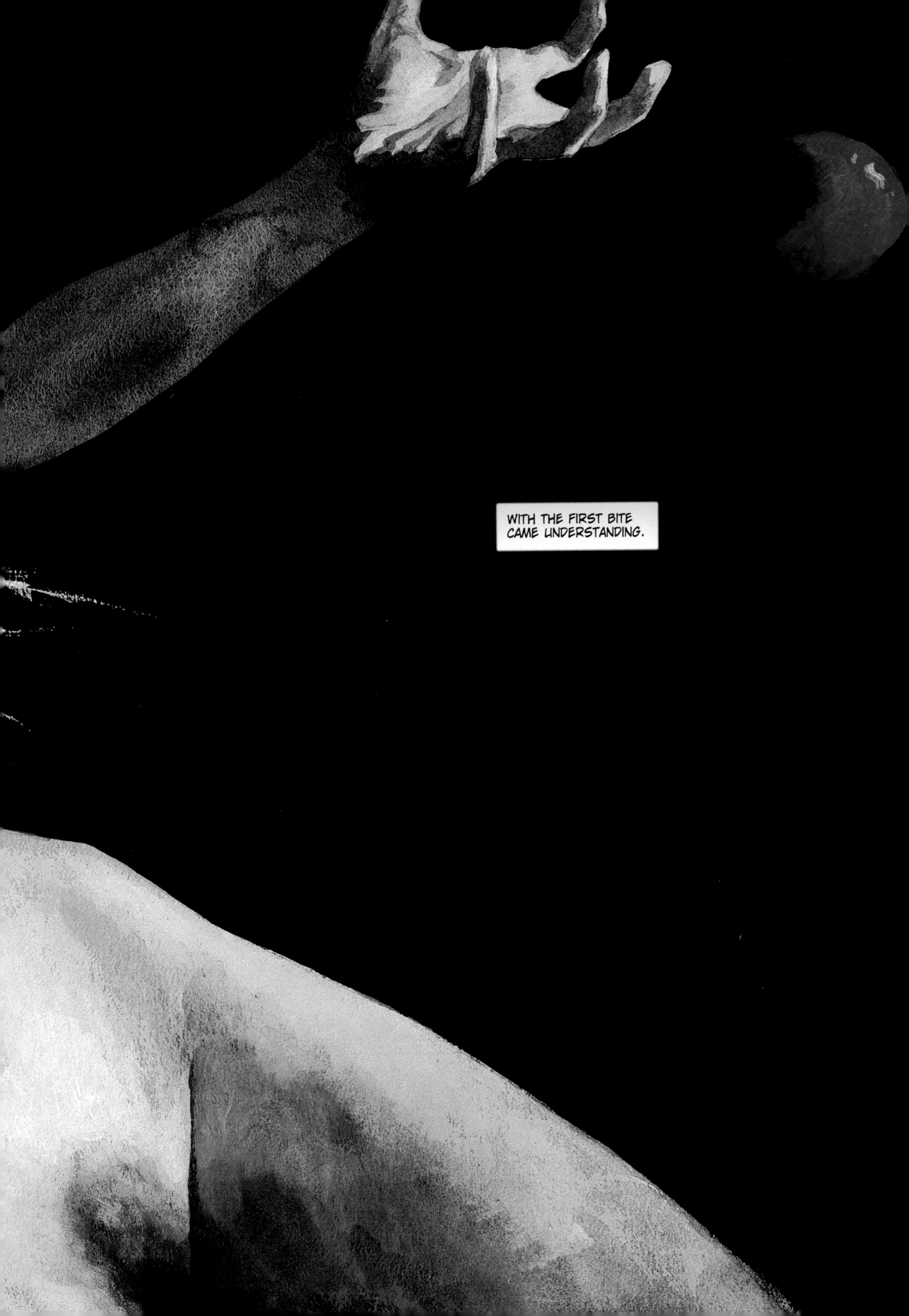
WITH THE FIRST BITE CAME UNDERSTANDING.

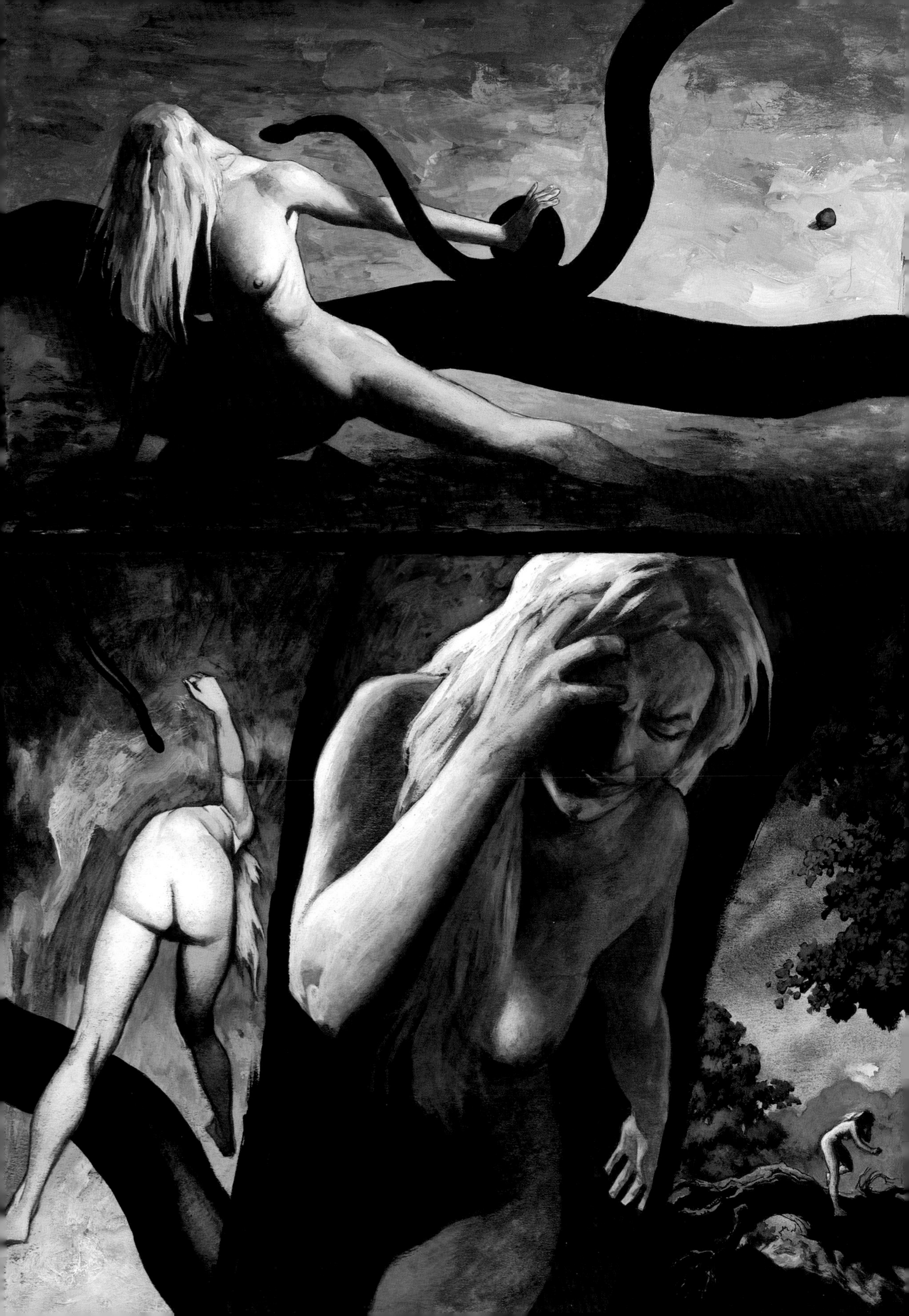

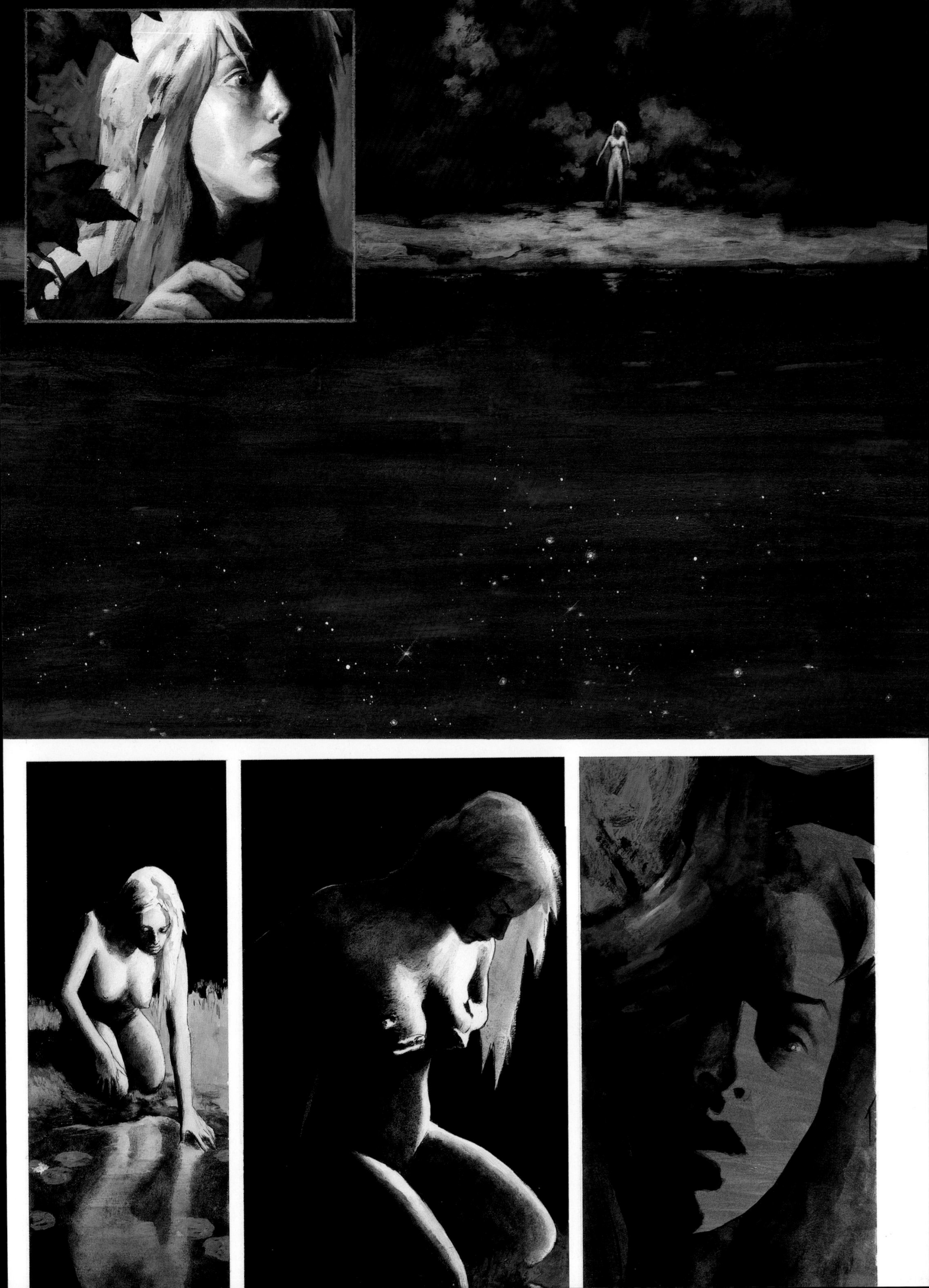

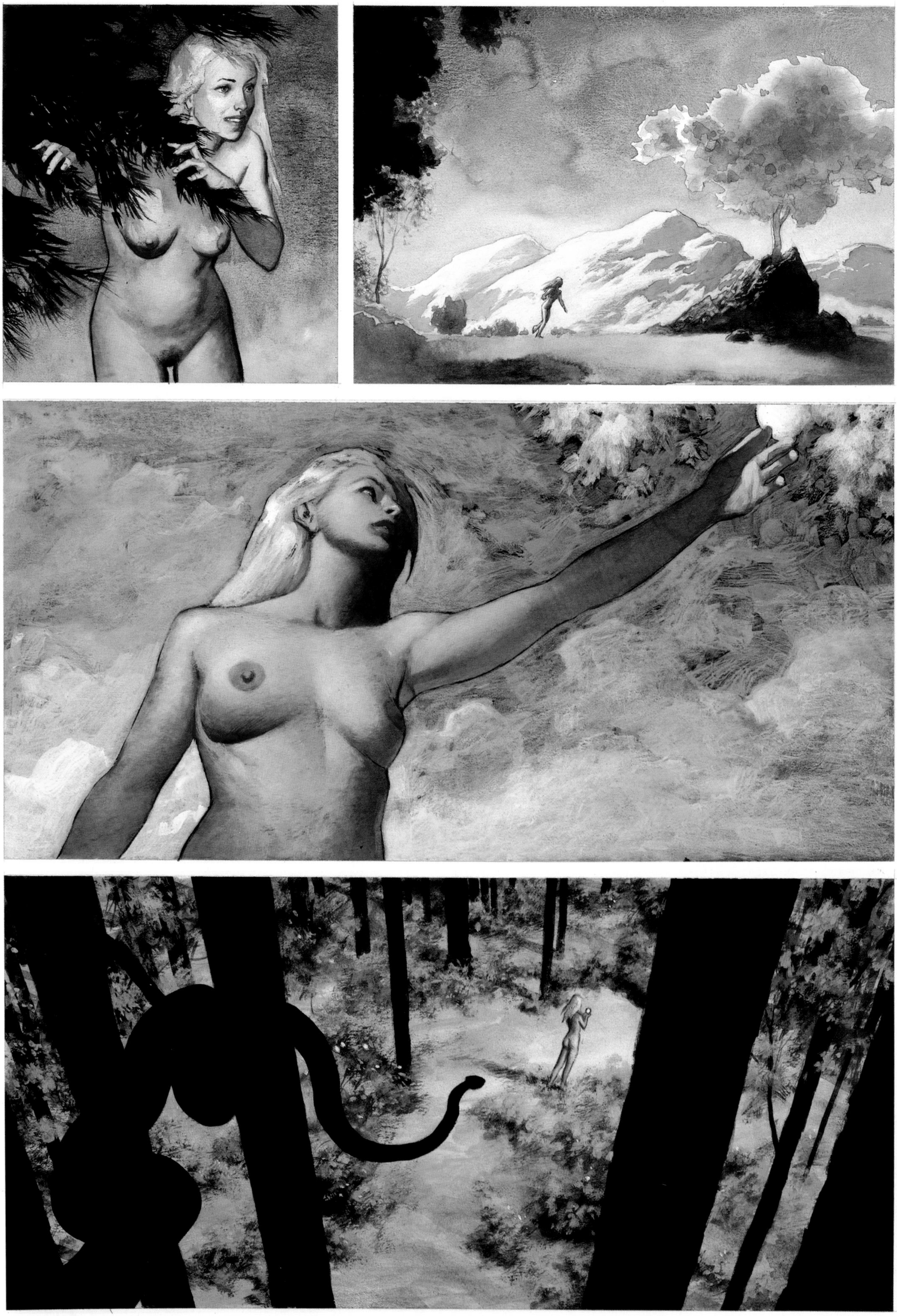

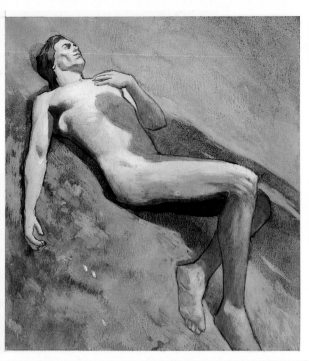

"I ATE OF THE FRUIT THAT WAS FORBIDDEN," SAID THE WOMAN TO THE MAN, "AND DID NOT DIE."

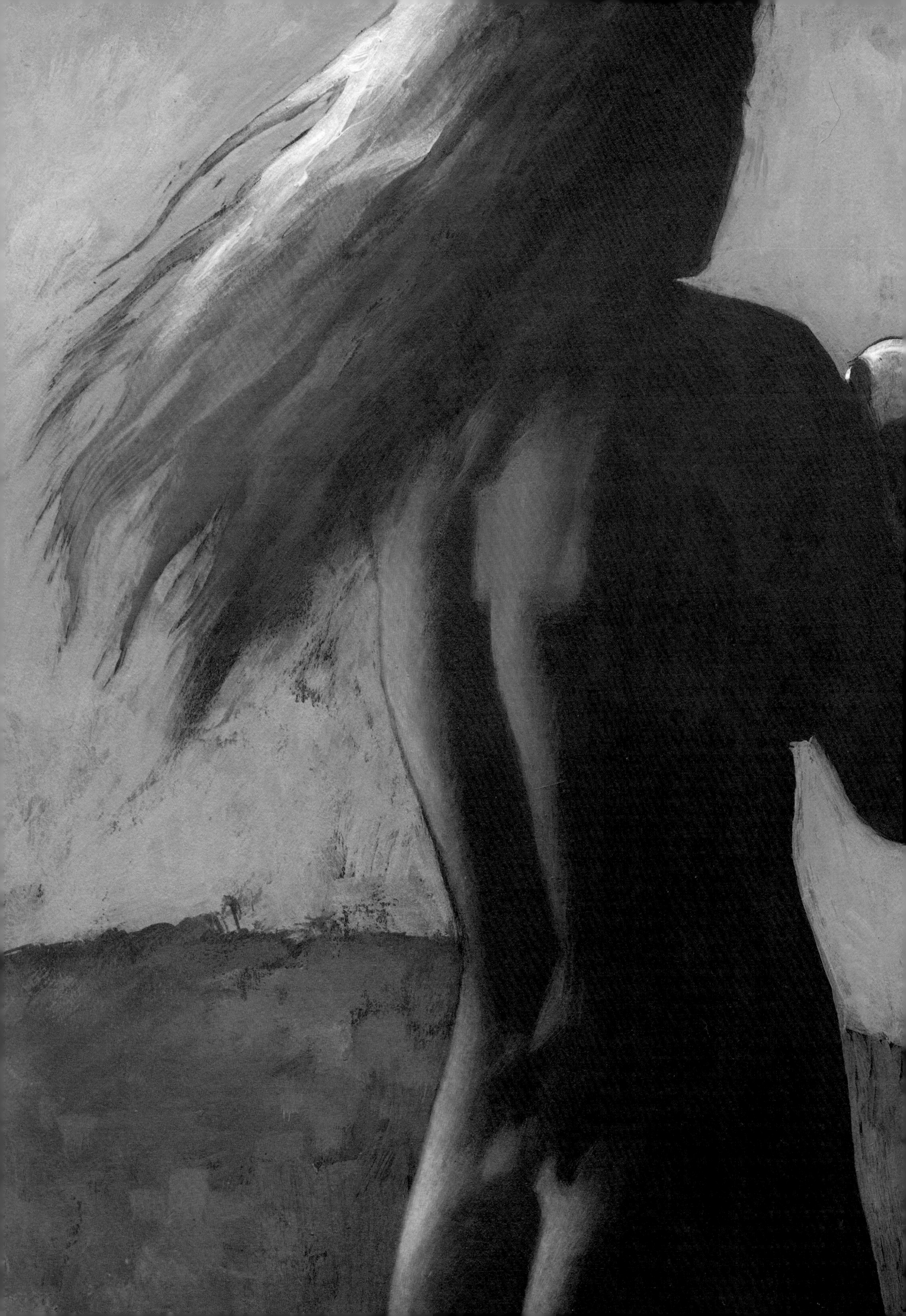

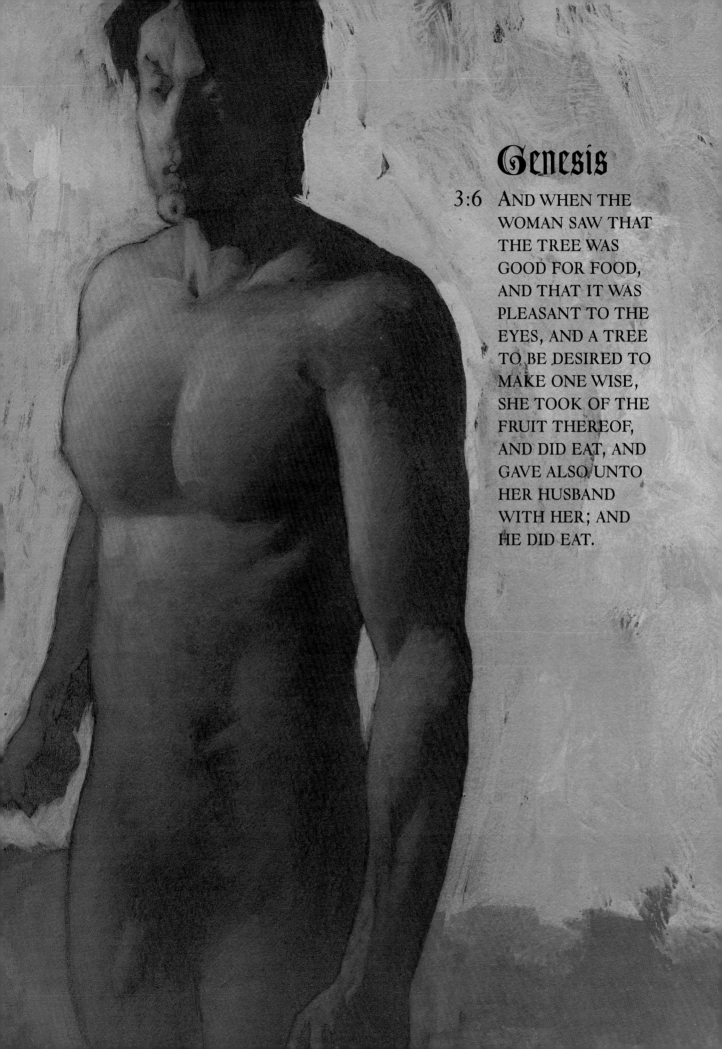

Genesis

3:6 AND WHEN THE WOMAN SAW THAT THE TREE WAS GOOD FOR FOOD, AND THAT IT WAS PLEASANT TO THE EYES, AND A TREE TO BE DESIRED TO MAKE ONE WISE, SHE TOOK OF THE FRUIT THEREOF, AND DID EAT, AND GAVE ALSO UNTO HER HUSBAND WITH HER; AND HE DID EAT.

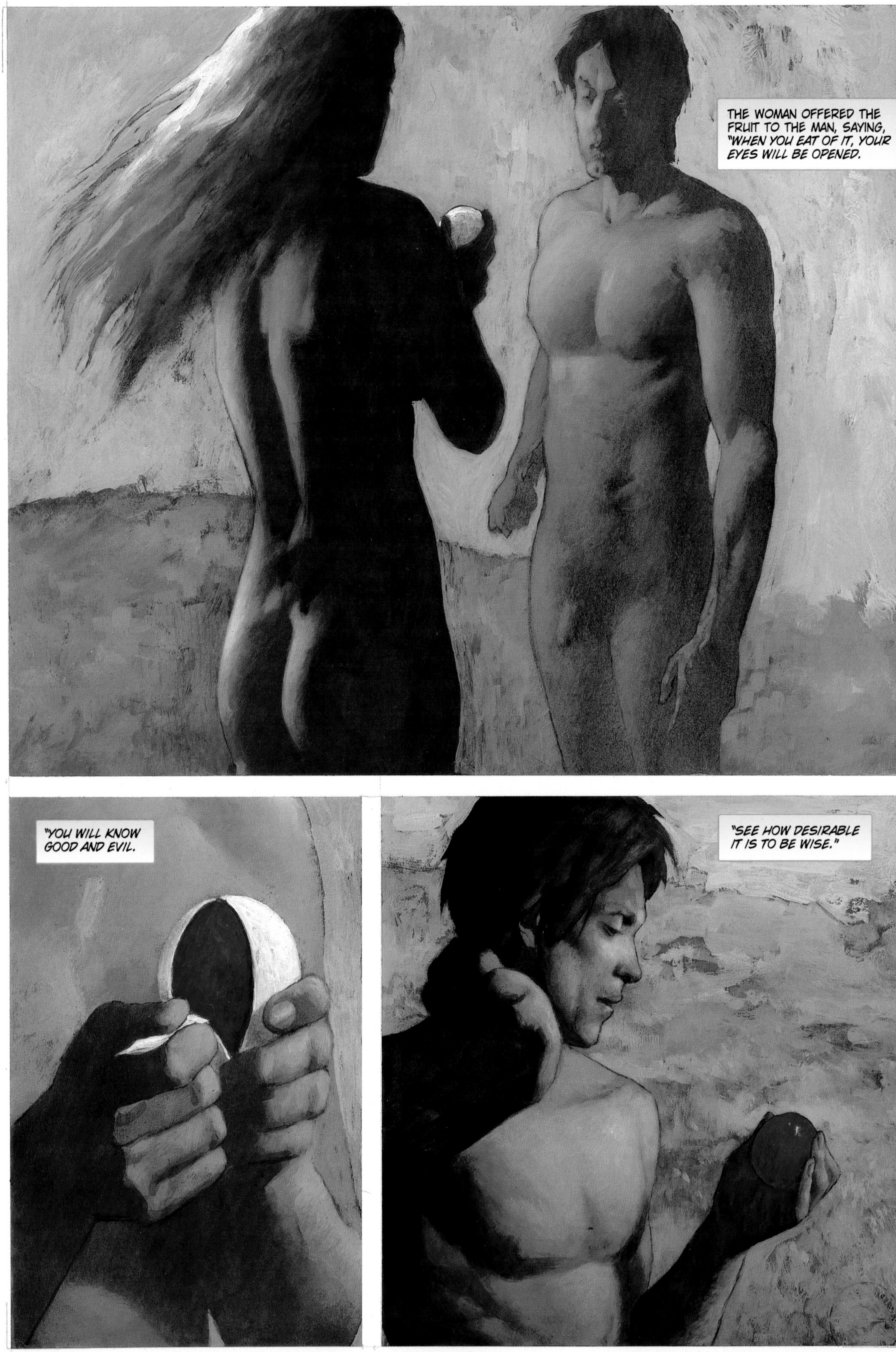
THE WOMAN OFFERED THE FRUIT TO THE MAN, SAYING, "WHEN YOU EAT OF IT, YOUR EYES WILL BE OPENED.
"YOU WILL KNOW GOOD AND EVIL.
"SEE HOW DESIRABLE IT IS TO BE WISE."

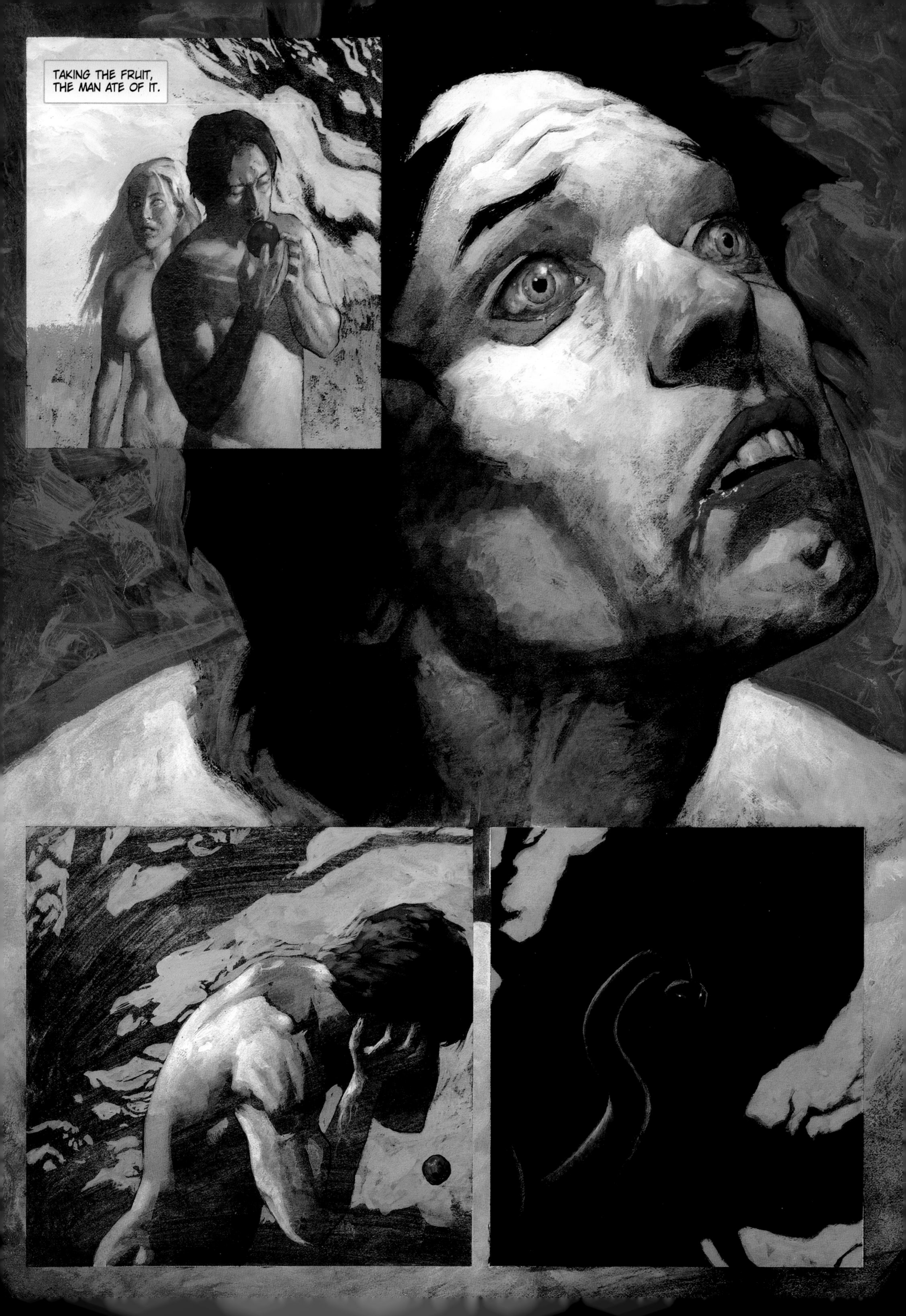
TAKING THE FRUIT, THE MAN ATE OF IT.

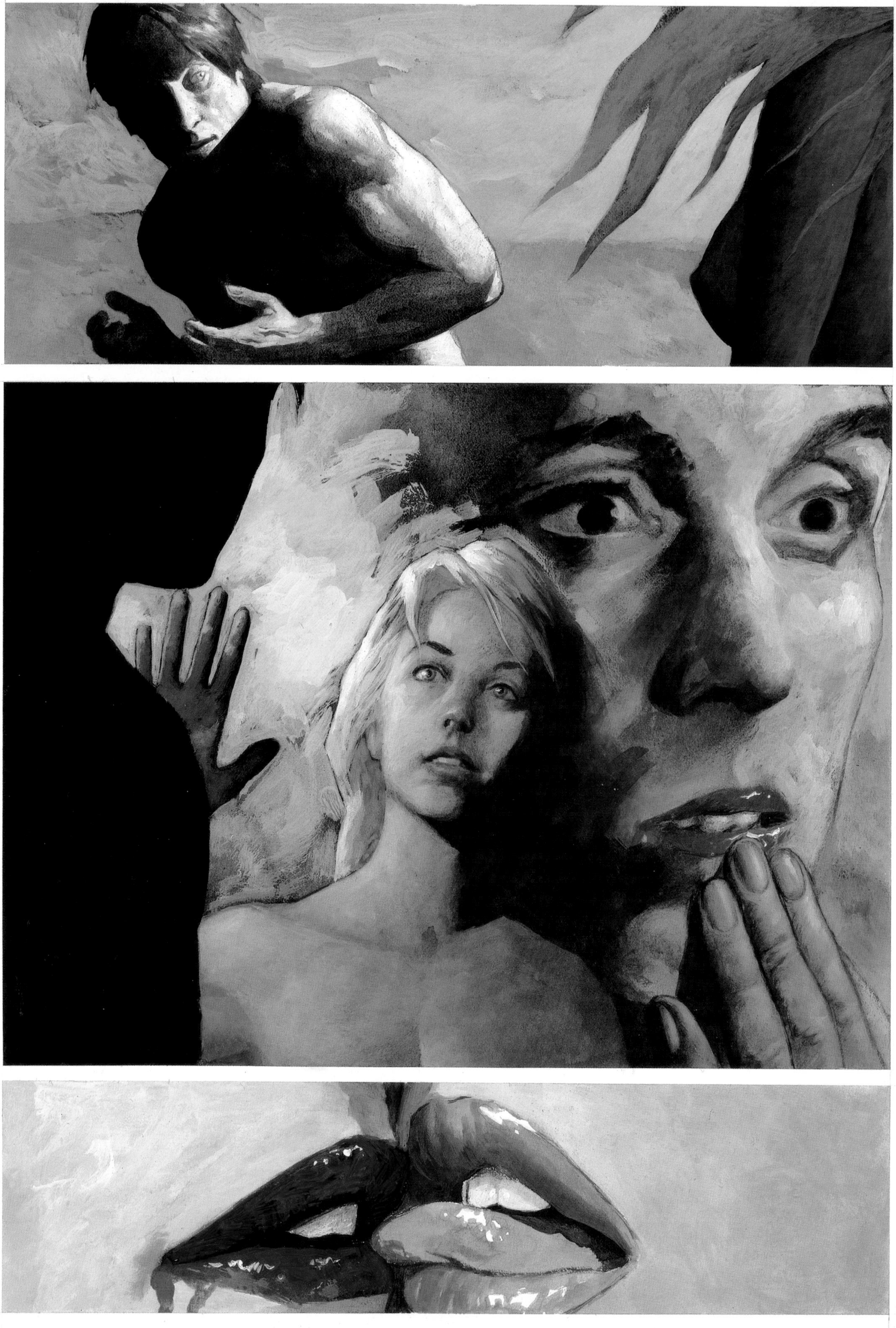

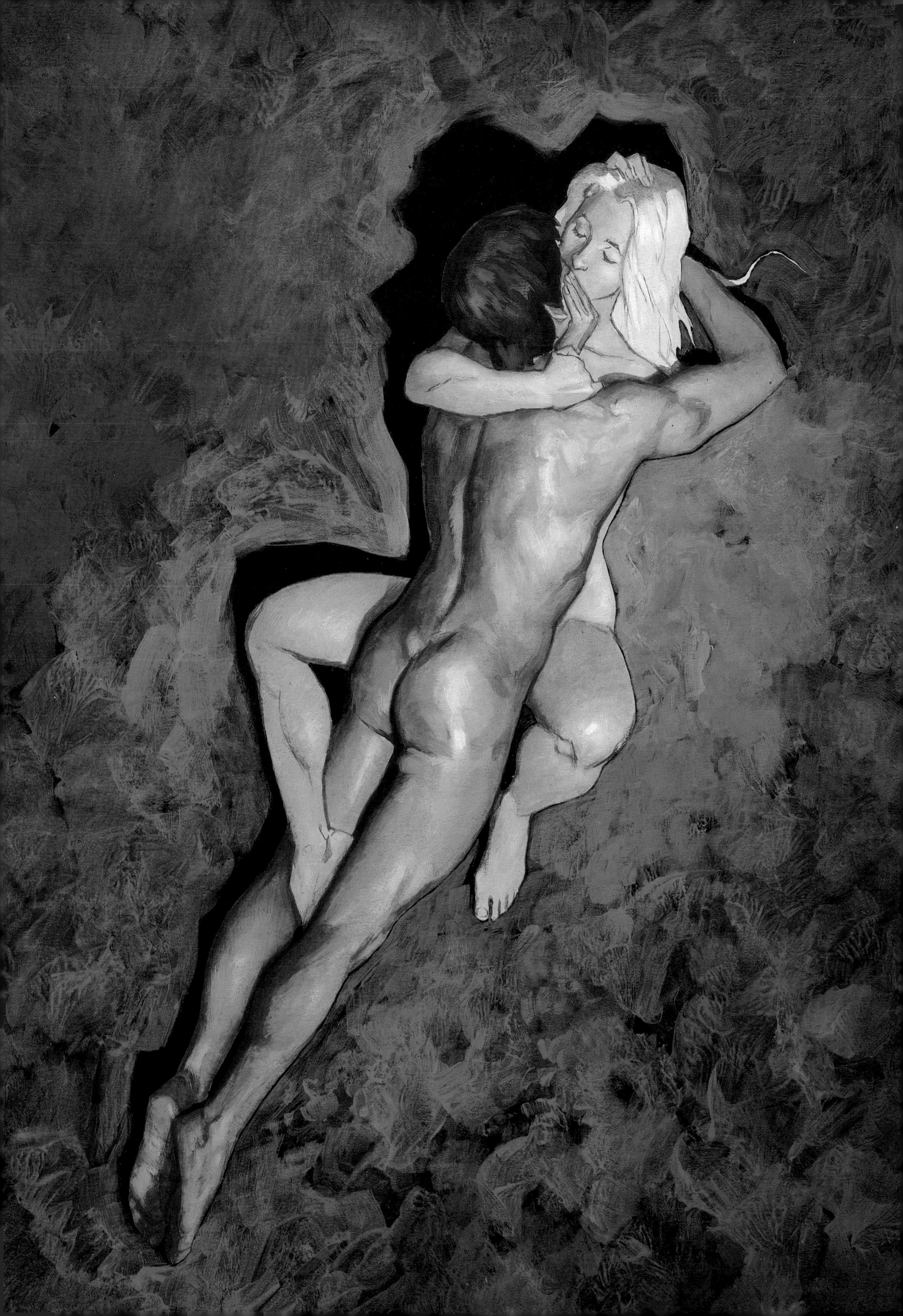

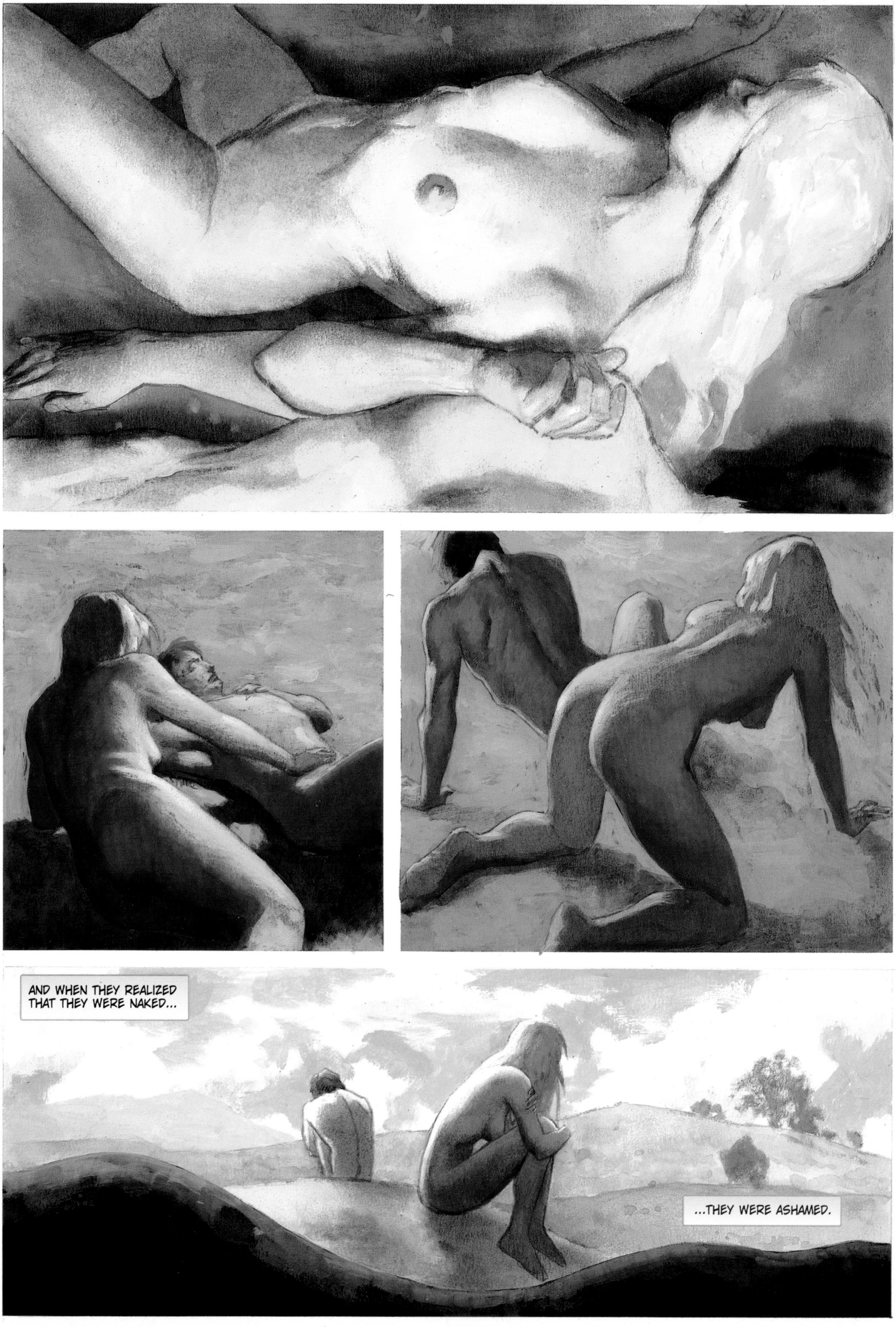
AND WHEN THEY REALIZED THAT THEY WERE NAKED...
...THEY WERE ASHAMED.

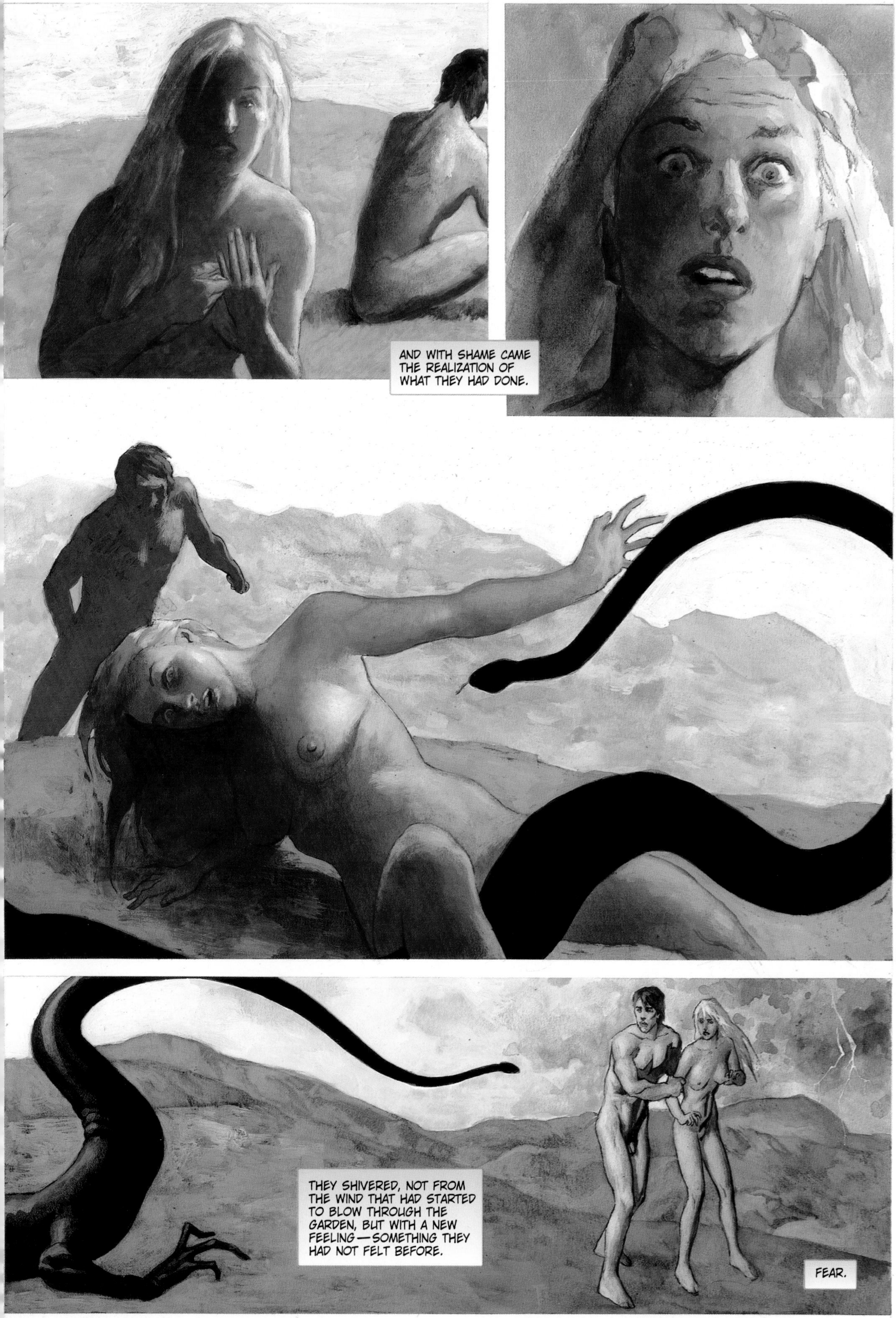
AND WITH SHAME CAME THE REALIZATION OF WHAT THEY HAD DONE.
THEY SHIVERED, NOT FROM THE WIND THAT HAD STARTED TO BLOW THROUGH THE GARDEN, BUT WITH A NEW FEELING—SOMETHING THEY HAD NOT FELT BEFORE.
FEAR.

Genesis

3:9 And the LORD GOD called unto Adam, and said unto him, "Where art thou?"

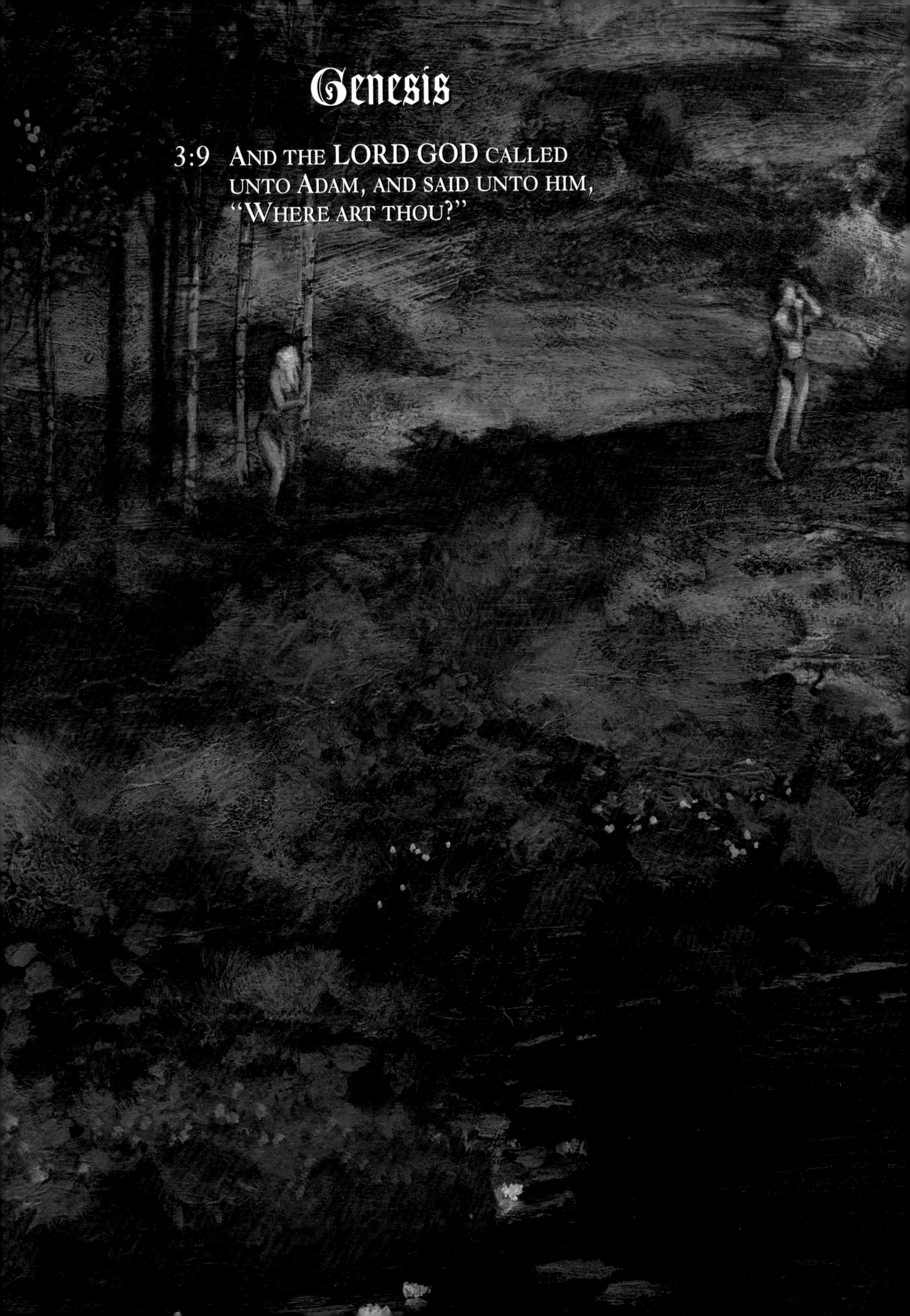

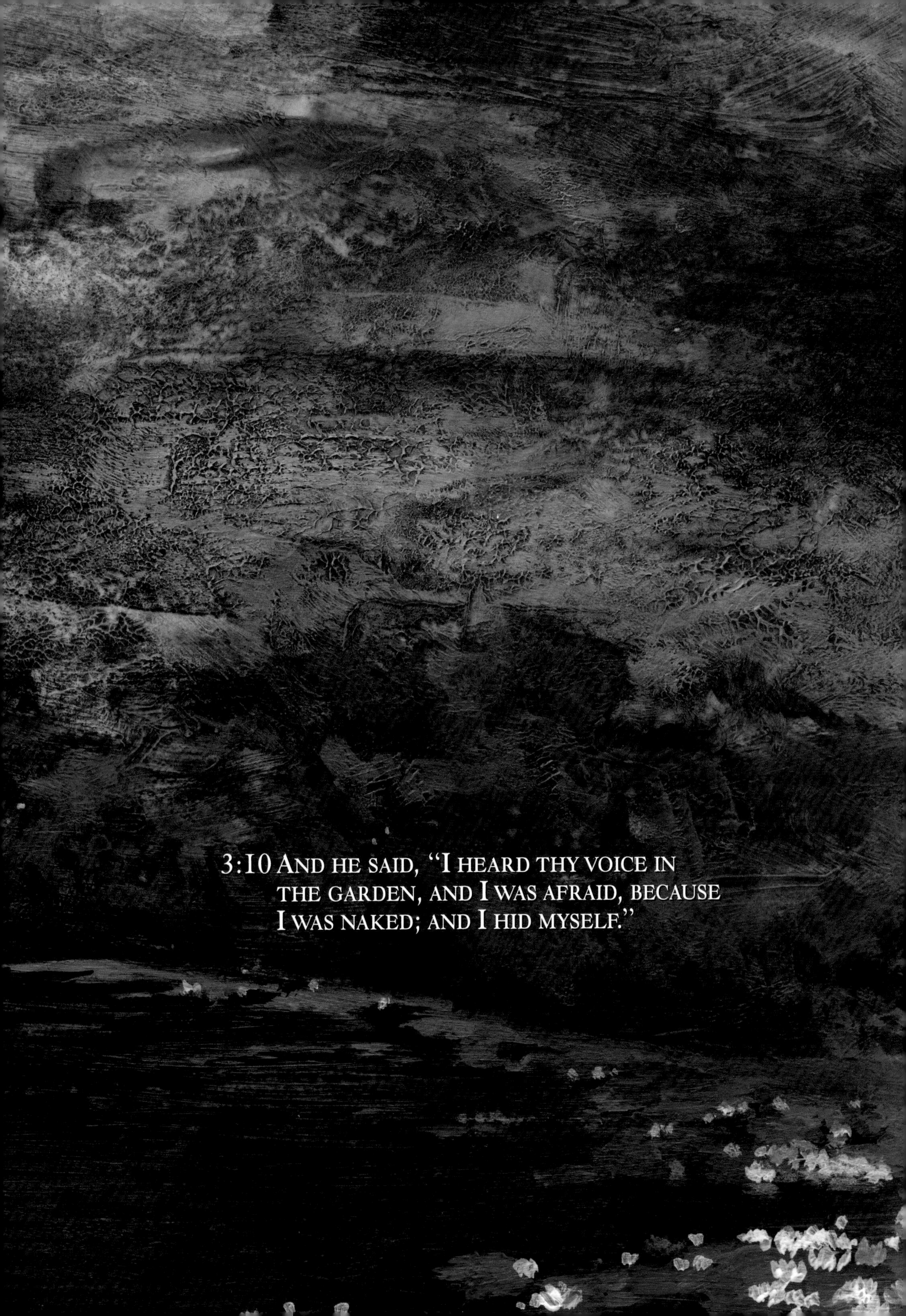

3:10 And he said, "I heard thy voice in
the garden, and I was afraid, because
I was naked; and I hid myself."

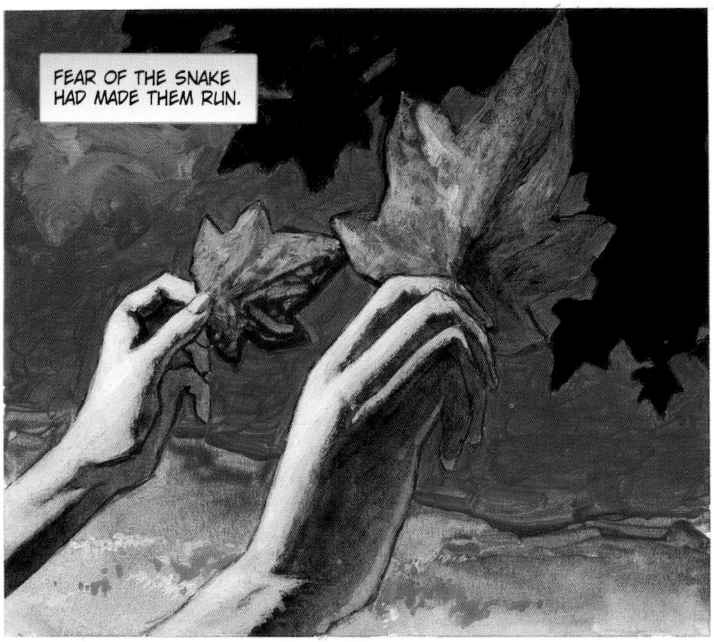
FEAR OF THE SNAKE HAD MADE THEM RUN.

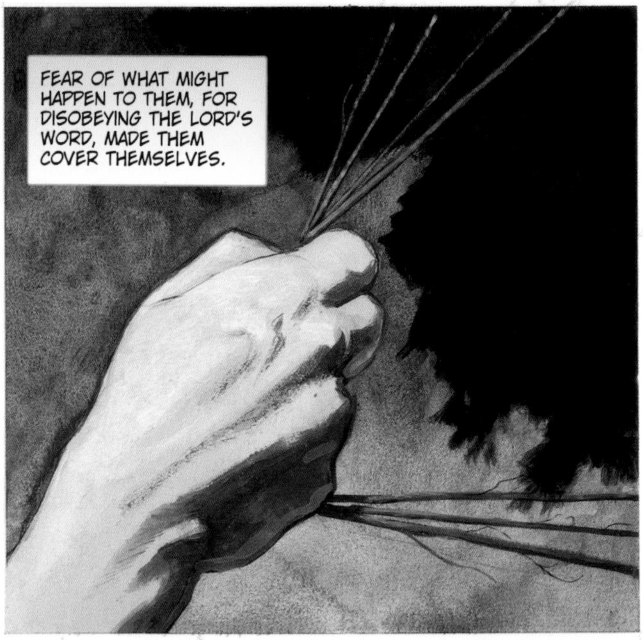
FEAR OF WHAT MIGHT HAPPEN TO THEM, FOR DISOBEYING THE LORD'S WORD, MADE THEM COVER THEMSELVES.

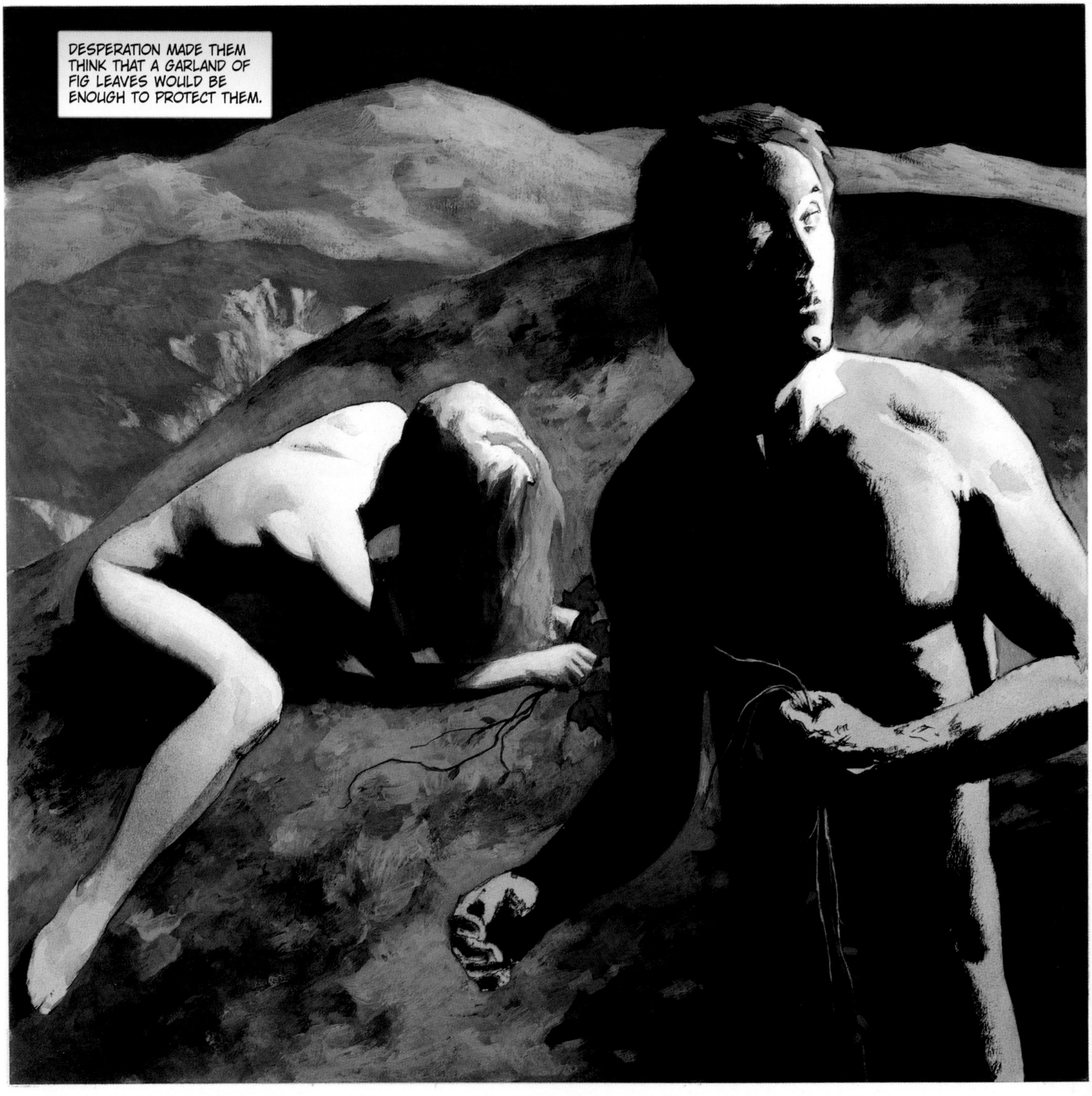
DESPERATION MADE THEM THINK THAT A GARLAND OF FIG LEAVES WOULD BE ENOUGH TO PROTECT THEM.

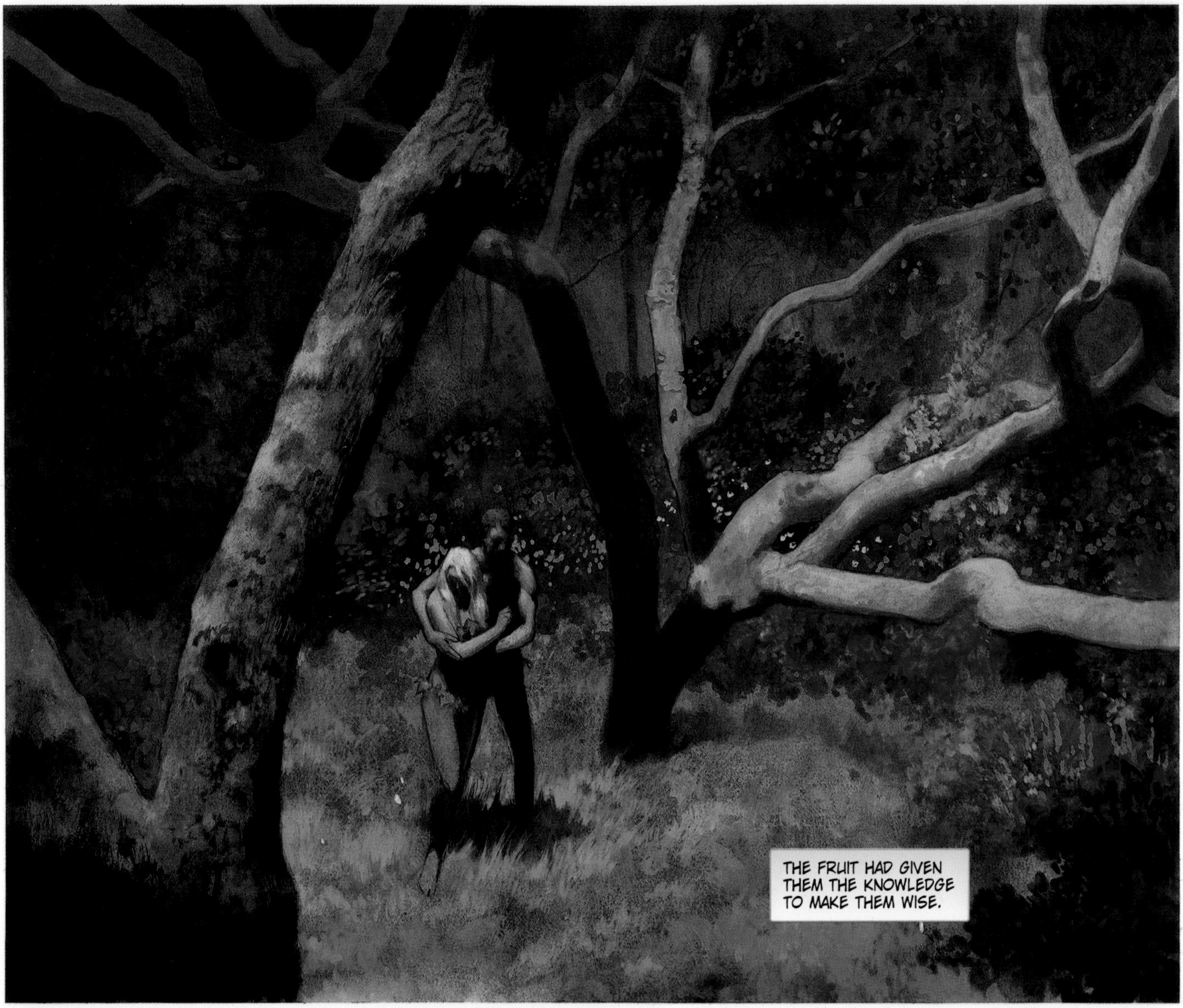
THE FRUIT HAD GIVEN
THEM THE KNOWLEDGE
TO MAKE THEM WISE.

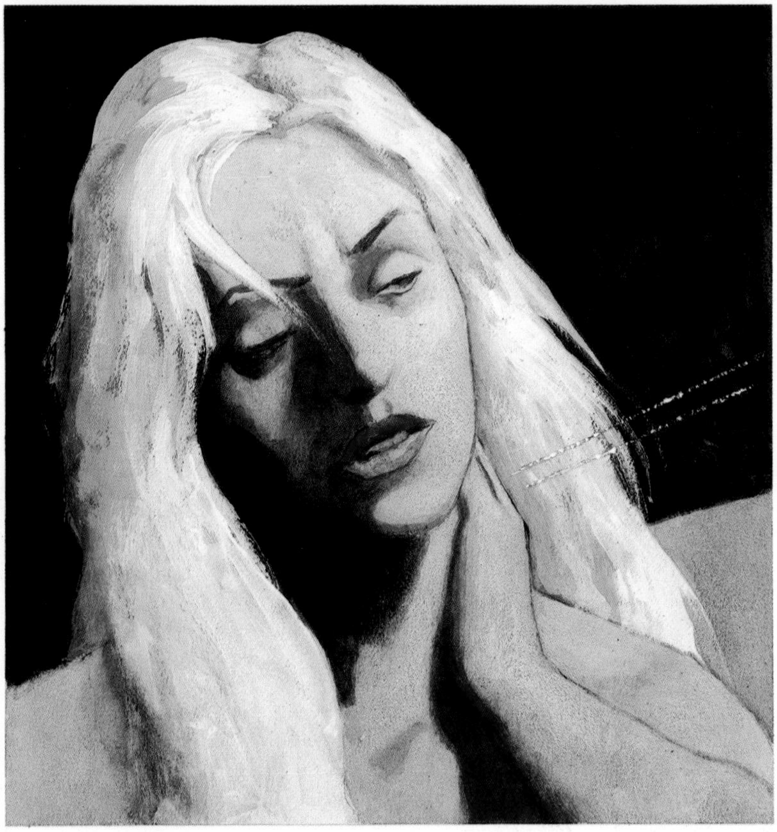

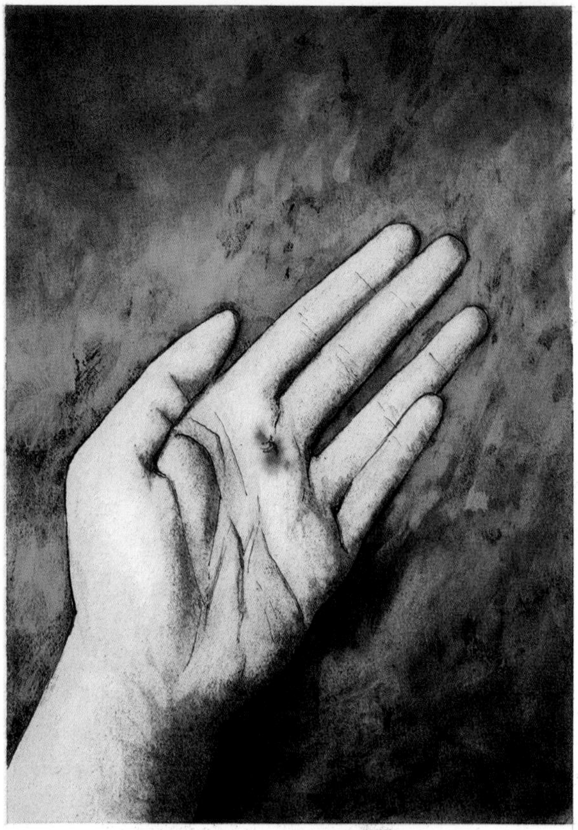

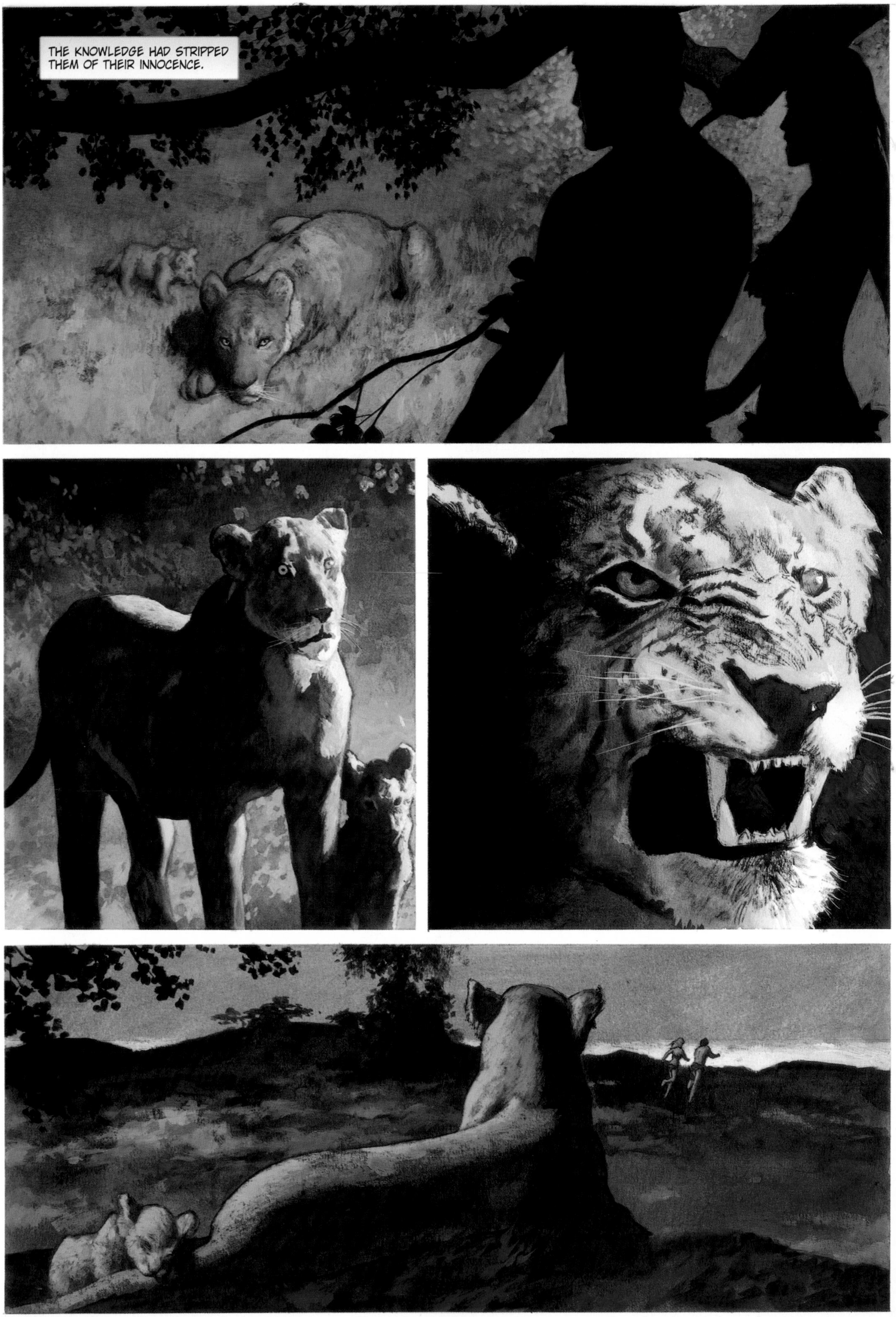
THE KNOWLEDGE HAD STRIPPED THEM OF THEIR INNOCENCE.

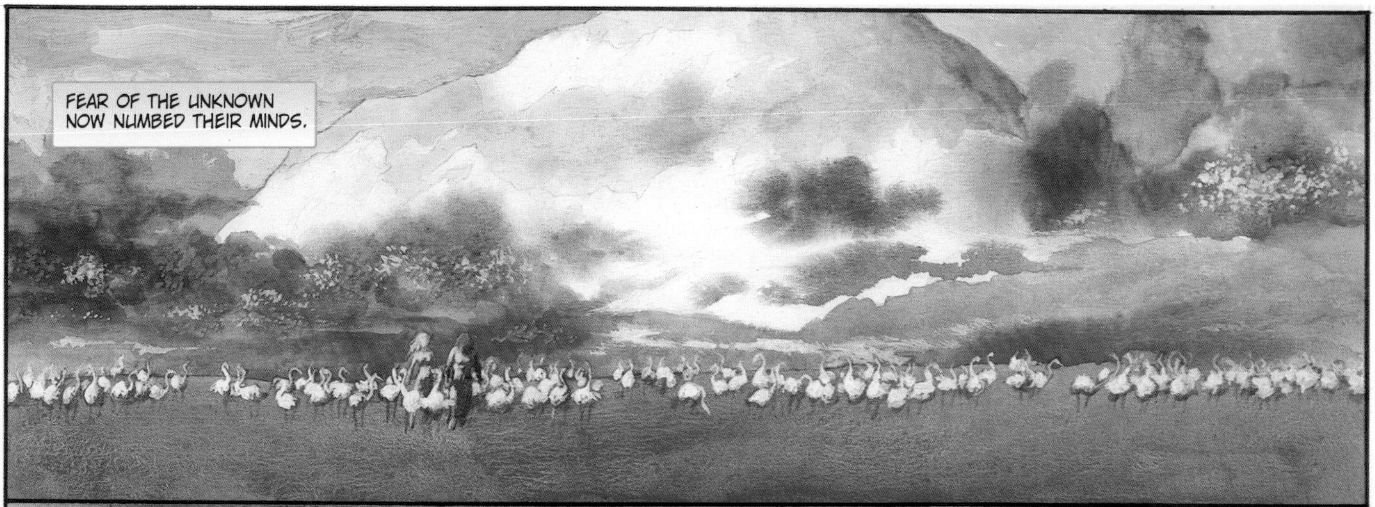
FEAR OF THE UNKNOWN
NOW NUMBED THEIR MINDS.

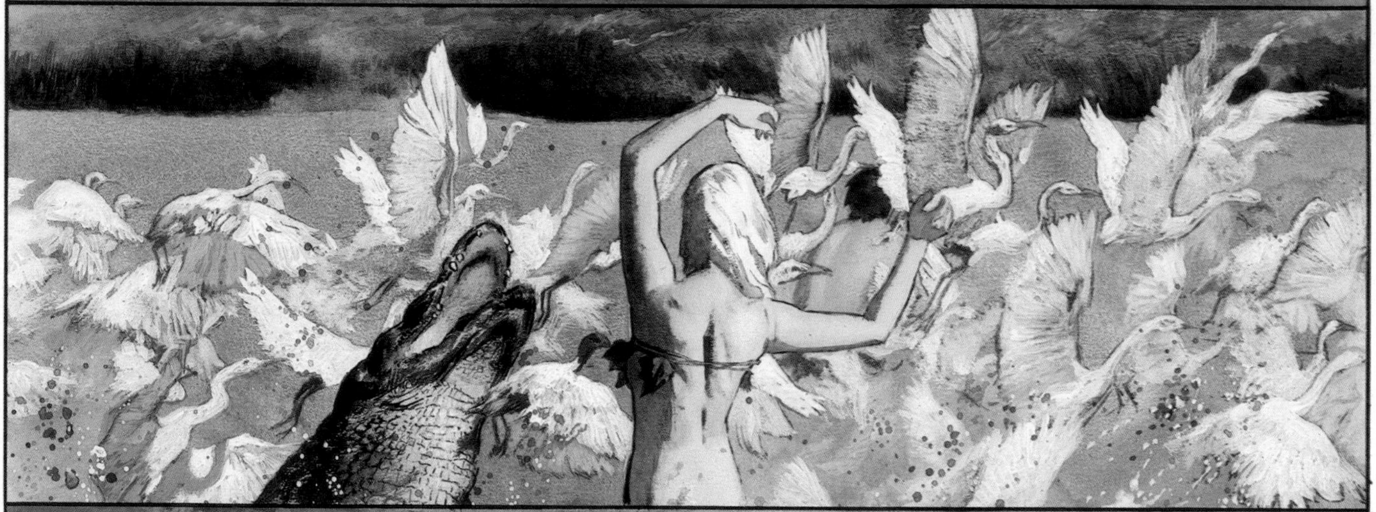

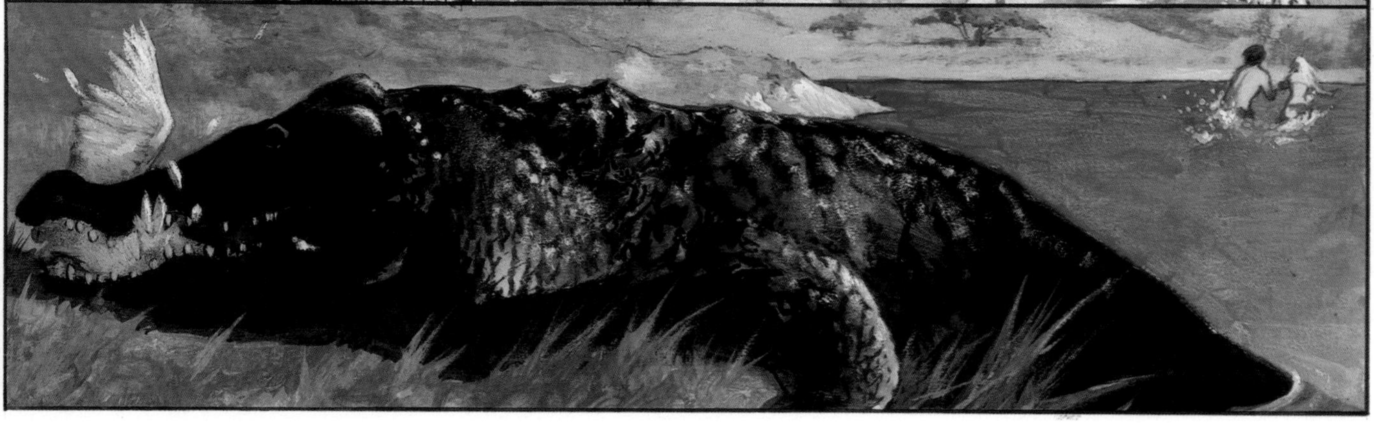

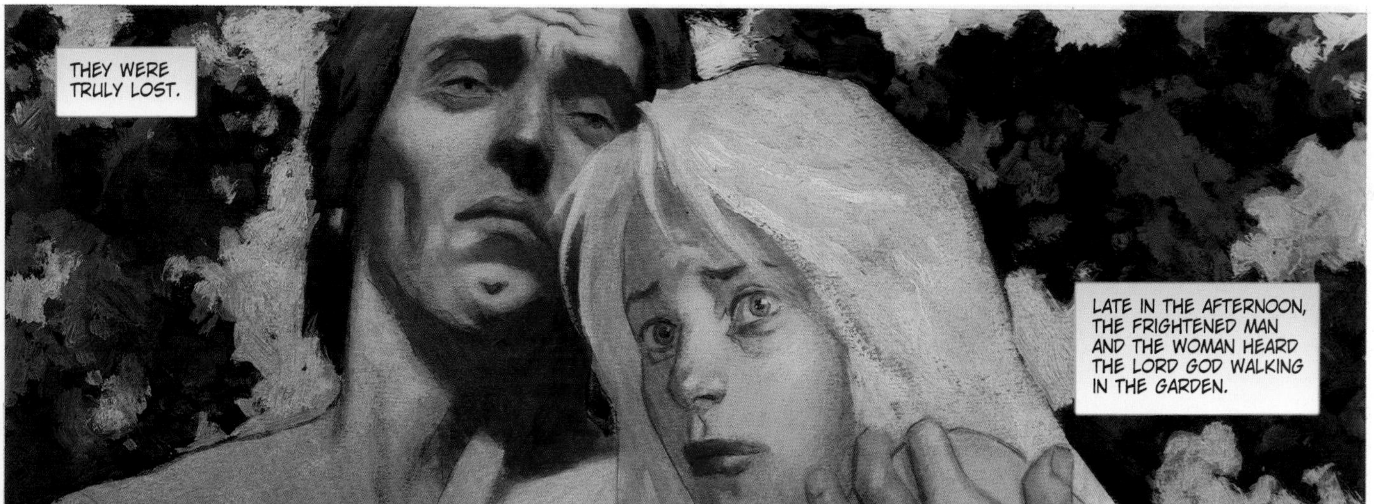
THEY WERE
TRULY LOST.
LATE IN THE AFTERNOON,
THE FRIGHTENED MAN
AND THE WOMAN HEARD
THE LORD GOD WALKING
IN THE GARDEN.

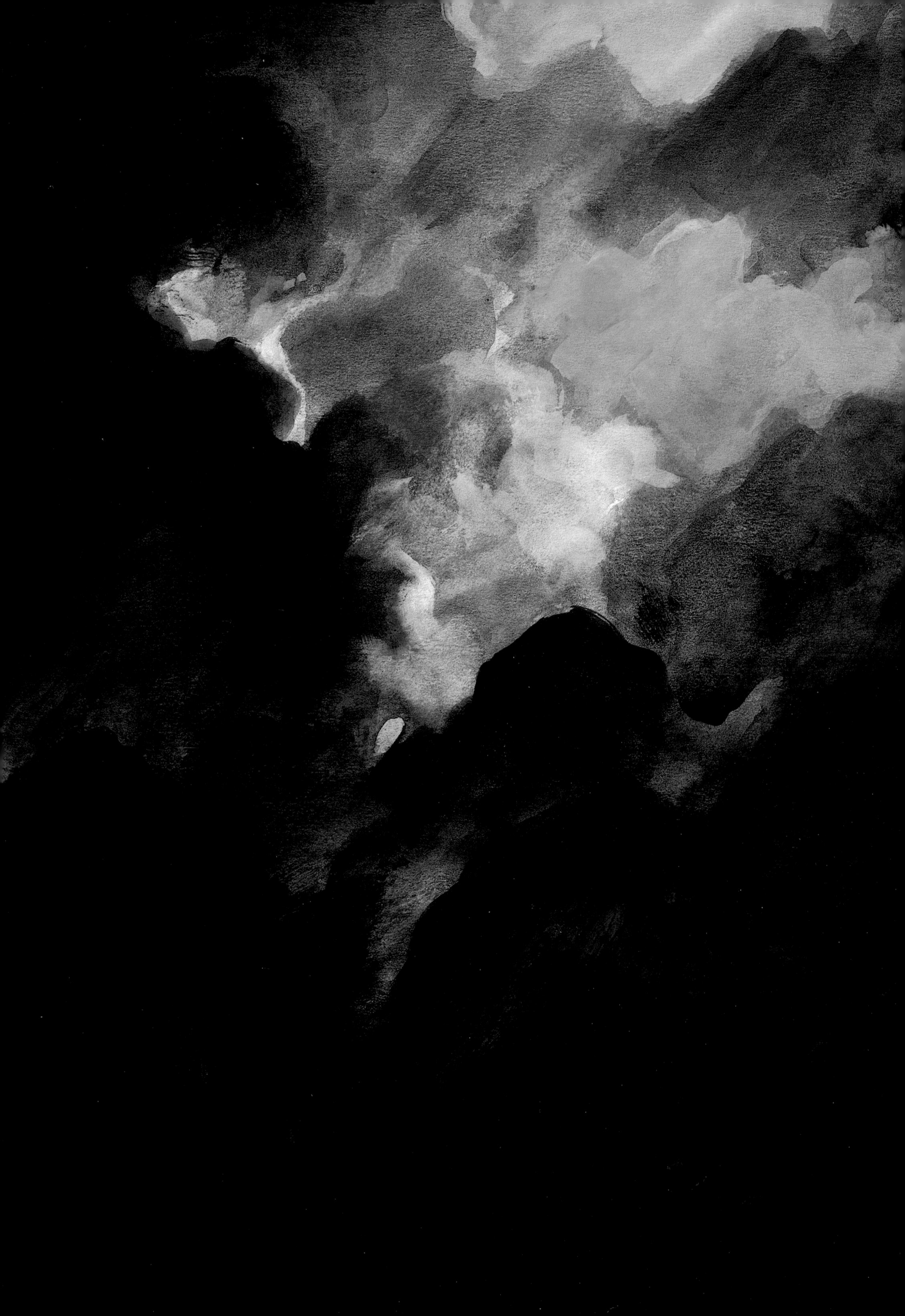

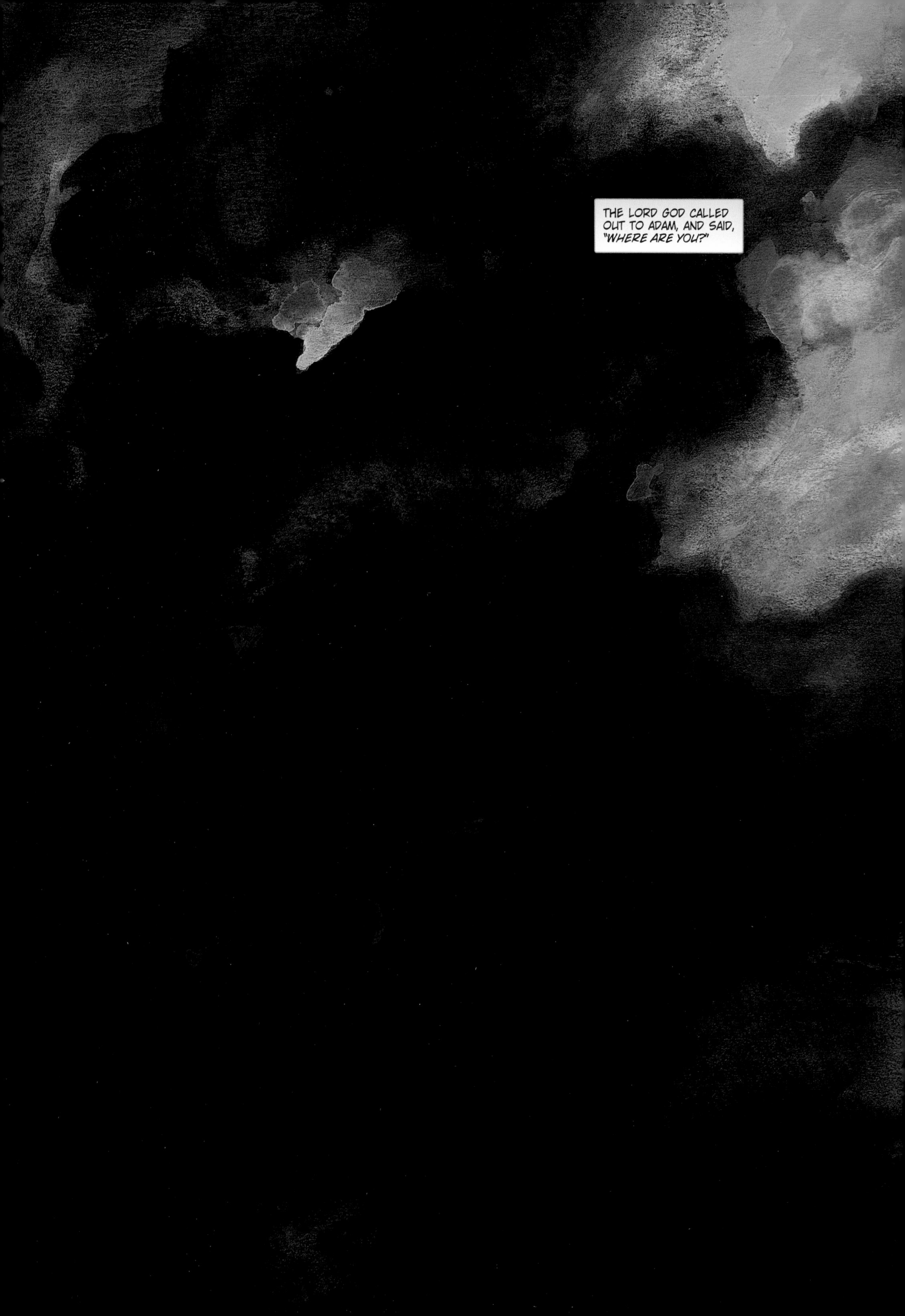
THE LORD GOD CALLED OUT TO ADAM, AND SAID, *"WHERE ARE YOU?"*

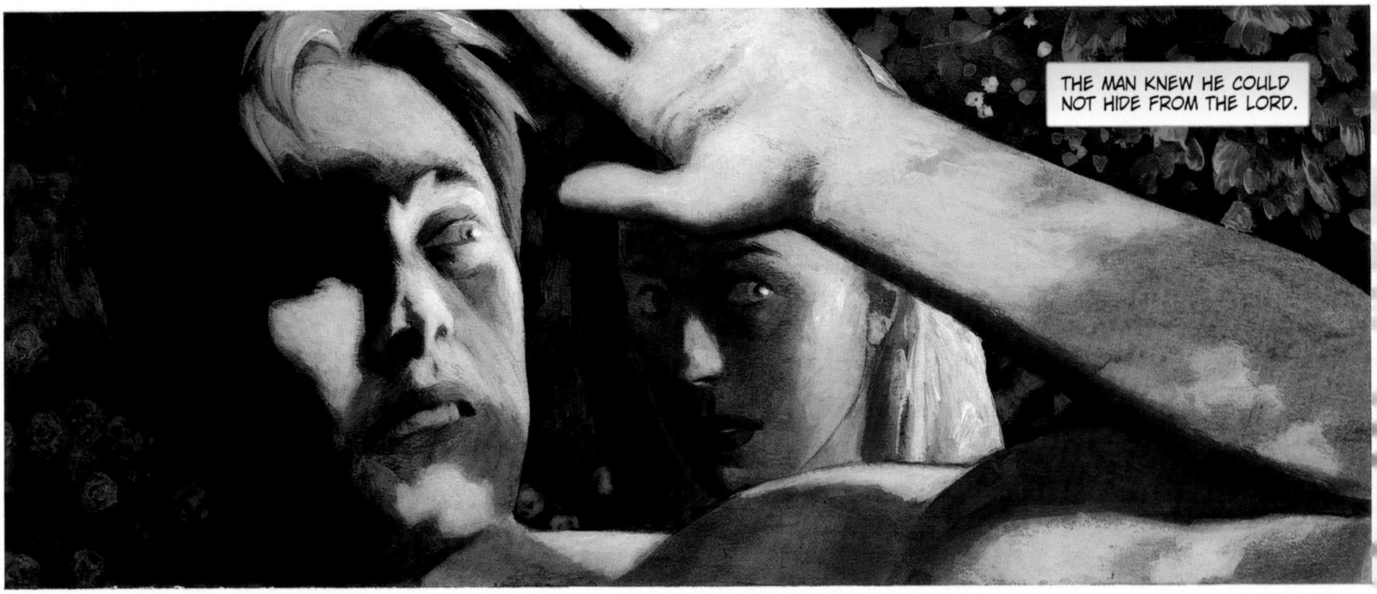
THE MAN KNEW HE COULD NOT HIDE FROM THE LORD.

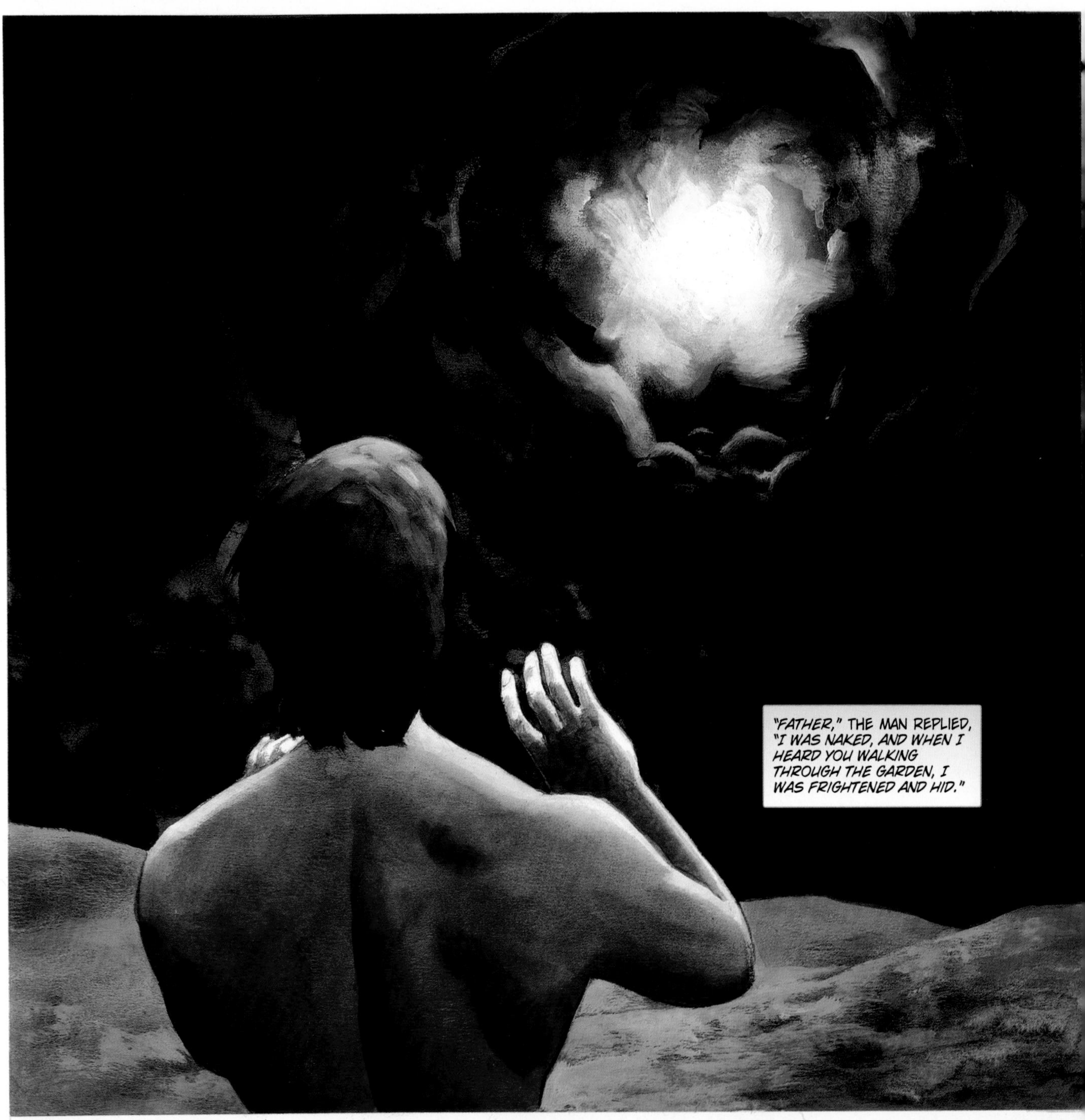
"FATHER," THE MAN REPLIED, "I WAS NAKED, AND WHEN I HEARD YOU WALKING THROUGH THE GARDEN, I WAS FRIGHTENED AND HID."

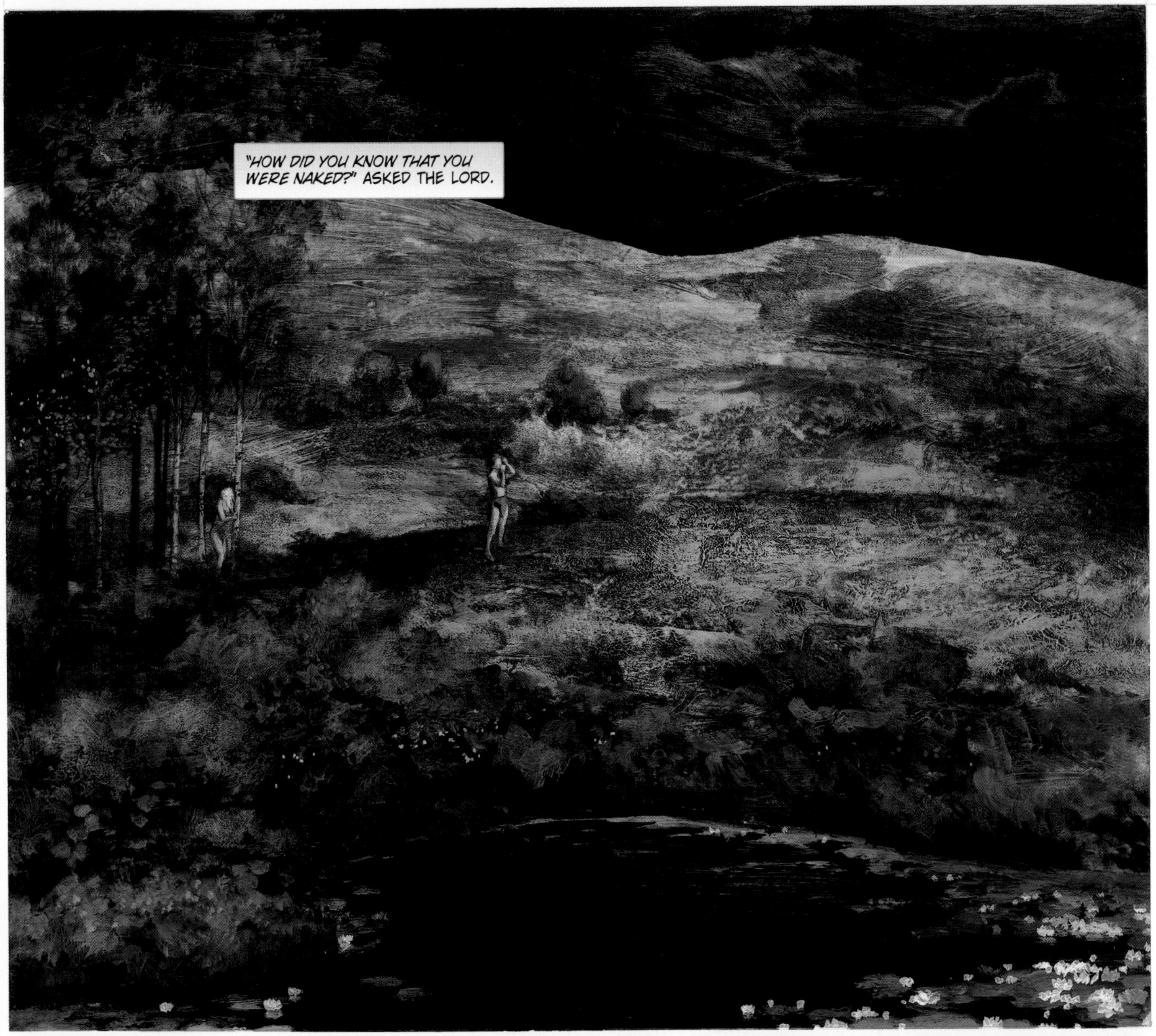
"HOW DID YOU KNOW THAT YOU WERE NAKED?" ASKED THE LORD.

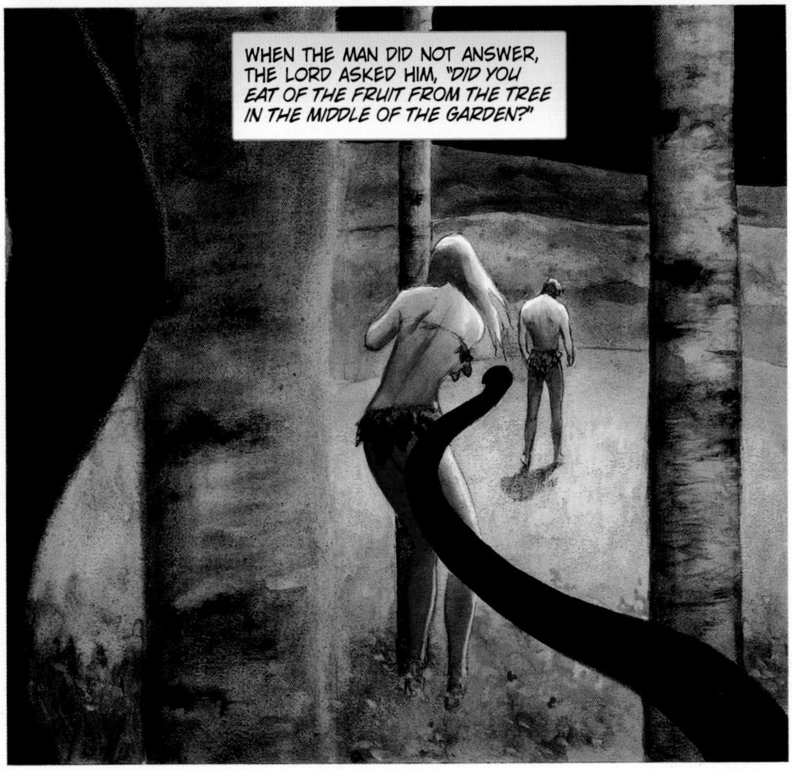
WHEN THE MAN DID NOT ANSWER, THE LORD ASKED HIM, "DID YOU EAT OF THE FRUIT FROM THE TREE IN THE MIDDLE OF THE GARDEN?"

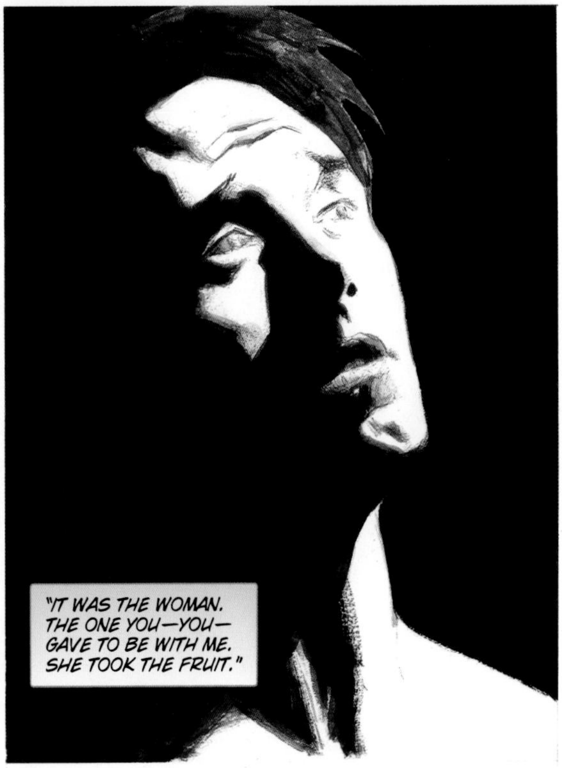
"IT WAS THE WOMAN. THE ONE YOU—YOU—GAVE TO BE WITH ME. SHE TOOK THE FRUIT."

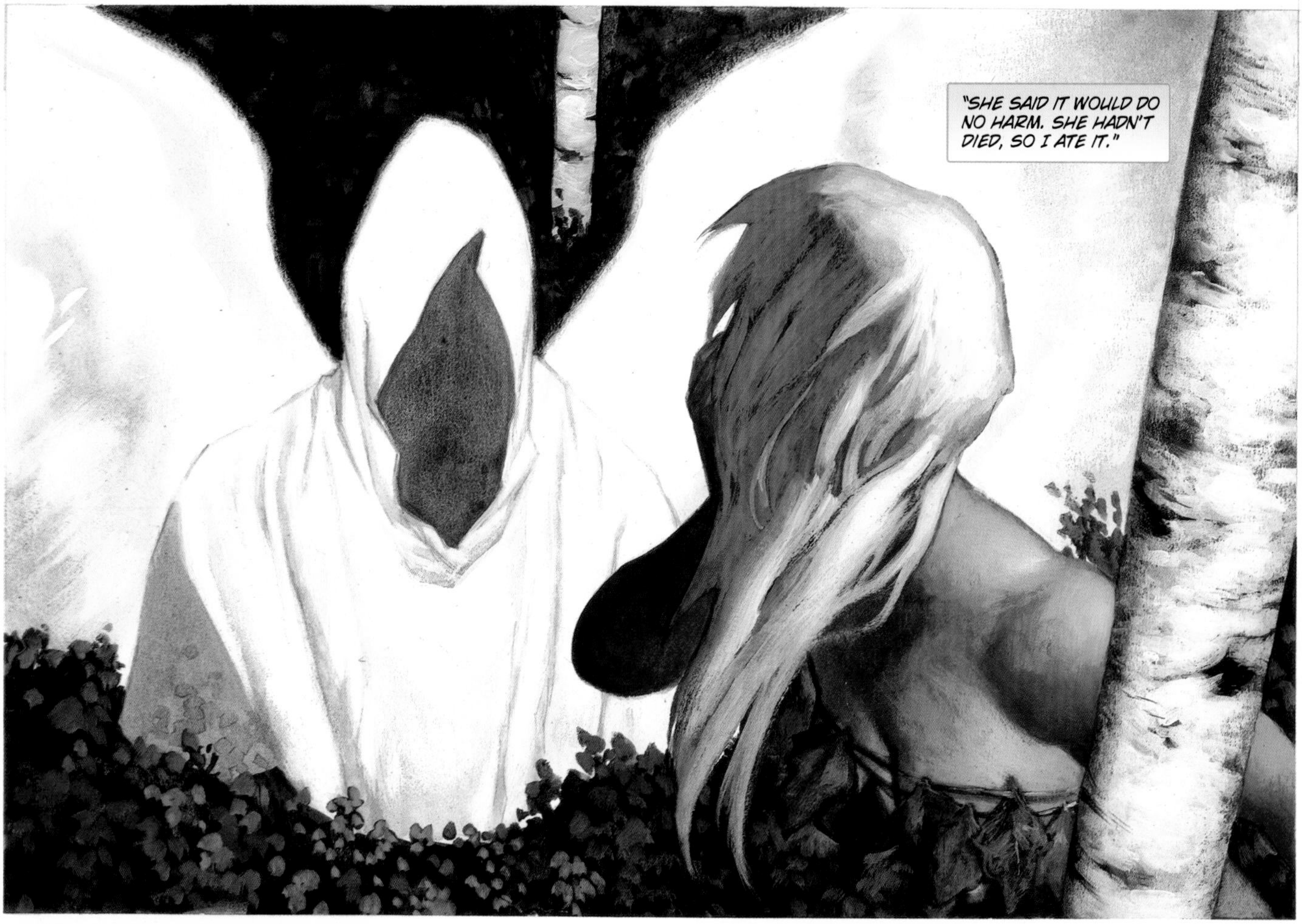
"SHE SAID IT WOULD DO NO HARM. SHE HADN'T DIED, SO I ATE IT."

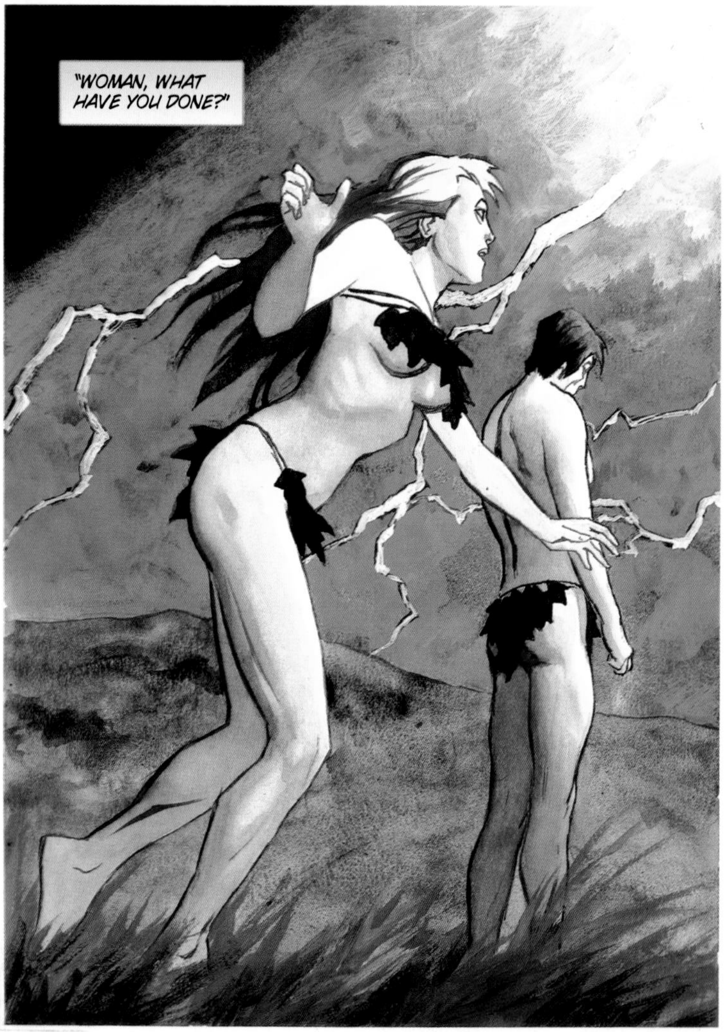
"WOMAN, WHAT HAVE YOU DONE?"

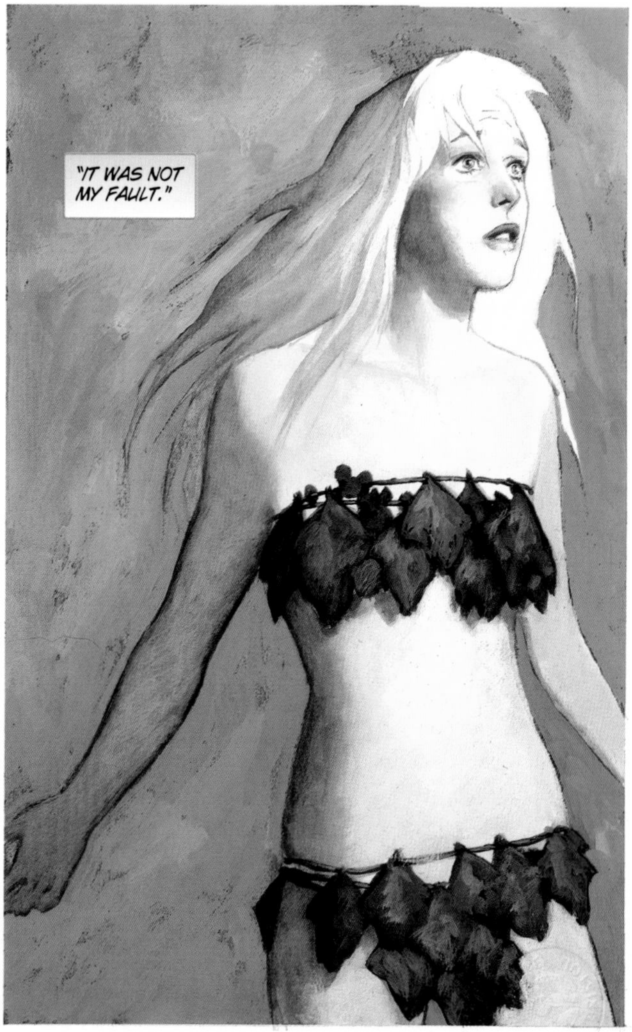
"IT WAS NOT MY FAULT."

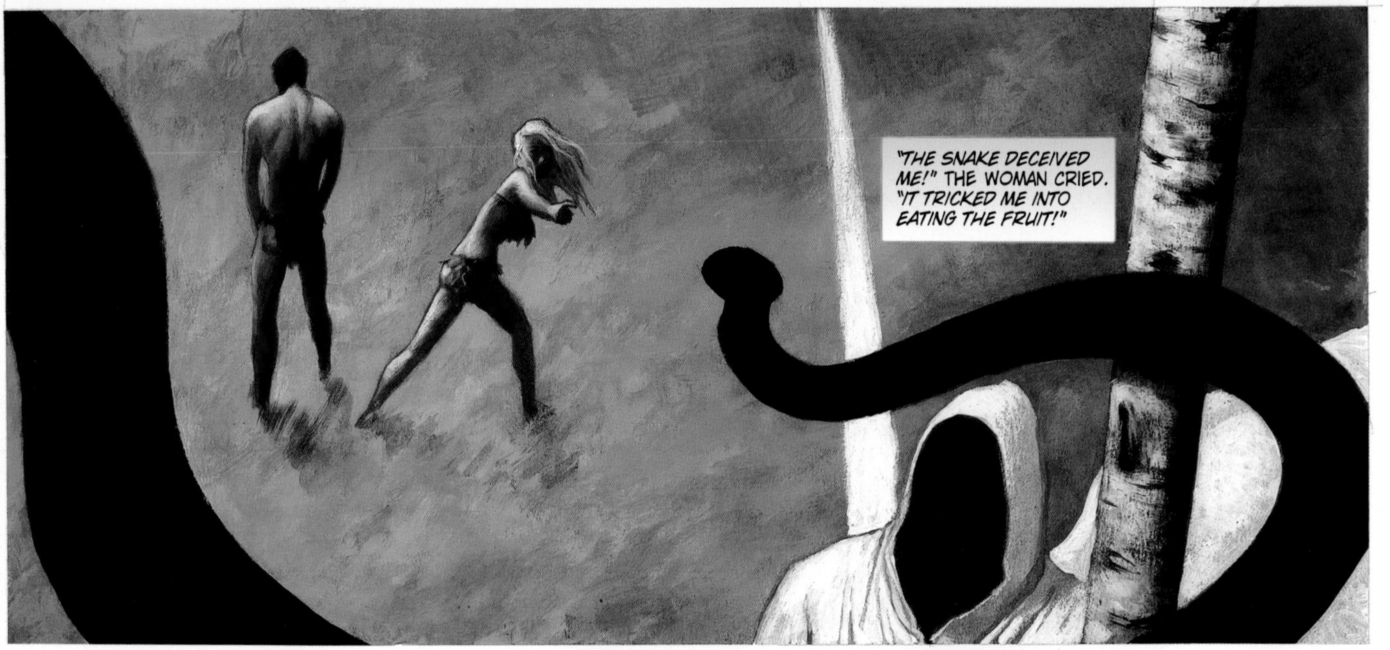
"THE SNAKE DECEIVED ME!" THE WOMAN CRIED. "IT TRICKED ME INTO EATING THE FRUIT!"

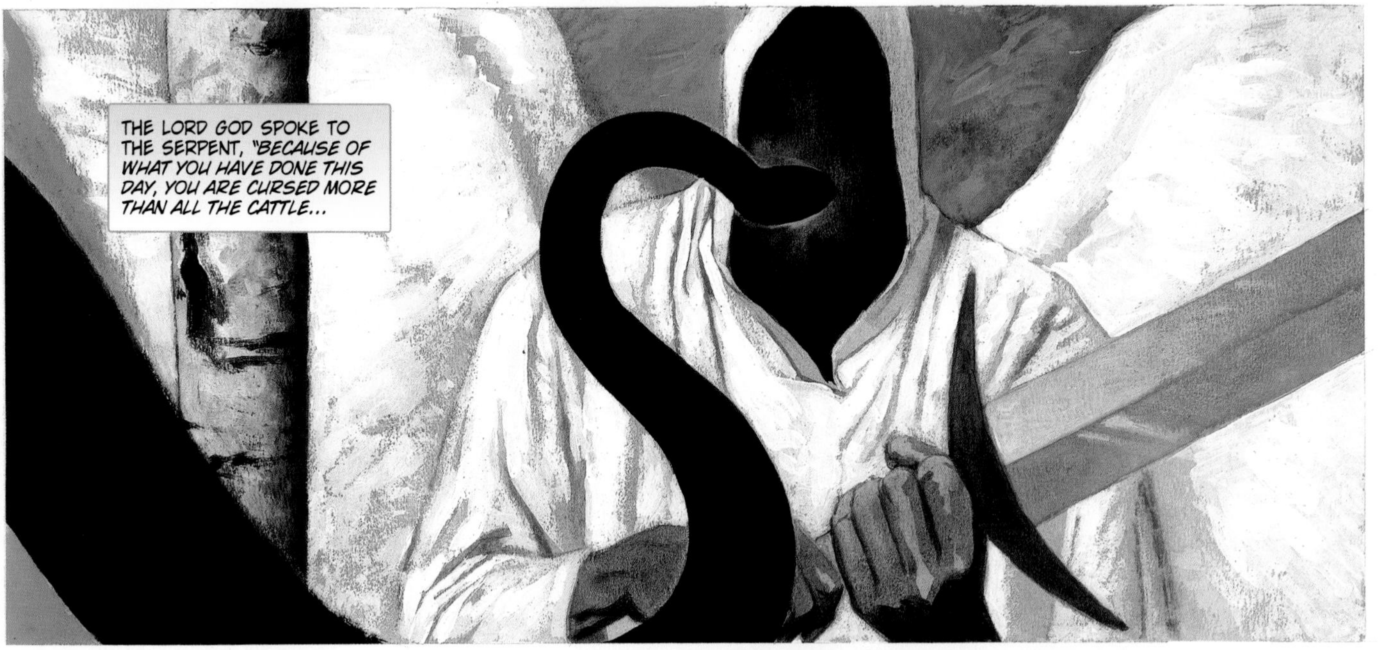
THE LORD GOD SPOKE TO THE SERPENT, "BECAUSE OF WHAT YOU HAVE DONE THIS DAY, YOU ARE CURSED MORE THAN ALL THE CATTLE...

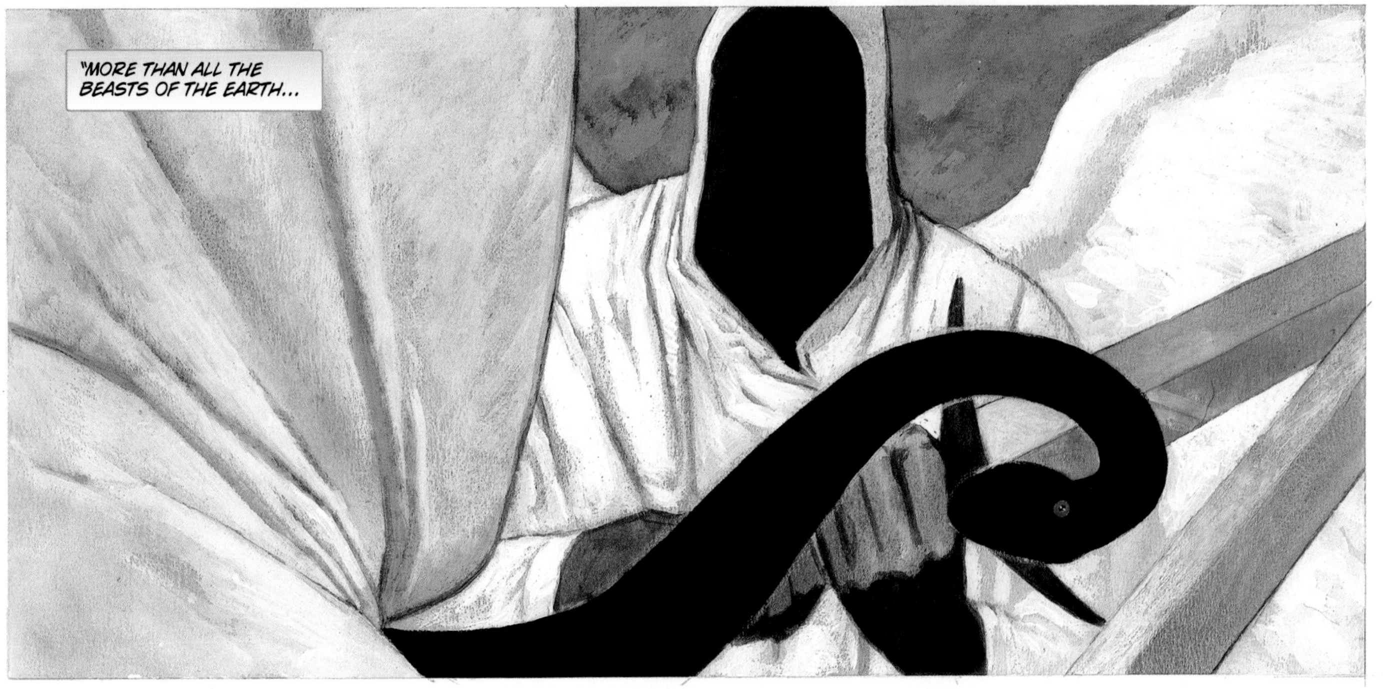
"MORE THAN ALL THE BEASTS OF THE EARTH...

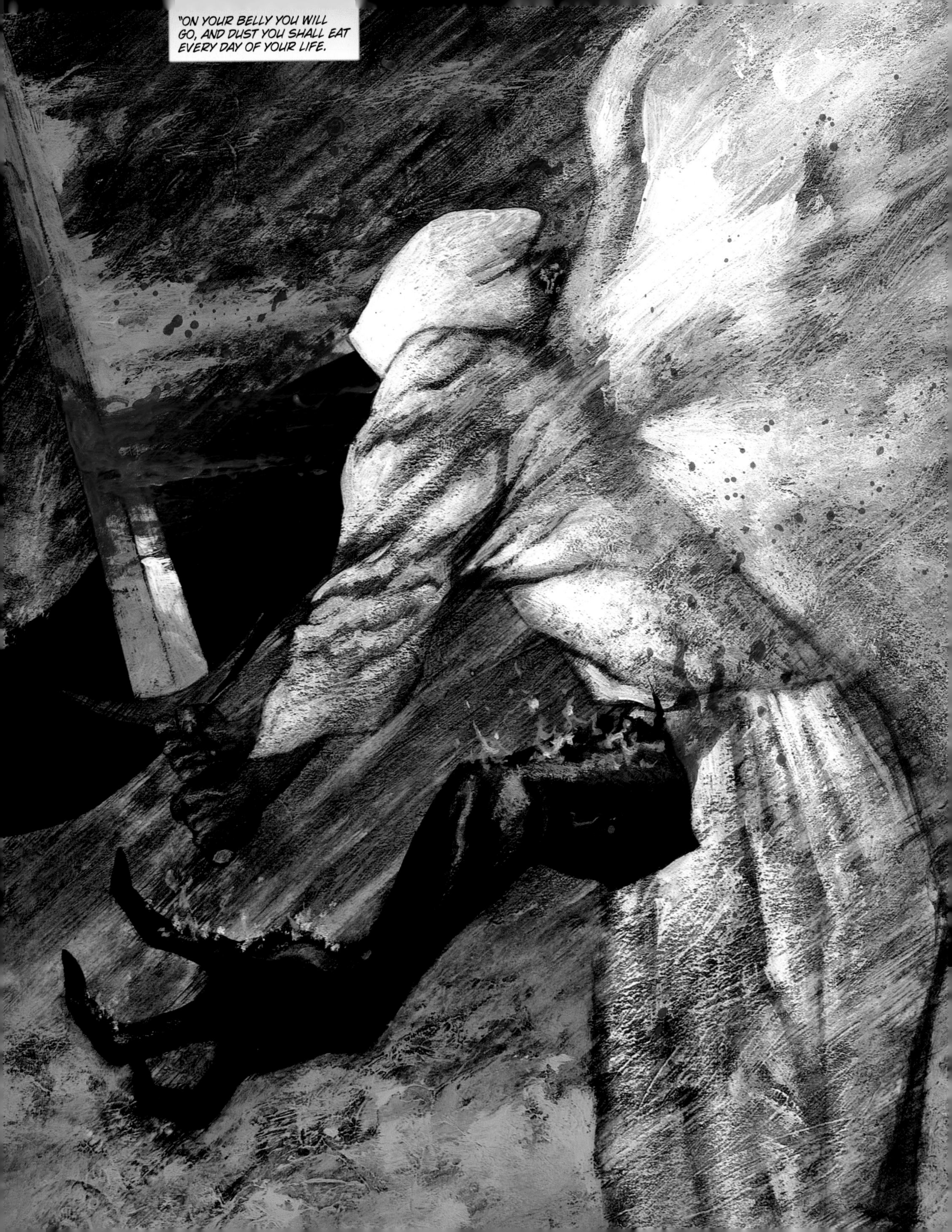
"ON YOUR BELLY YOU WILL GO, AND DUST YOU SHALL EAT EVERY DAY OF YOUR LIFE.

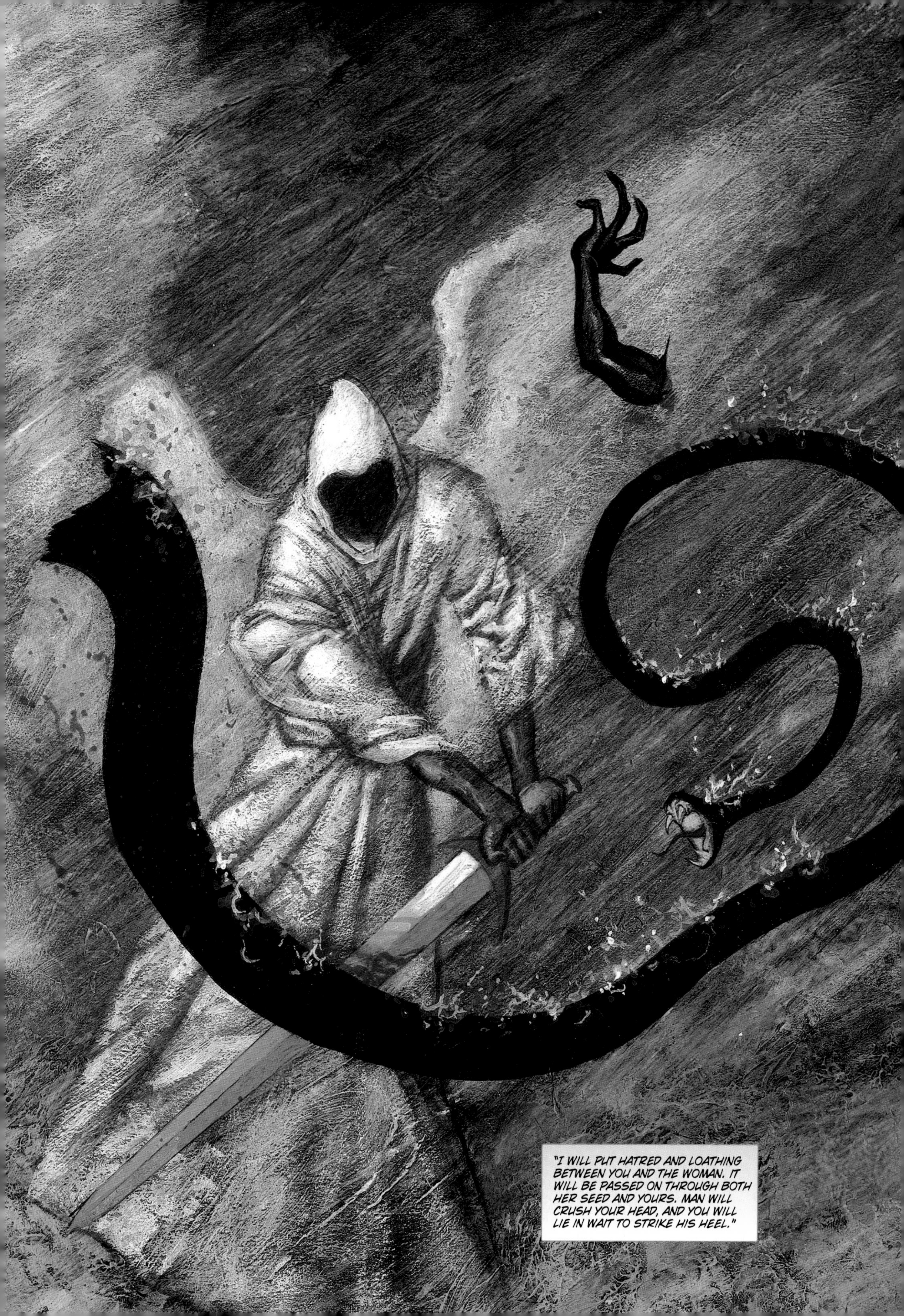
"I WILL PUT HATRED AND LOATHING BETWEEN YOU AND THE WOMAN. IT WILL BE PASSED ON THROUGH BOTH HER SEED AND YOURS. MAN WILL CRUSH YOUR HEAD, AND YOU WILL LIE IN WAIT TO STRIKE HIS HEEL."

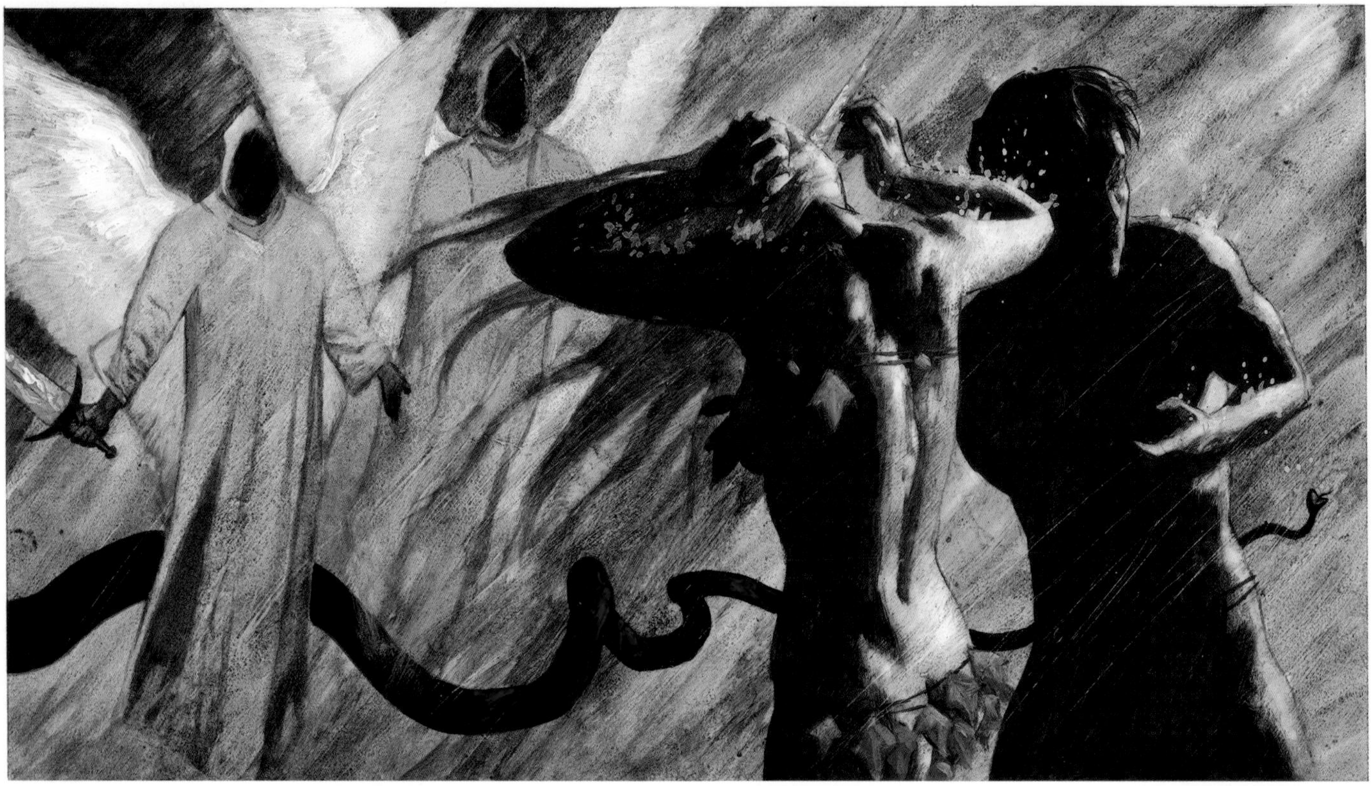

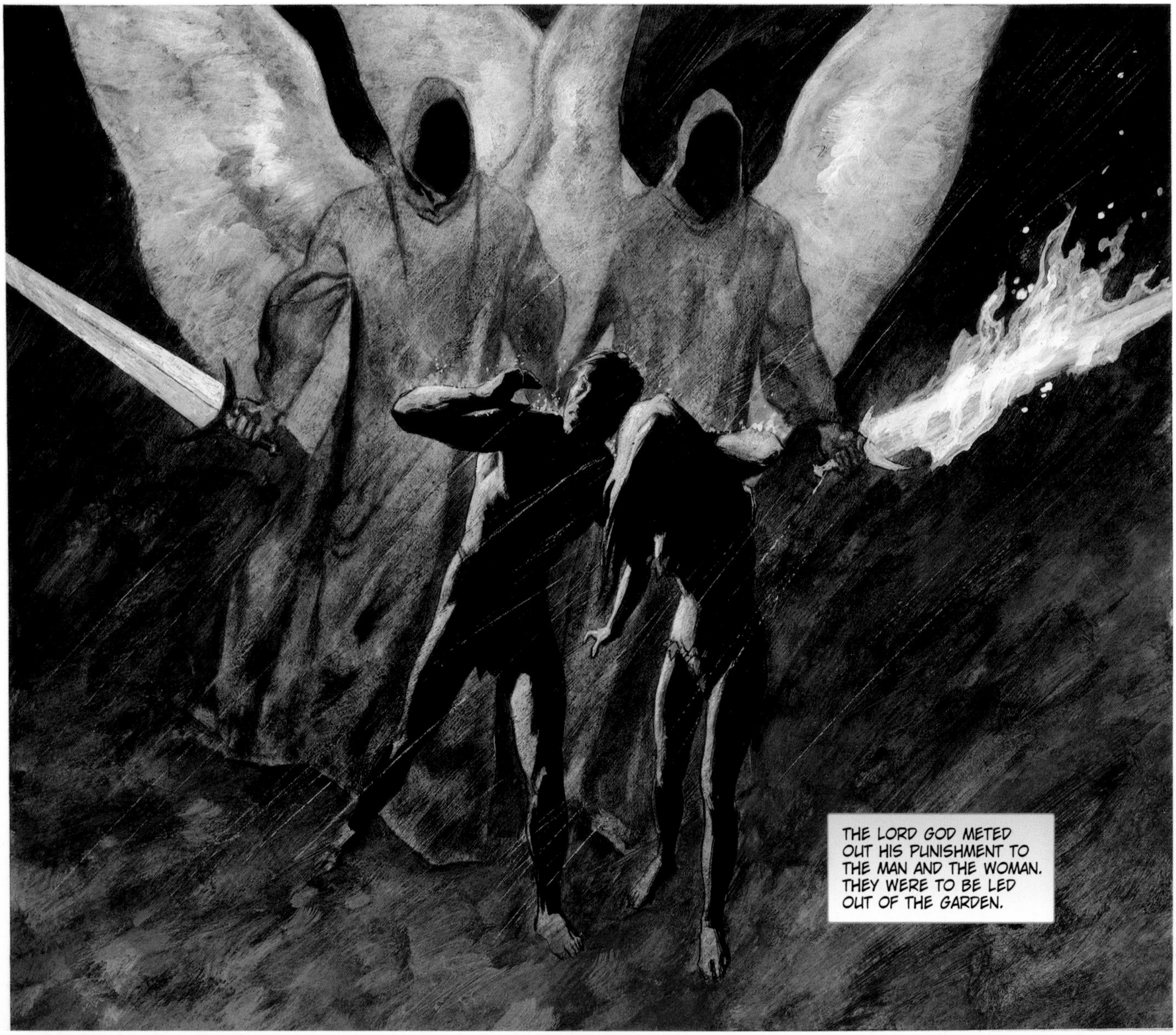
THE LORD GOD METED OUT HIS PUNISHMENT TO THE MAN AND THE WOMAN. THEY WERE TO BE LED OUT OF THE GARDEN.

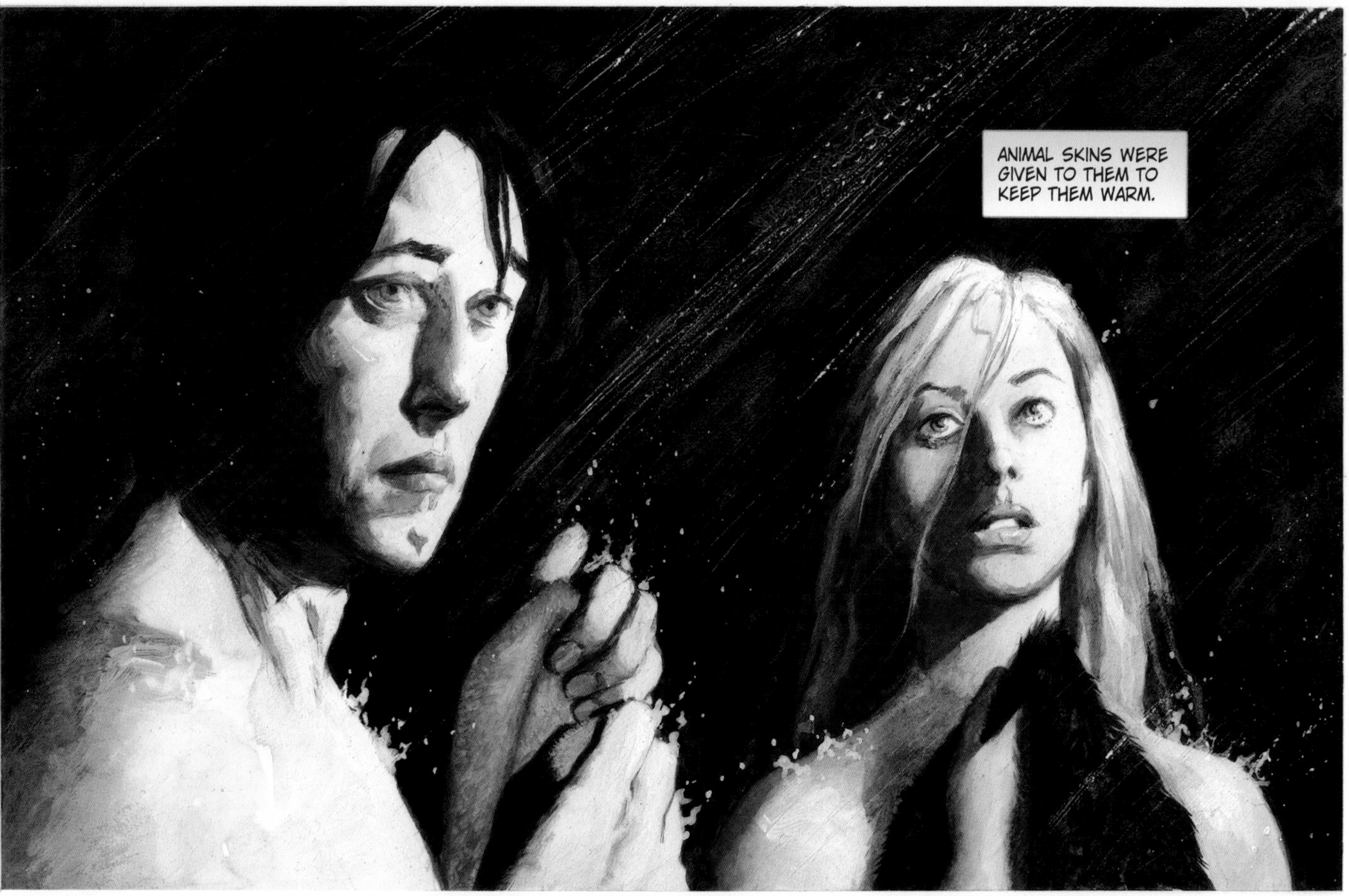
ANIMAL SKINS WERE GIVEN TO THEM TO KEEP THEM WARM.

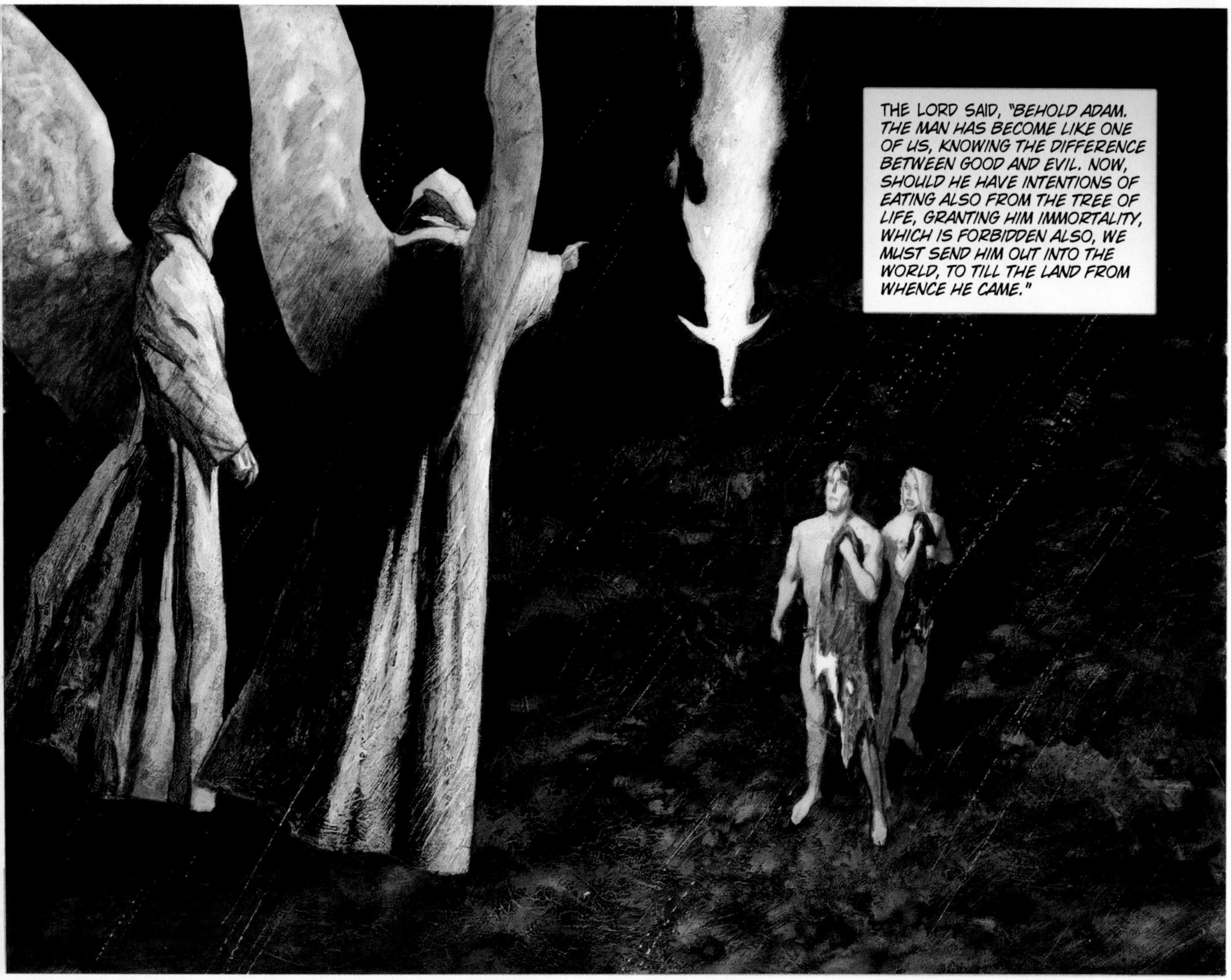
THE LORD SAID, "BEHOLD ADAM. THE MAN HAS BECOME LIKE ONE OF US, KNOWING THE DIFFERENCE BETWEEN GOOD AND EVIL. NOW, SHOULD HE HAVE INTENTIONS OF EATING ALSO FROM THE TREE OF LIFE, GRANTING HIM IMMORTALITY, WHICH IS FORBIDDEN ALSO, WE MUST SEND HIM OUT INTO THE WORLD, TO TILL THE LAND FROM WHENCE HE CAME."

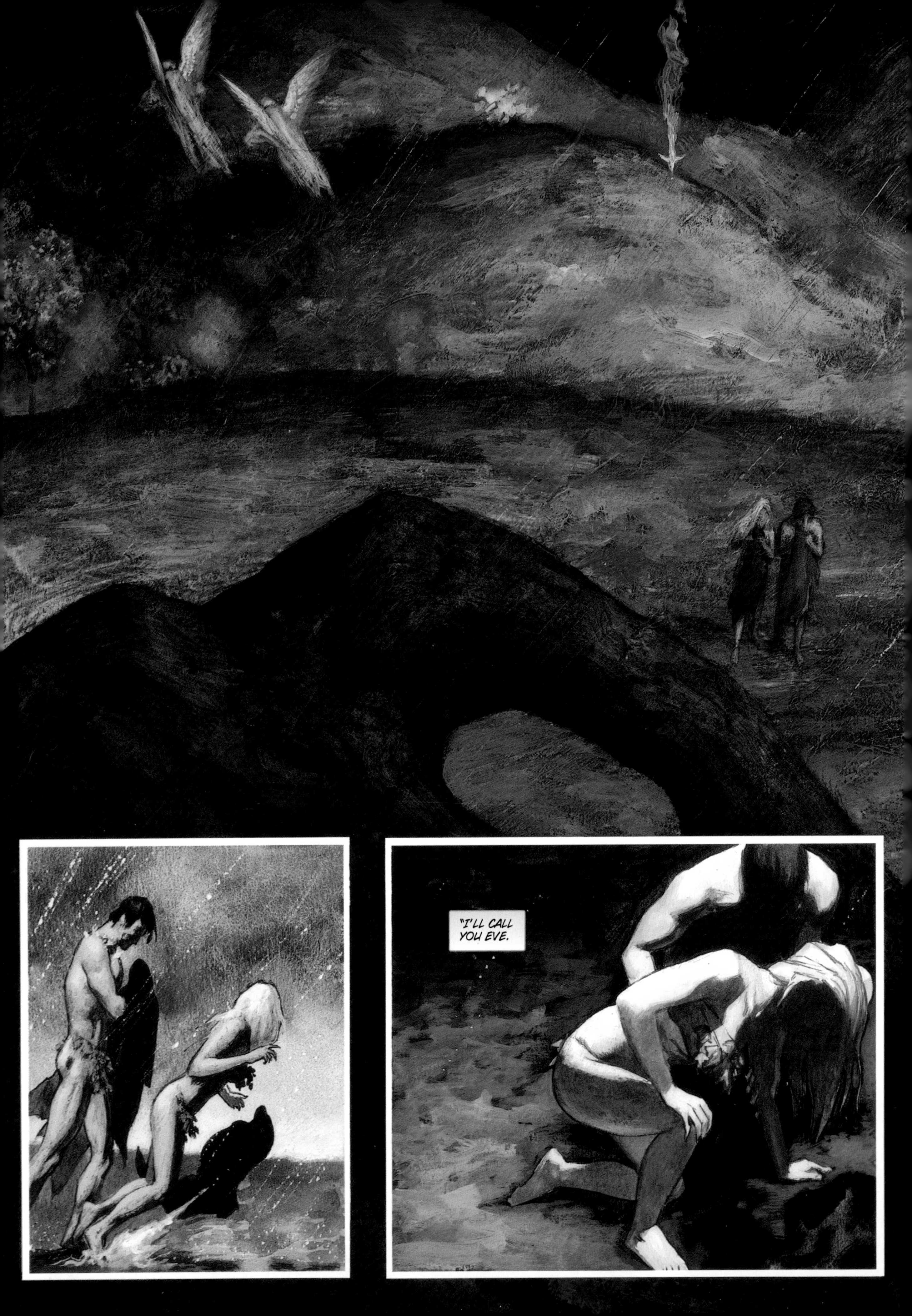
"I'LL CALL YOU EVE.

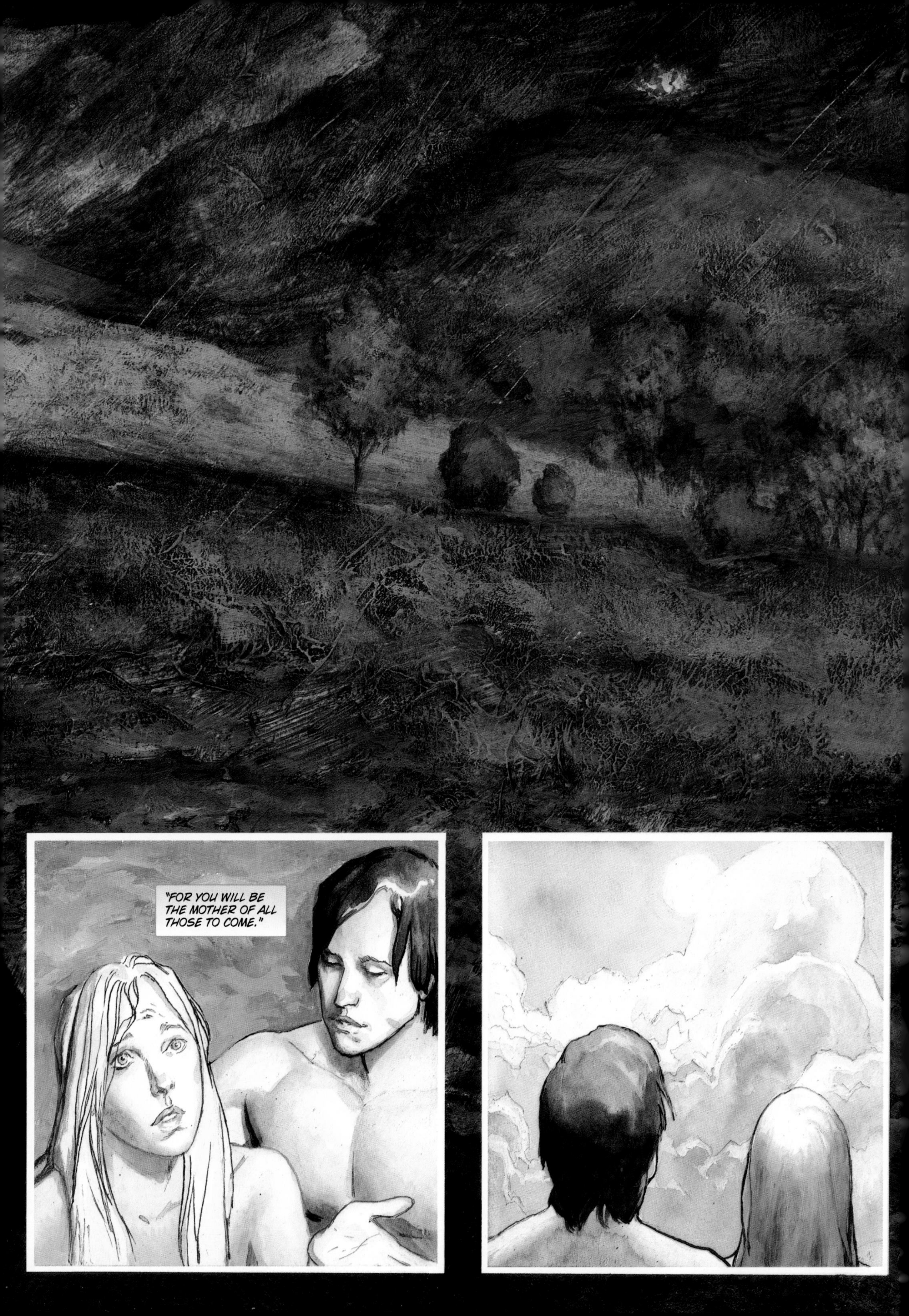
"FOR YOU WILL BE THE MOTHER OF ALL THOSE TO COME."

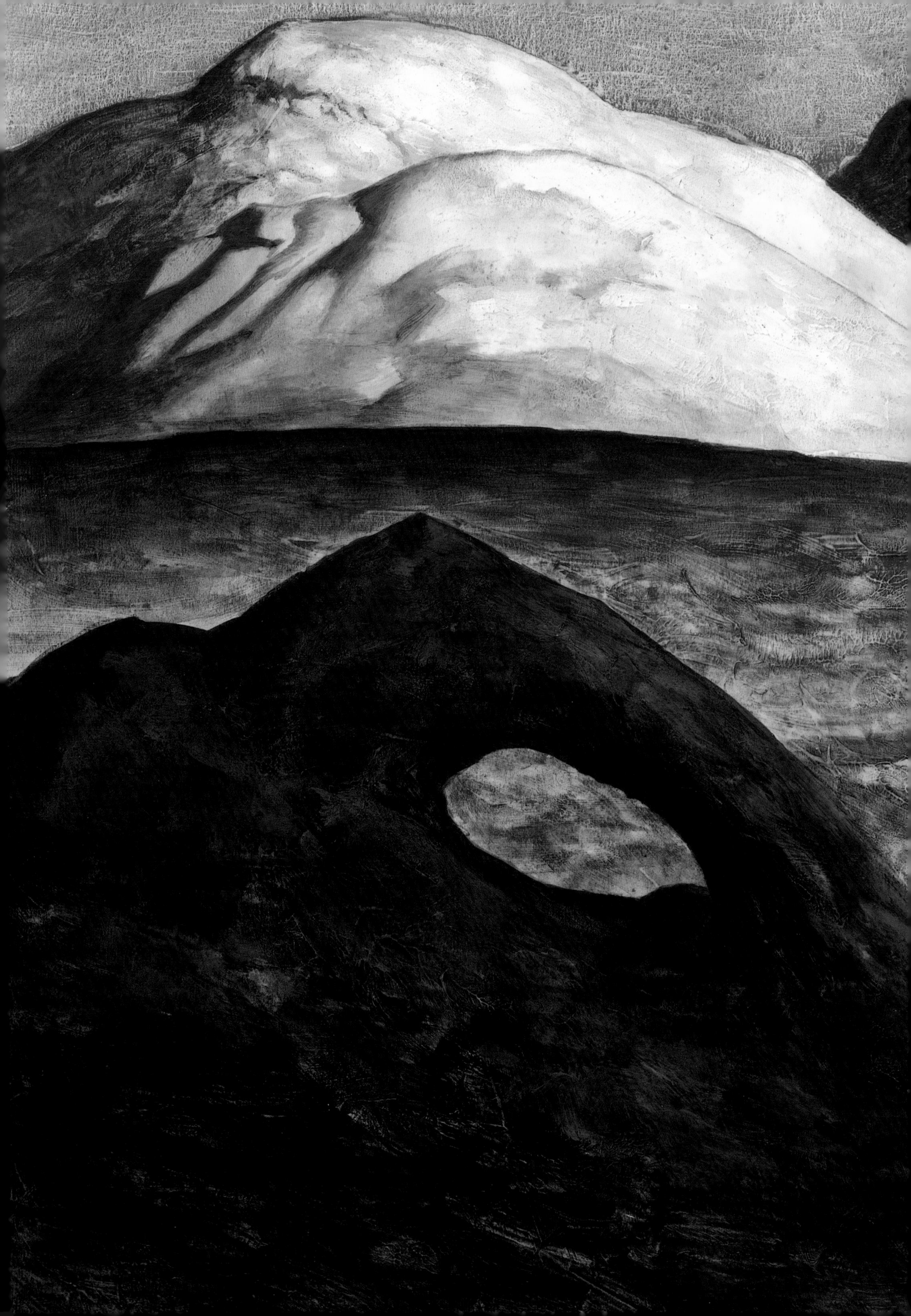

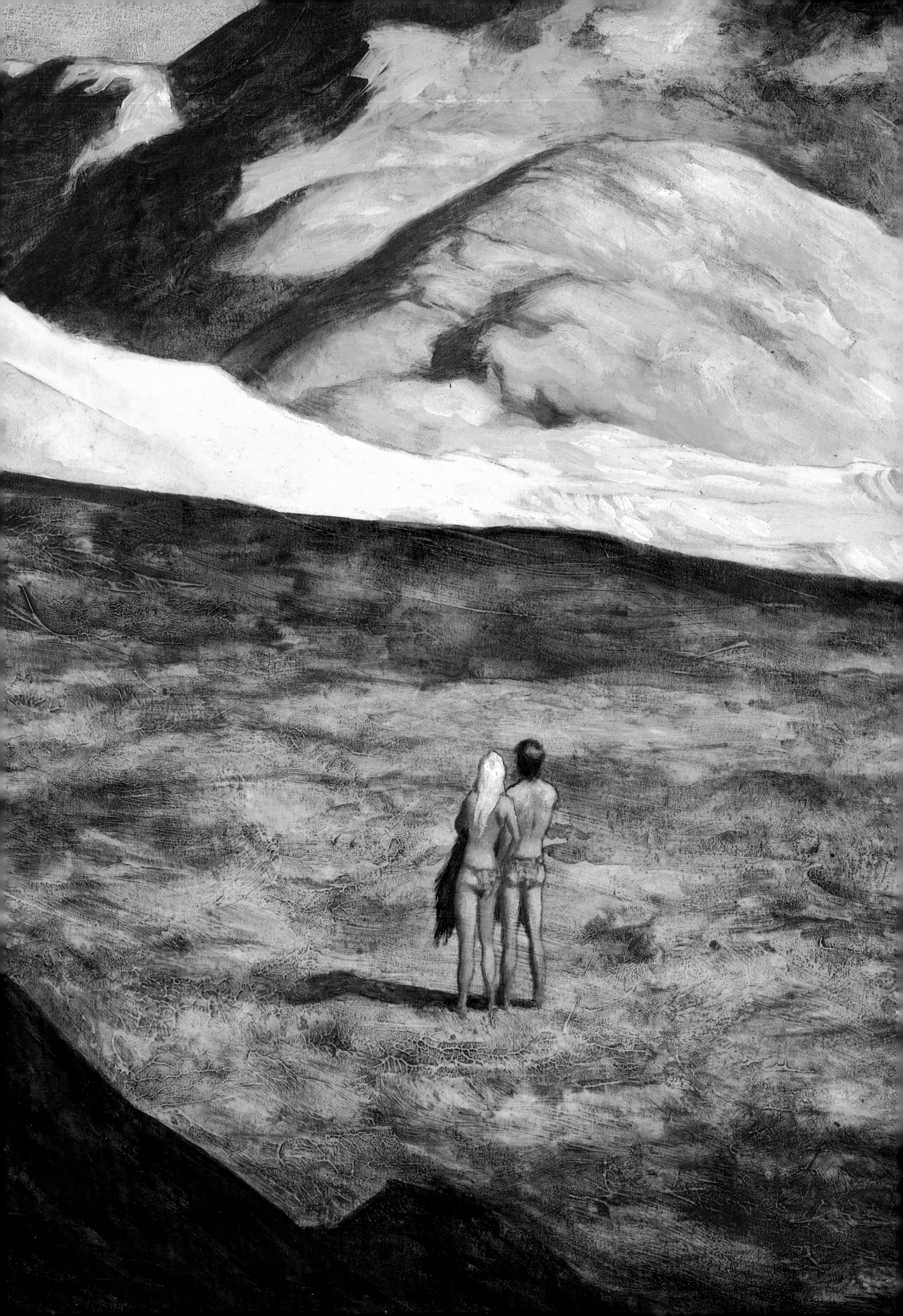

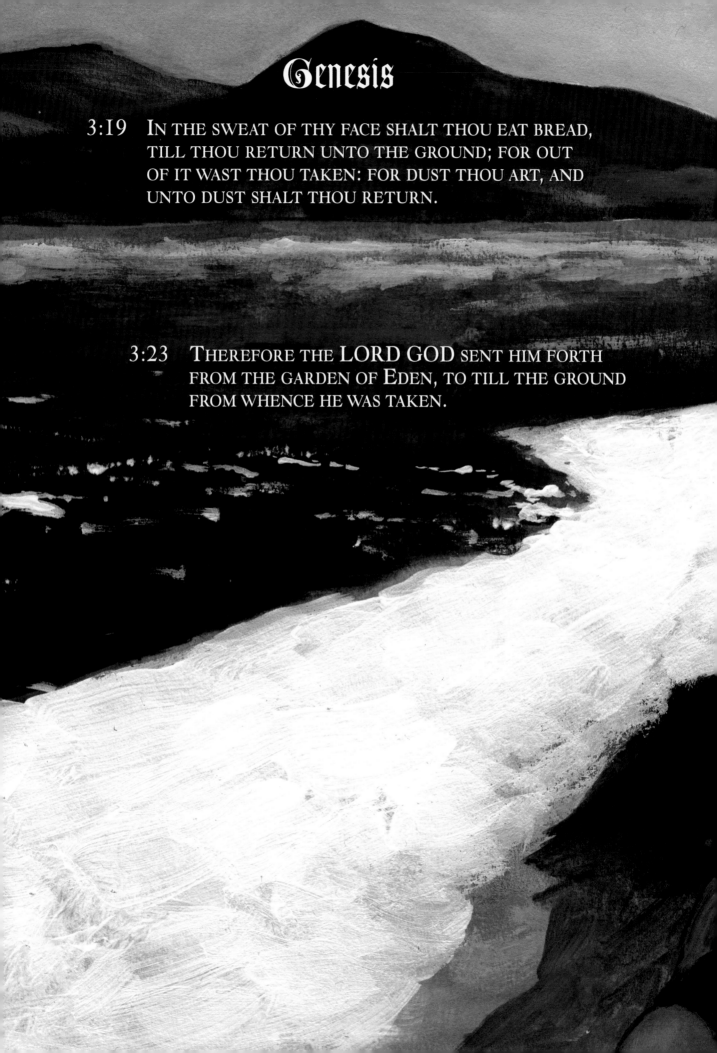

Genesis

3:19   In the sweat of thy face shalt thou eat bread, till thou return unto the ground; for out of it wast thou taken: for dust thou art, and unto dust shalt thou return.

3:23   Therefore the LORD GOD sent him forth from the garden of Eden, to till the ground from whence he was taken.

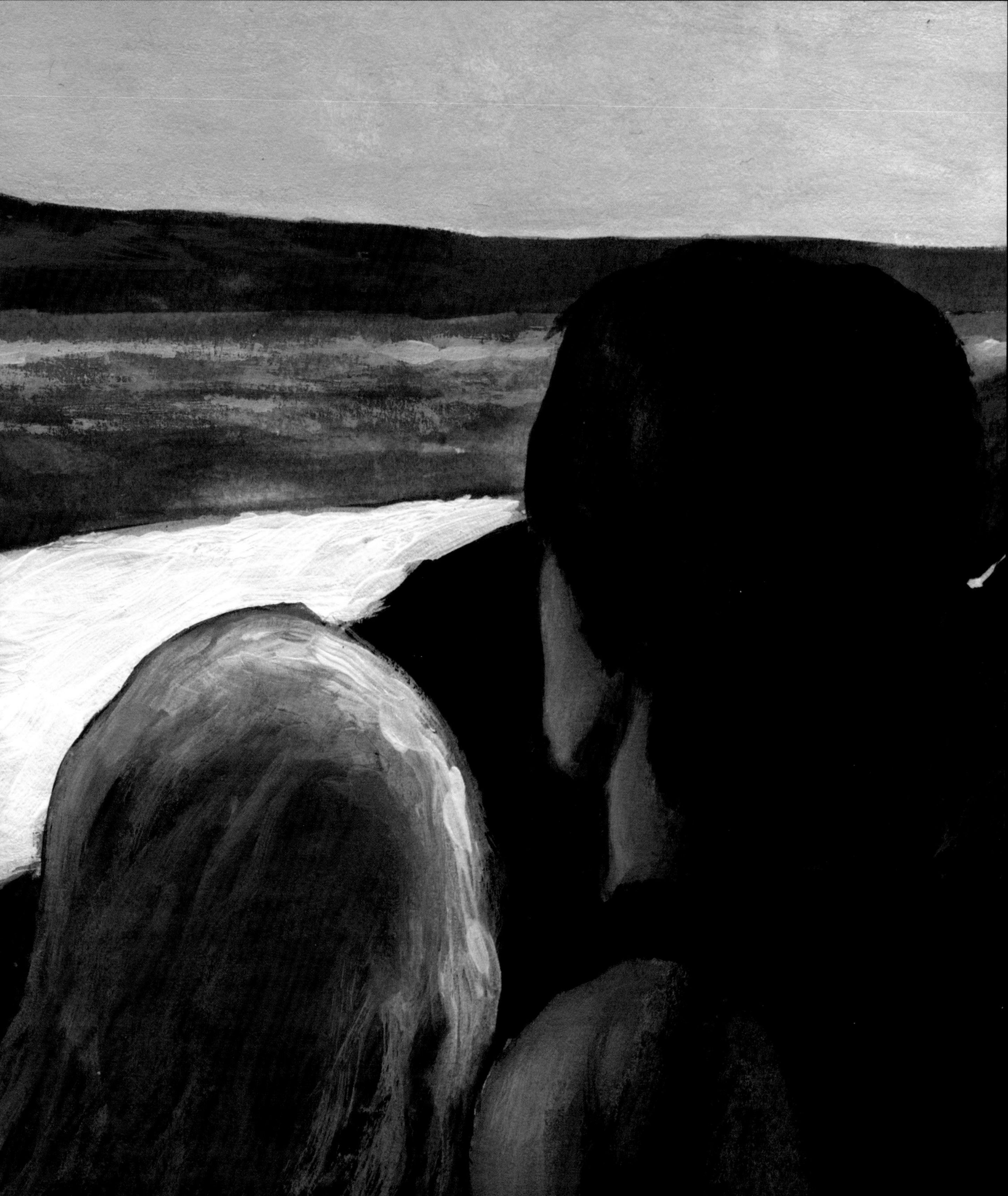

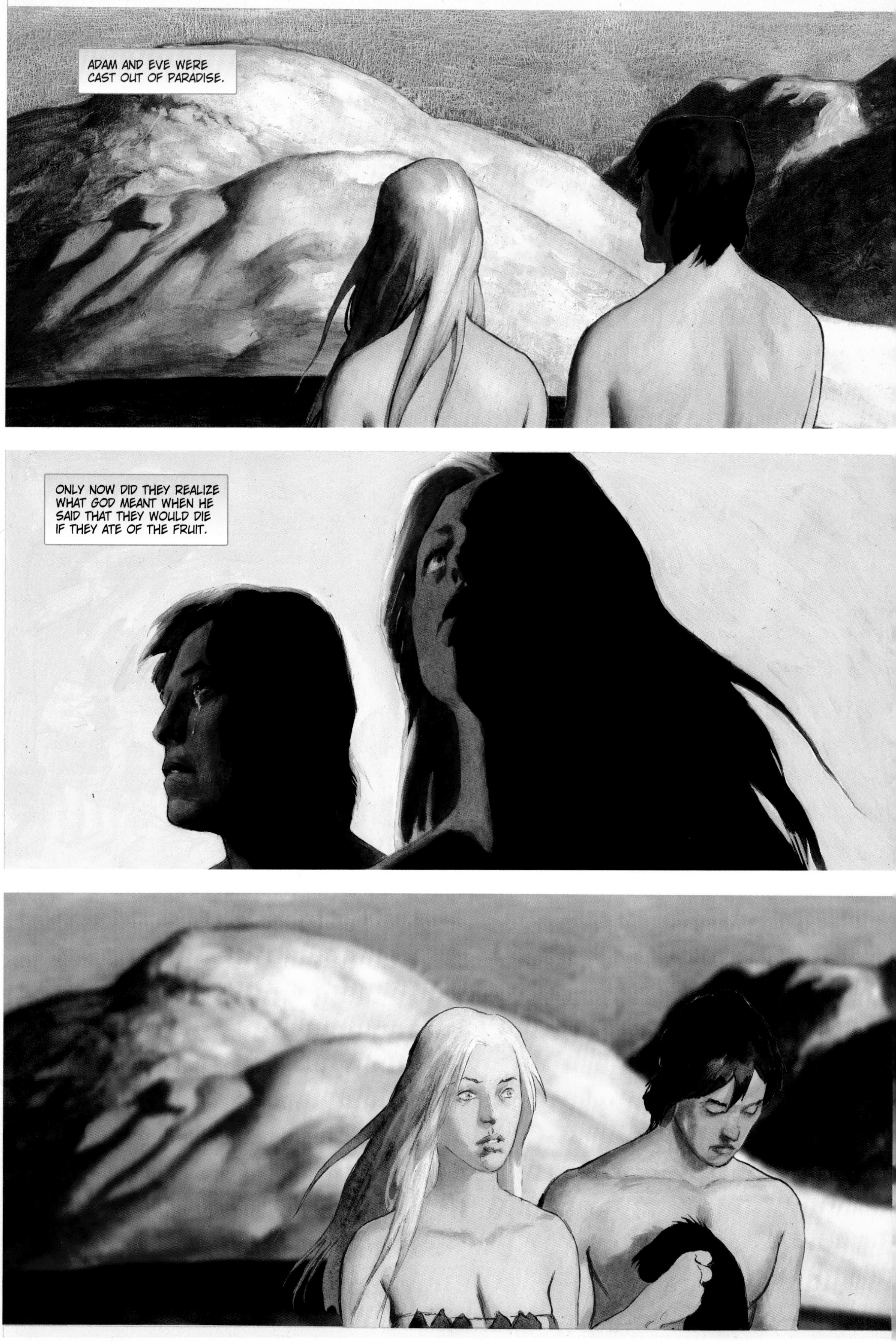
ADAM AND EVE WERE CAST OUT OF PARADISE.
ONLY NOW DID THEY REALIZE WHAT GOD MEANT WHEN HE SAID THAT THEY WOULD DIE IF THEY ATE OF THE FRUIT.

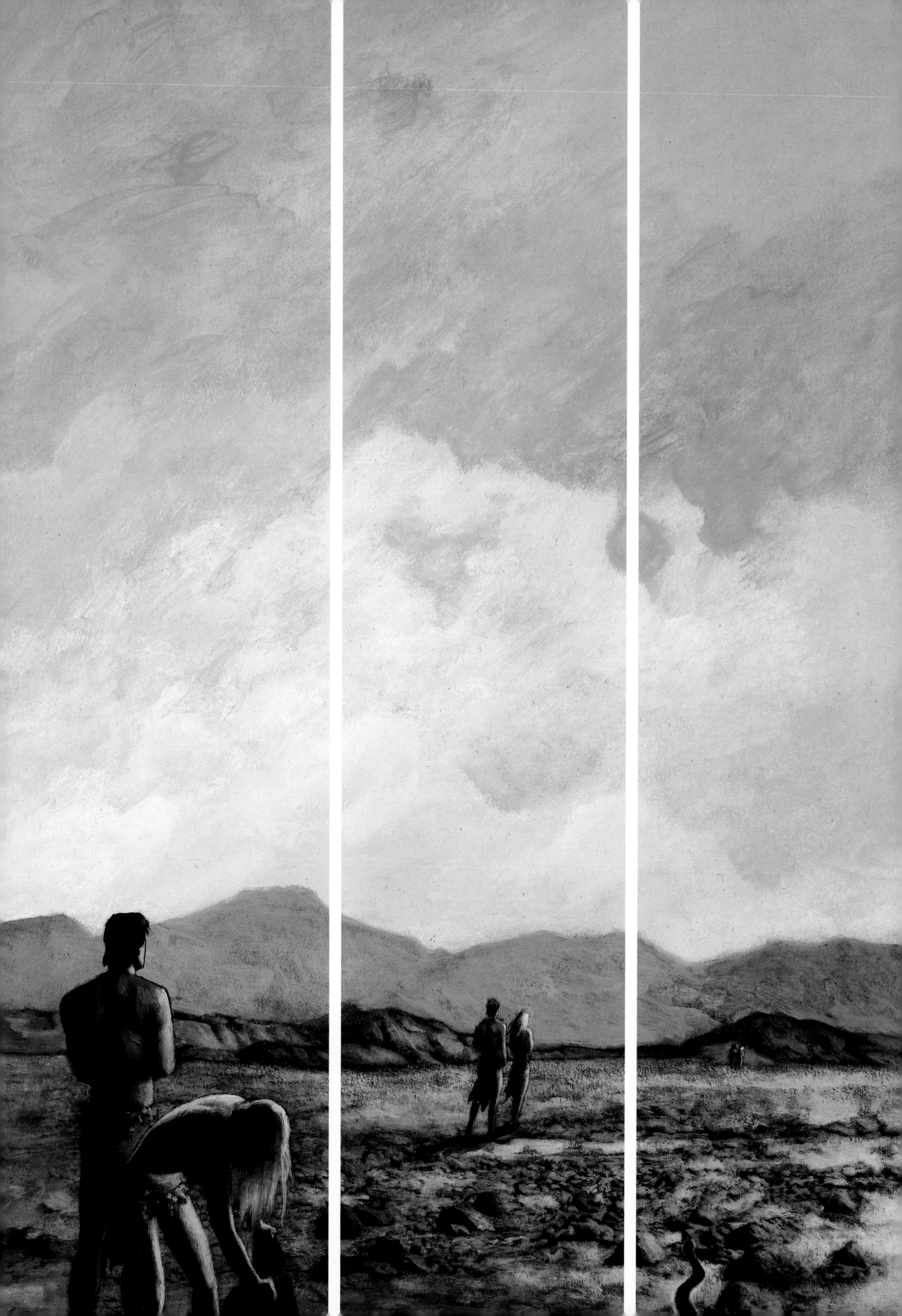

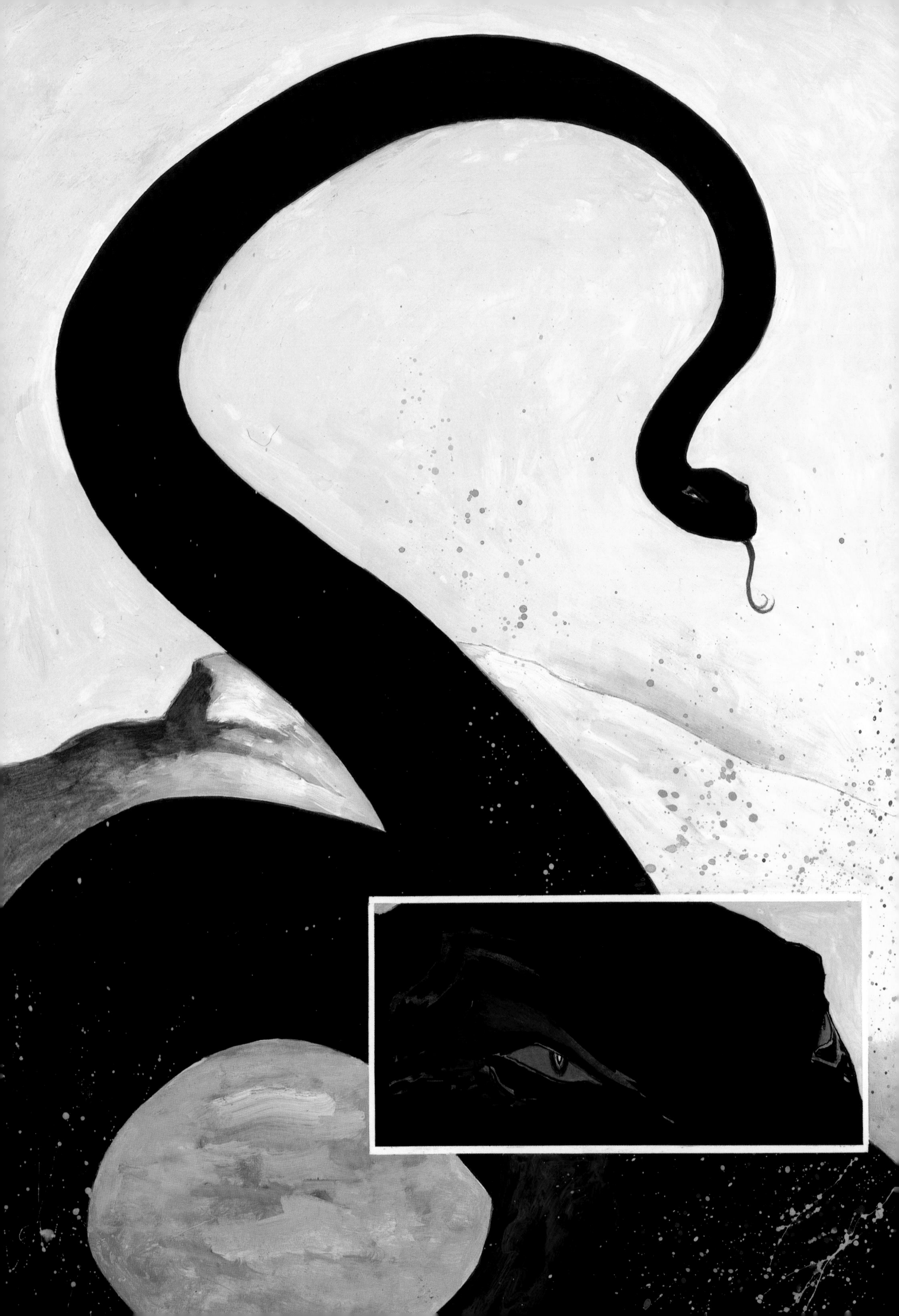

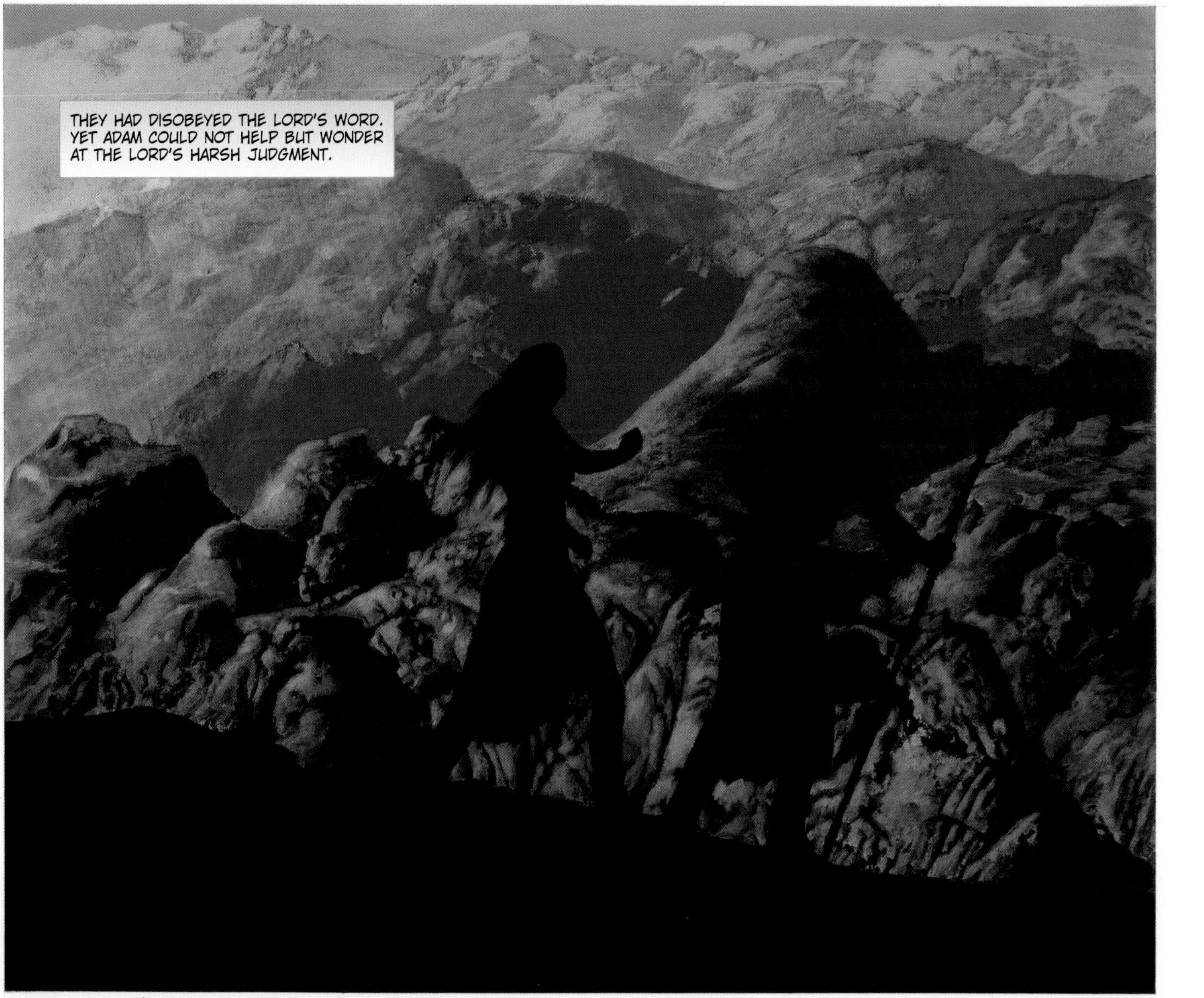
THEY HAD DISOBEYED THE LORD'S WORD. YET ADAM COULD NOT HELP BUT WONDER AT THE LORD'S HARSH JUDGMENT.

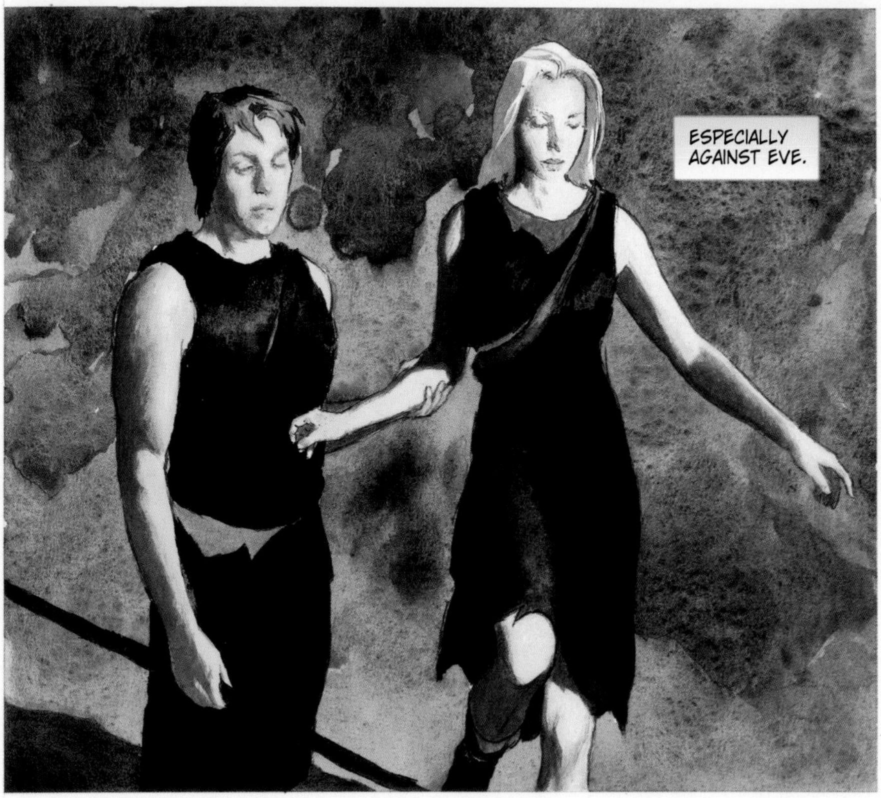
ESPECIALLY AGAINST EVE.

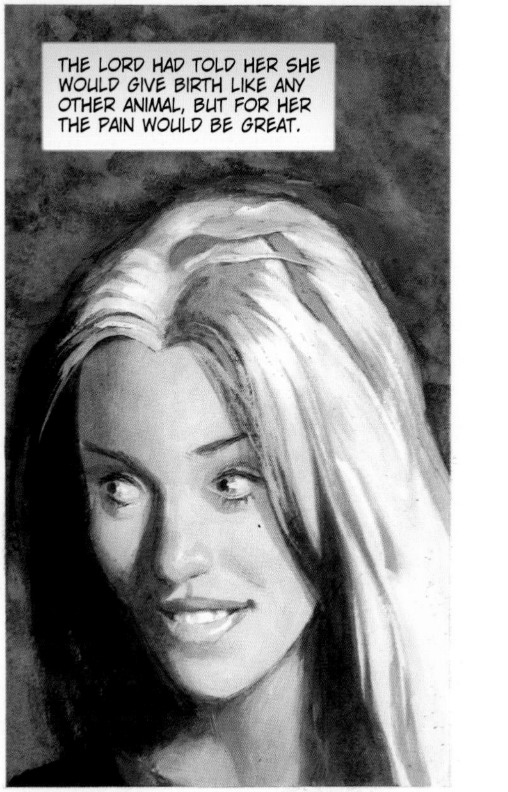
THE LORD HAD TOLD HER SHE WOULD GIVE BIRTH LIKE ANY OTHER ANIMAL, BUT FOR HER THE PAIN WOULD BE GREAT.

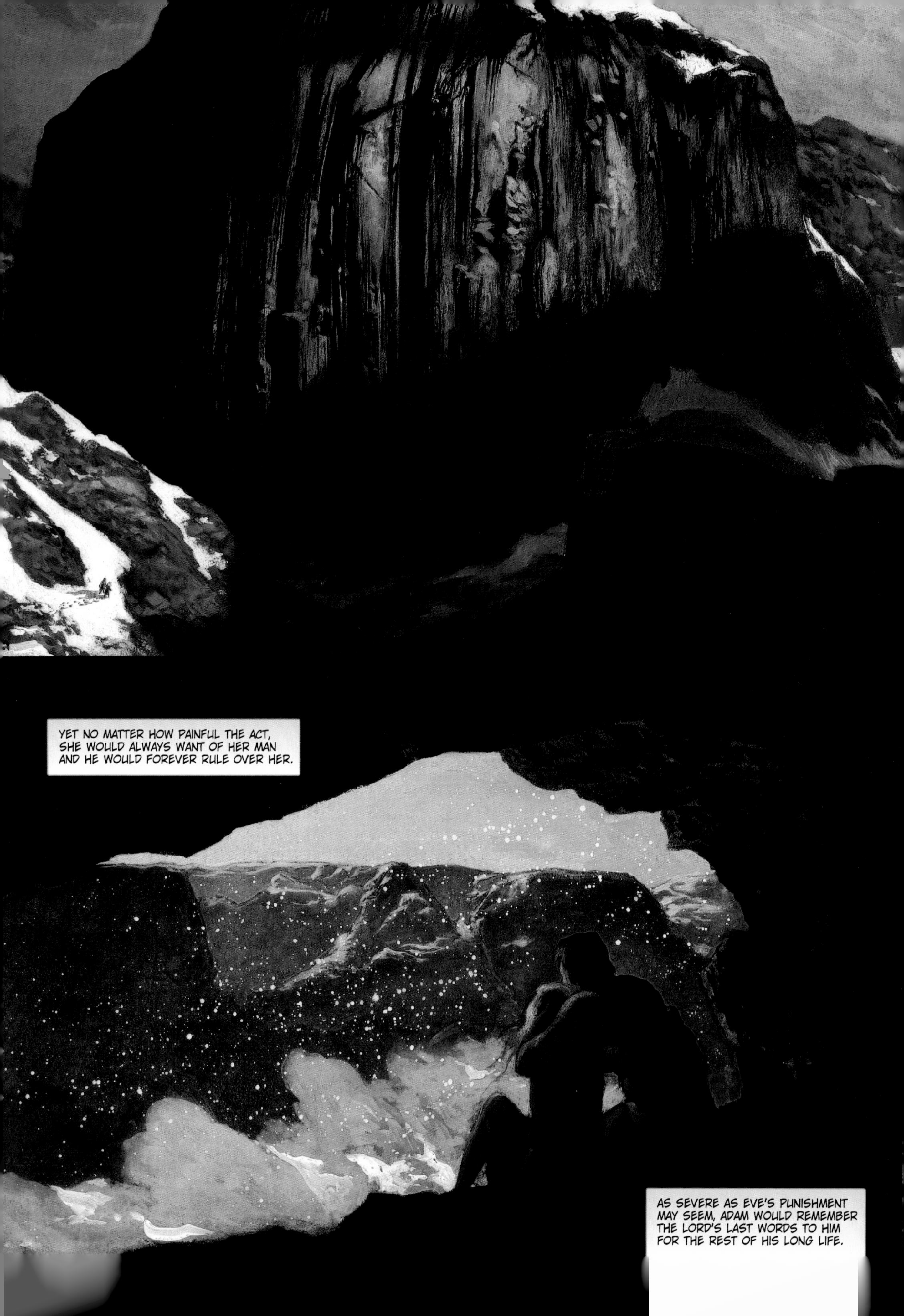

YET NO MATTER HOW PAINFUL THE ACT, SHE WOULD ALWAYS WANT OF HER MAN AND HE WOULD FOREVER RULE OVER HER.
AS SEVERE AS EVE'S PUNISHMENT MAY SEEM, ADAM WOULD REMEMBER THE LORD'S LAST WORDS TO HIM FOR THE REST OF HIS LONG LIFE.

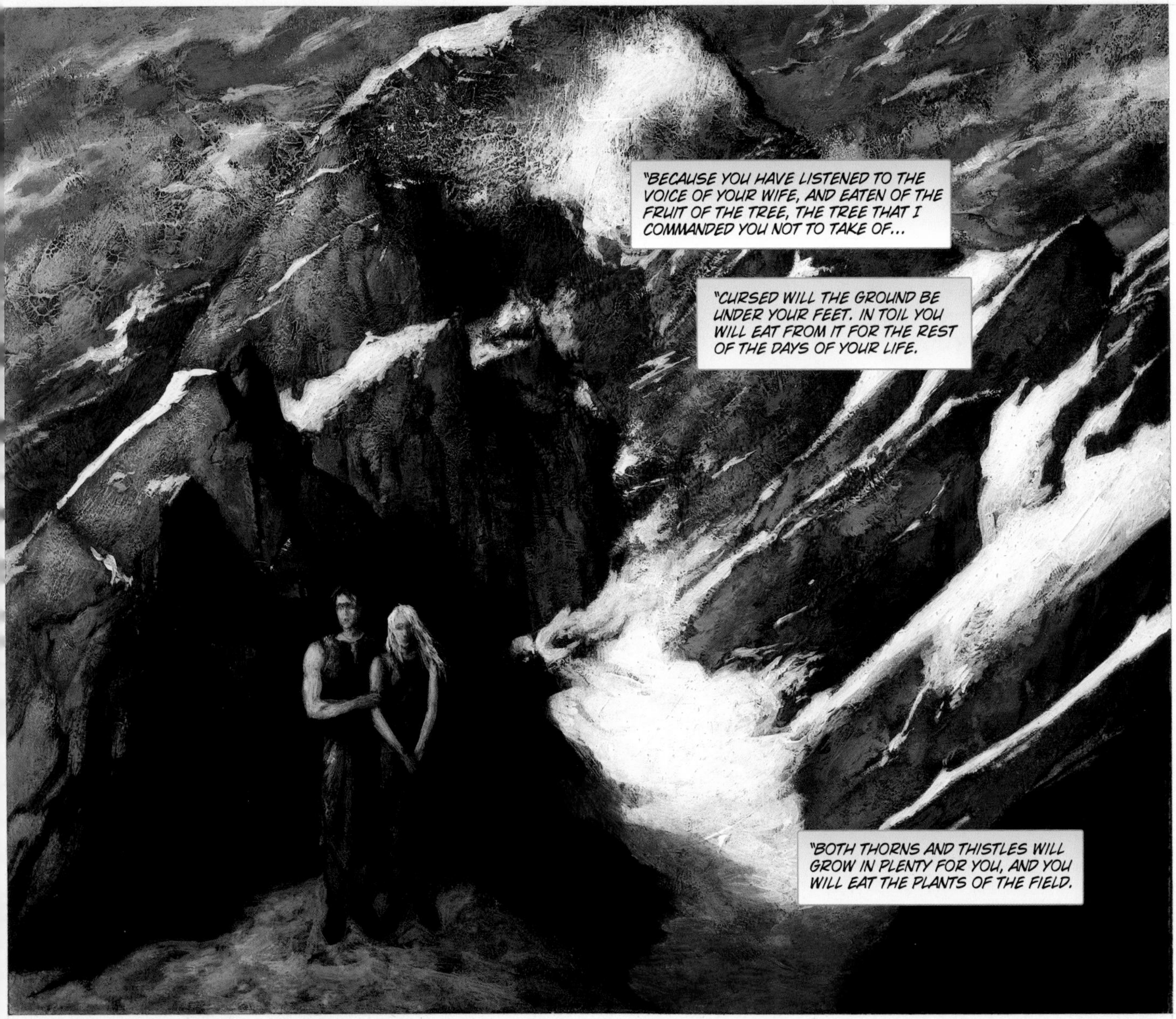
"BECAUSE YOU HAVE LISTENED TO THE VOICE OF YOUR WIFE, AND EATEN OF THE FRUIT OF THE TREE, THE TREE THAT I COMMANDED YOU NOT TO TAKE OF...
"CURSED WILL THE GROUND BE UNDER YOUR FEET. IN TOIL YOU WILL EAT FROM IT FOR THE REST OF THE DAYS OF YOUR LIFE.
"BOTH THORNS AND THISTLES WILL GROW IN PLENTY FOR YOU, AND YOU WILL EAT THE PLANTS OF THE FIELD.

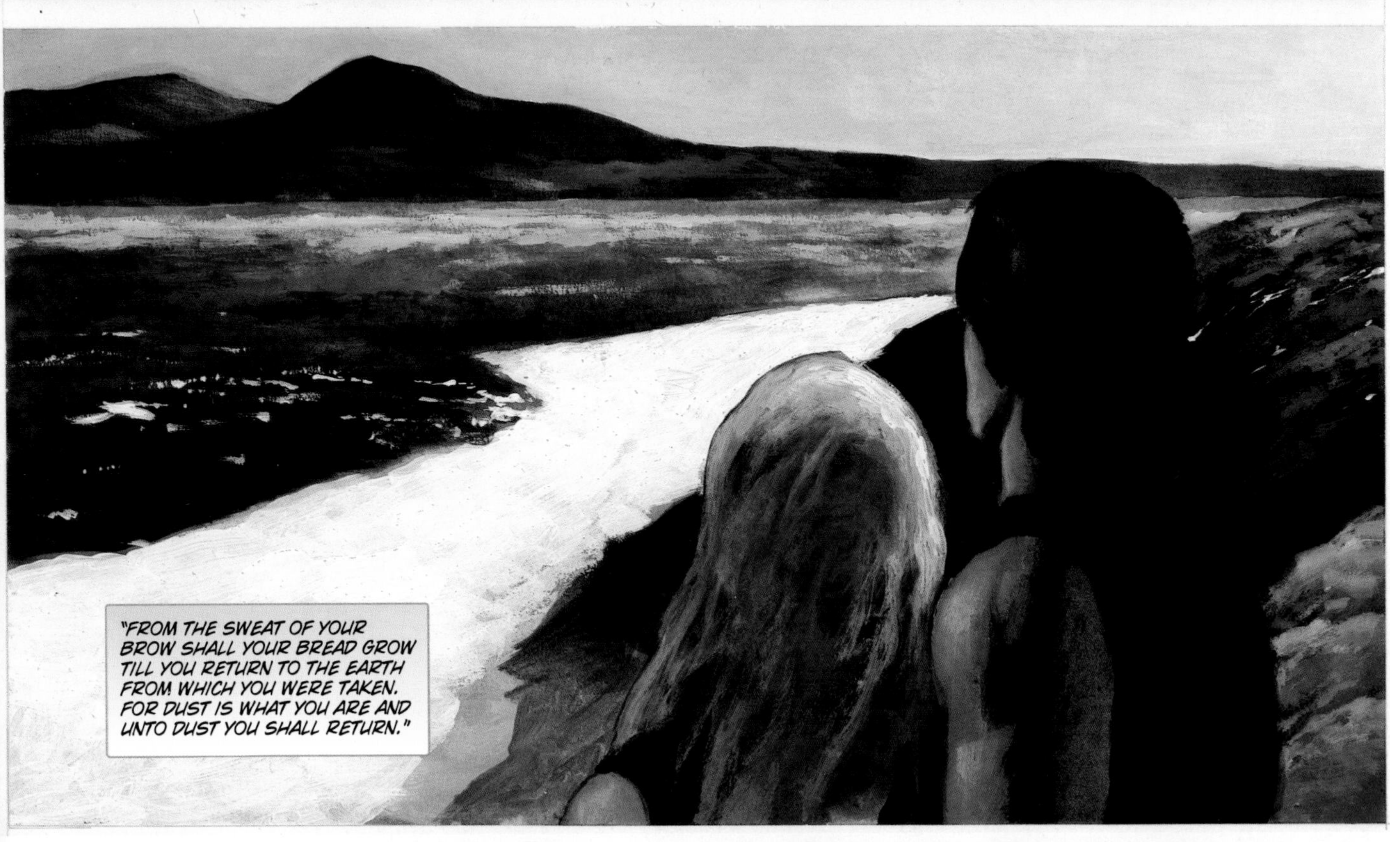
"FROM THE SWEAT OF YOUR BROW SHALL YOUR BREAD GROW TILL YOU RETURN TO THE EARTH FROM WHICH YOU WERE TAKEN. FOR DUST IS WHAT YOU ARE AND UNTO DUST YOU SHALL RETURN."

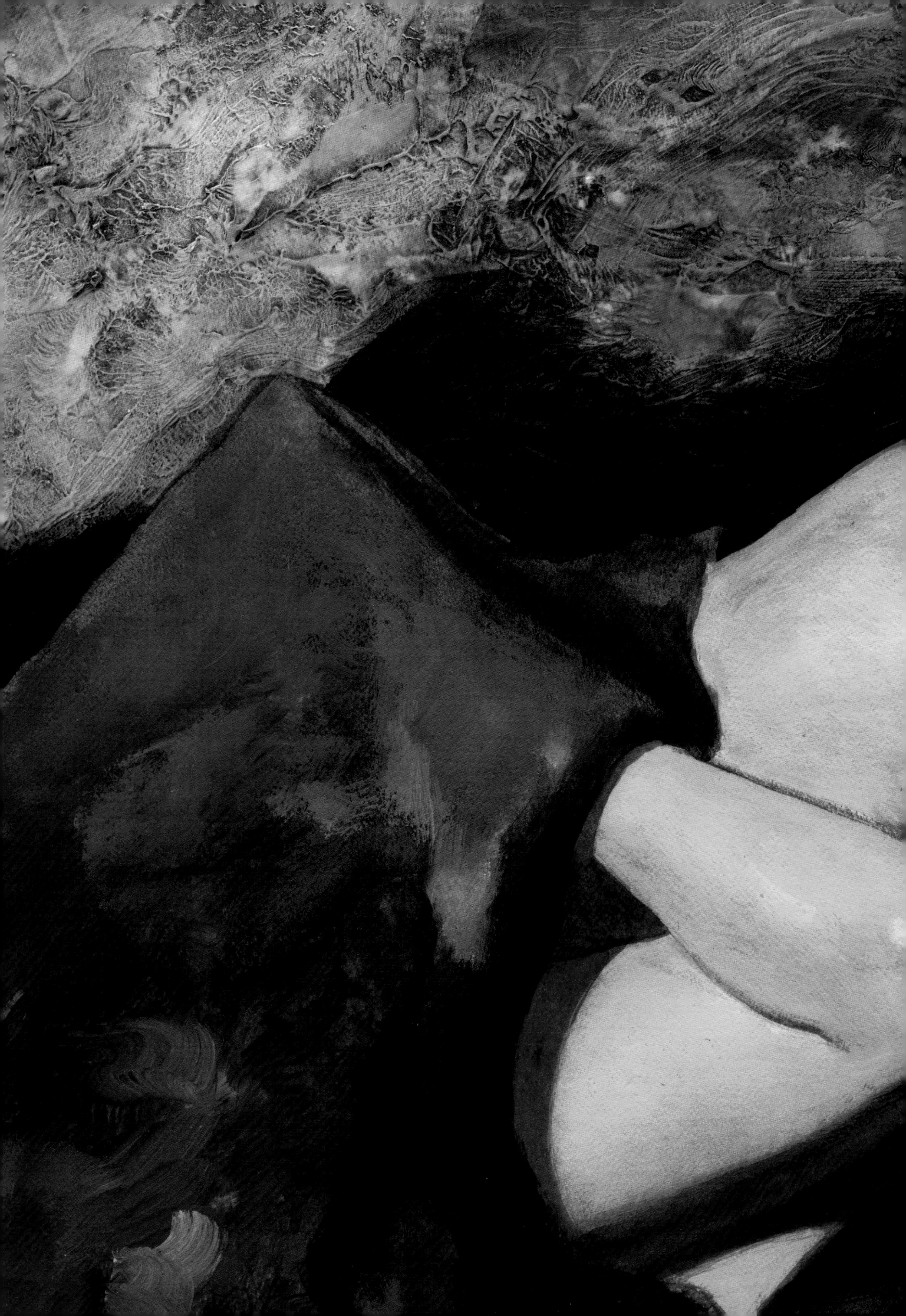

Genesis

4:1 AND ADAM KNEW EVE HIS WIFE; AND SHE
CONCEIVED, AND BARE CAIN, AND SAID, "I
HAVE GOTTEN A MAN FROM THE LORD."

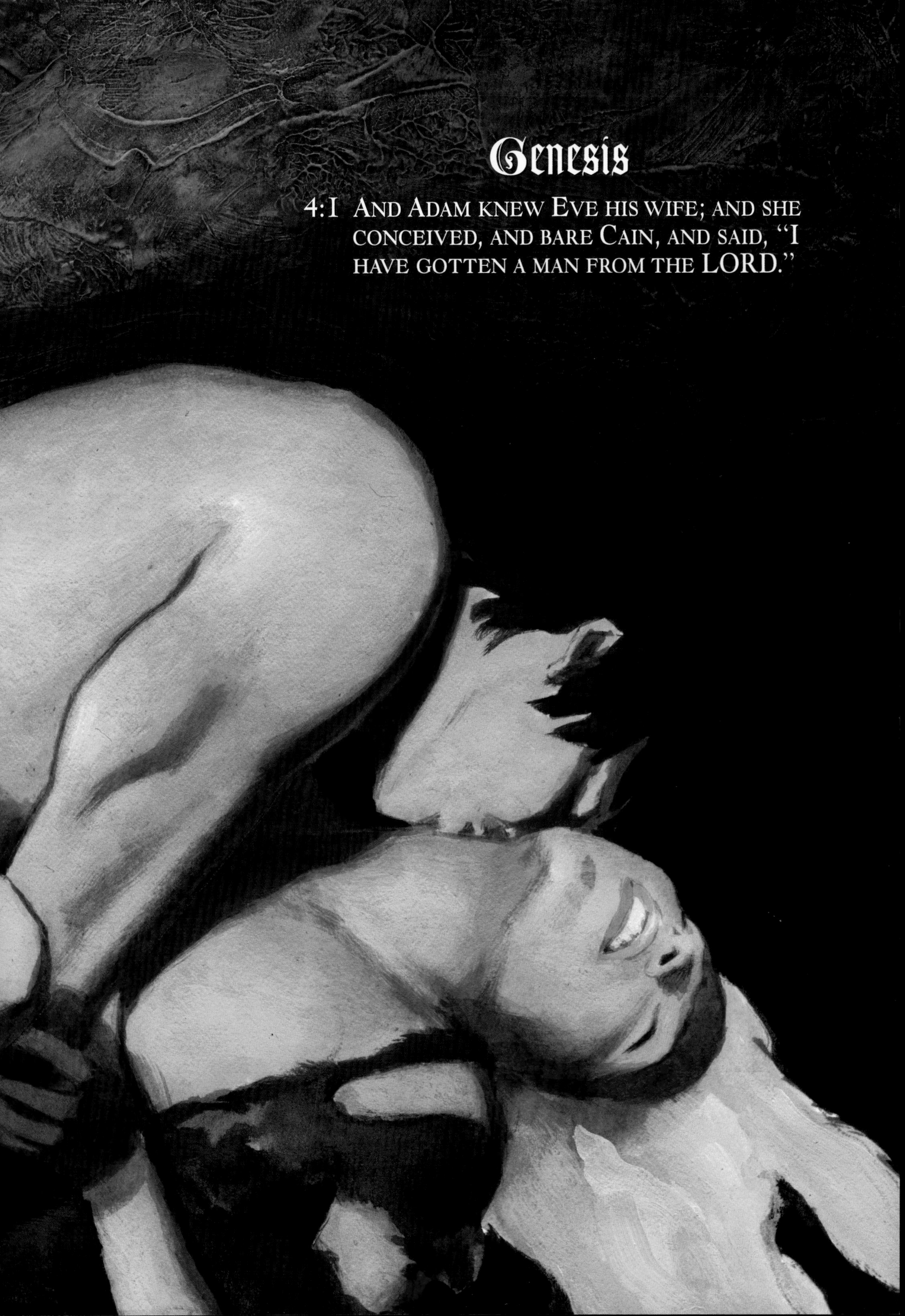

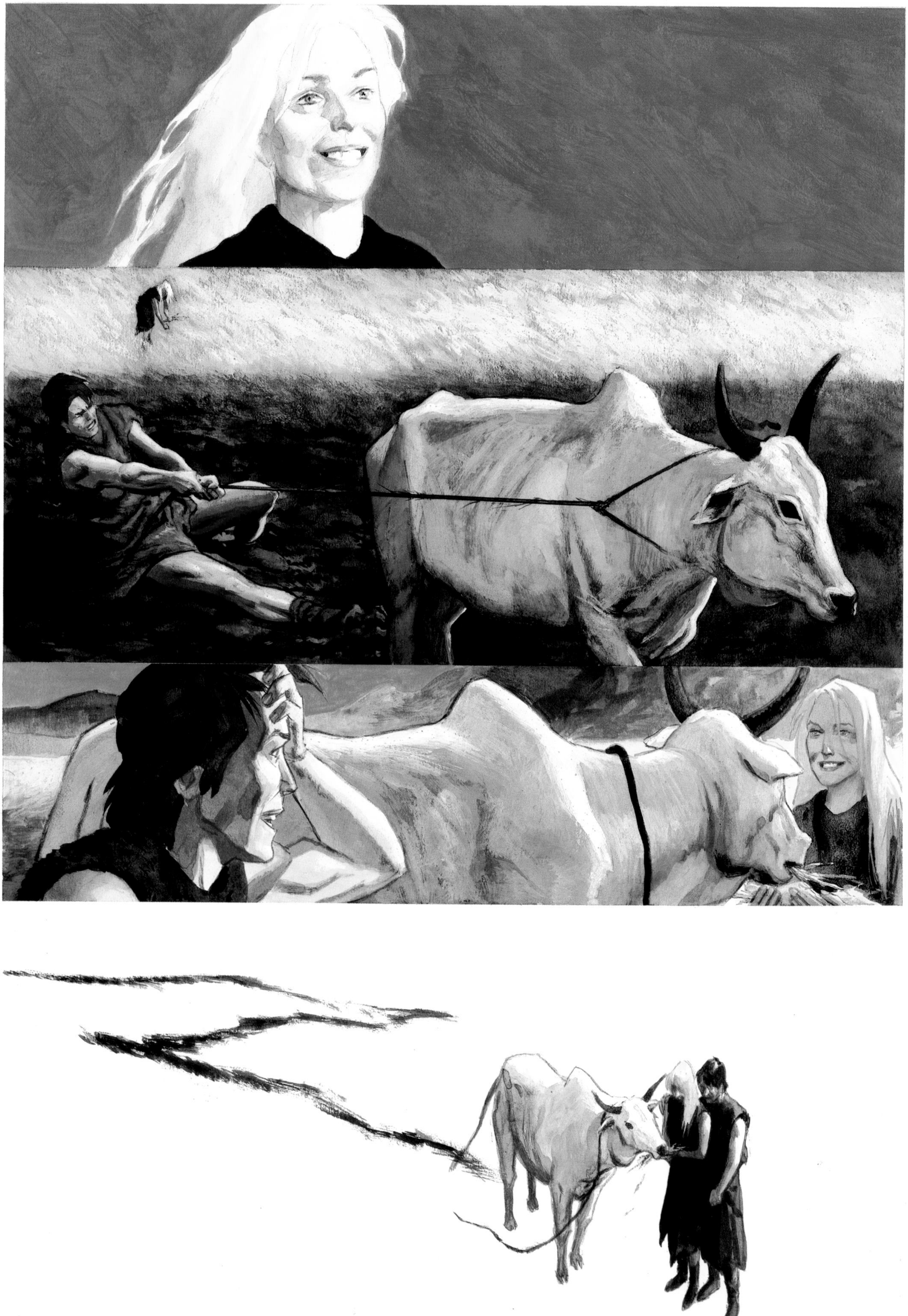

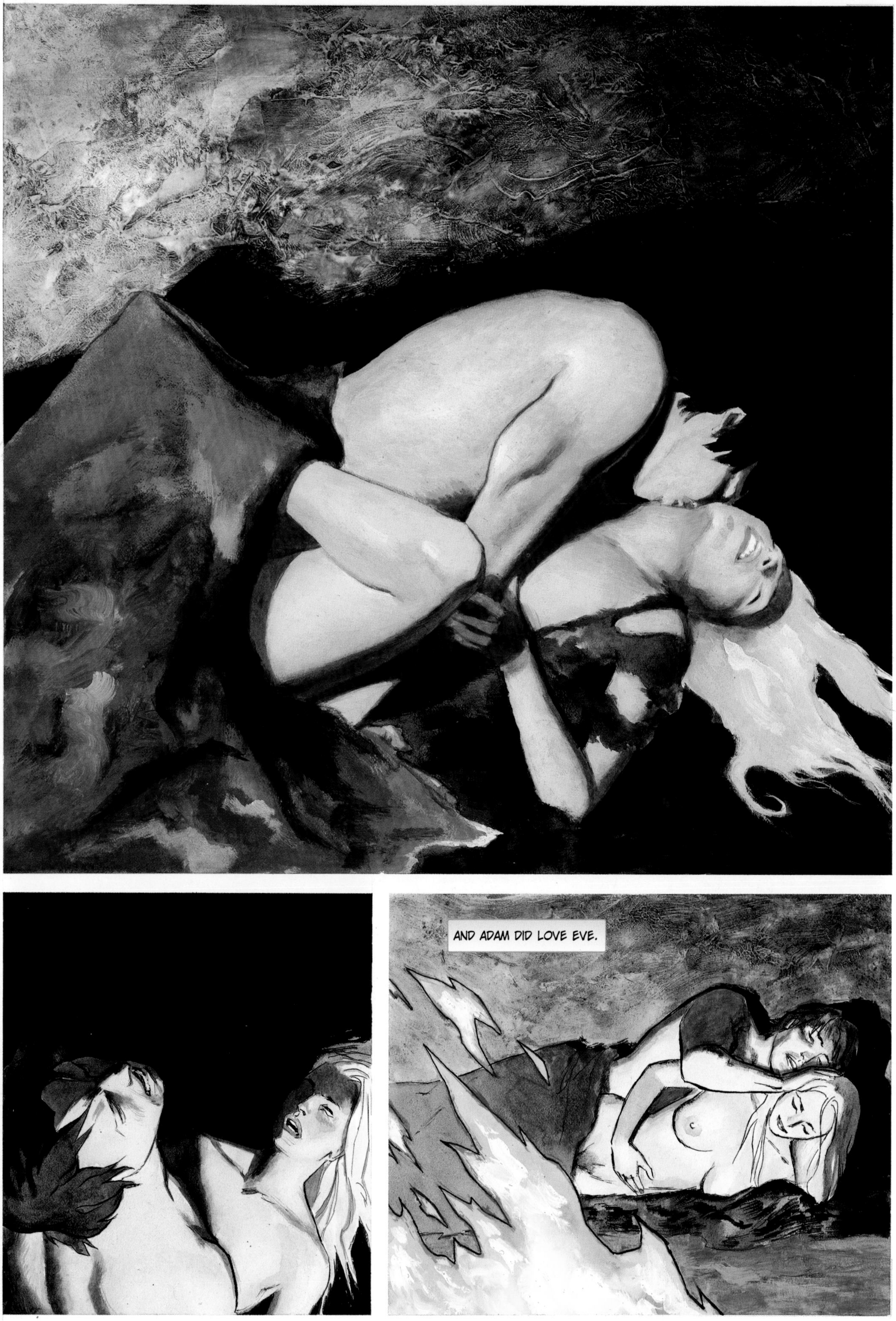
AND ADAM DID LOVE EVE.

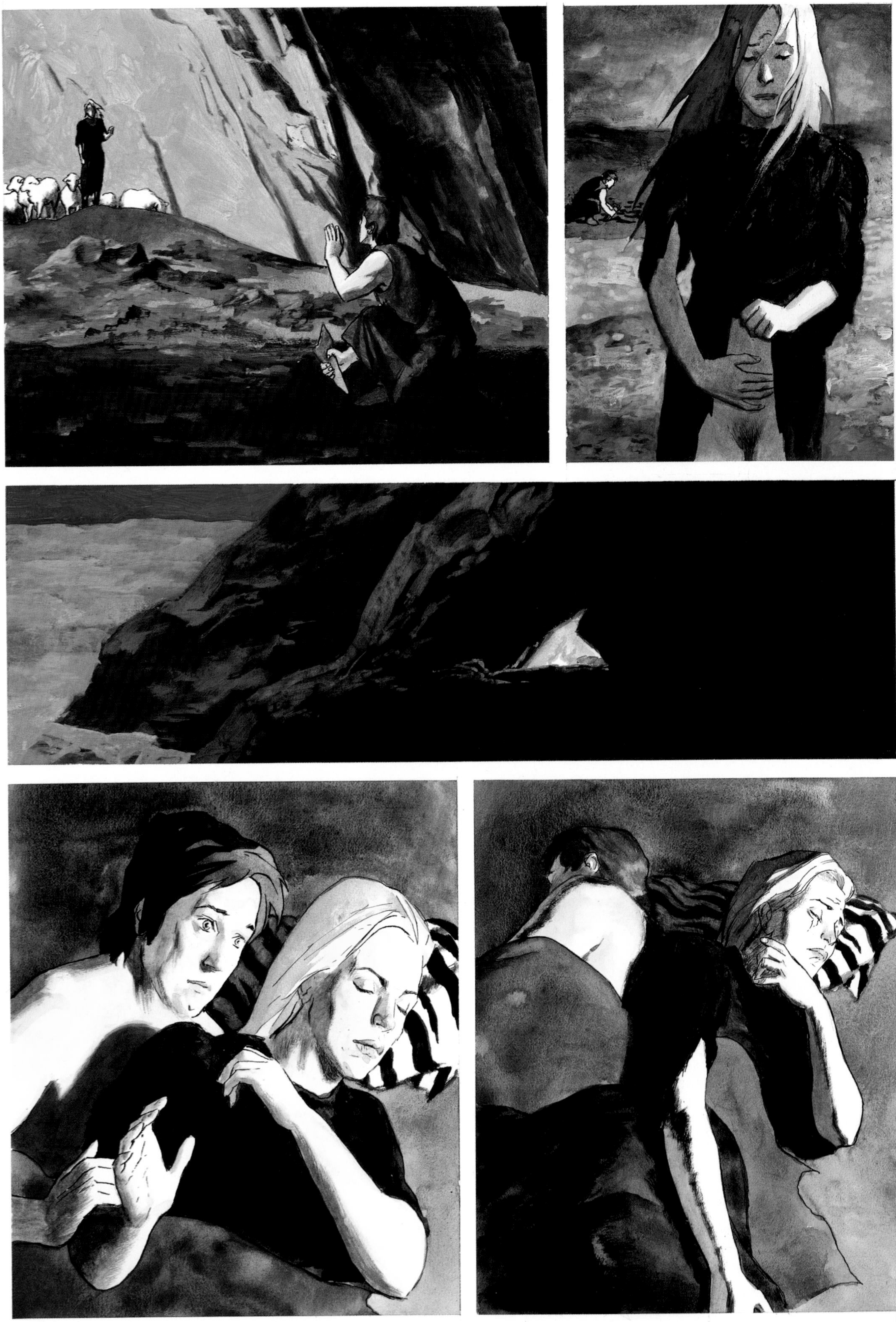

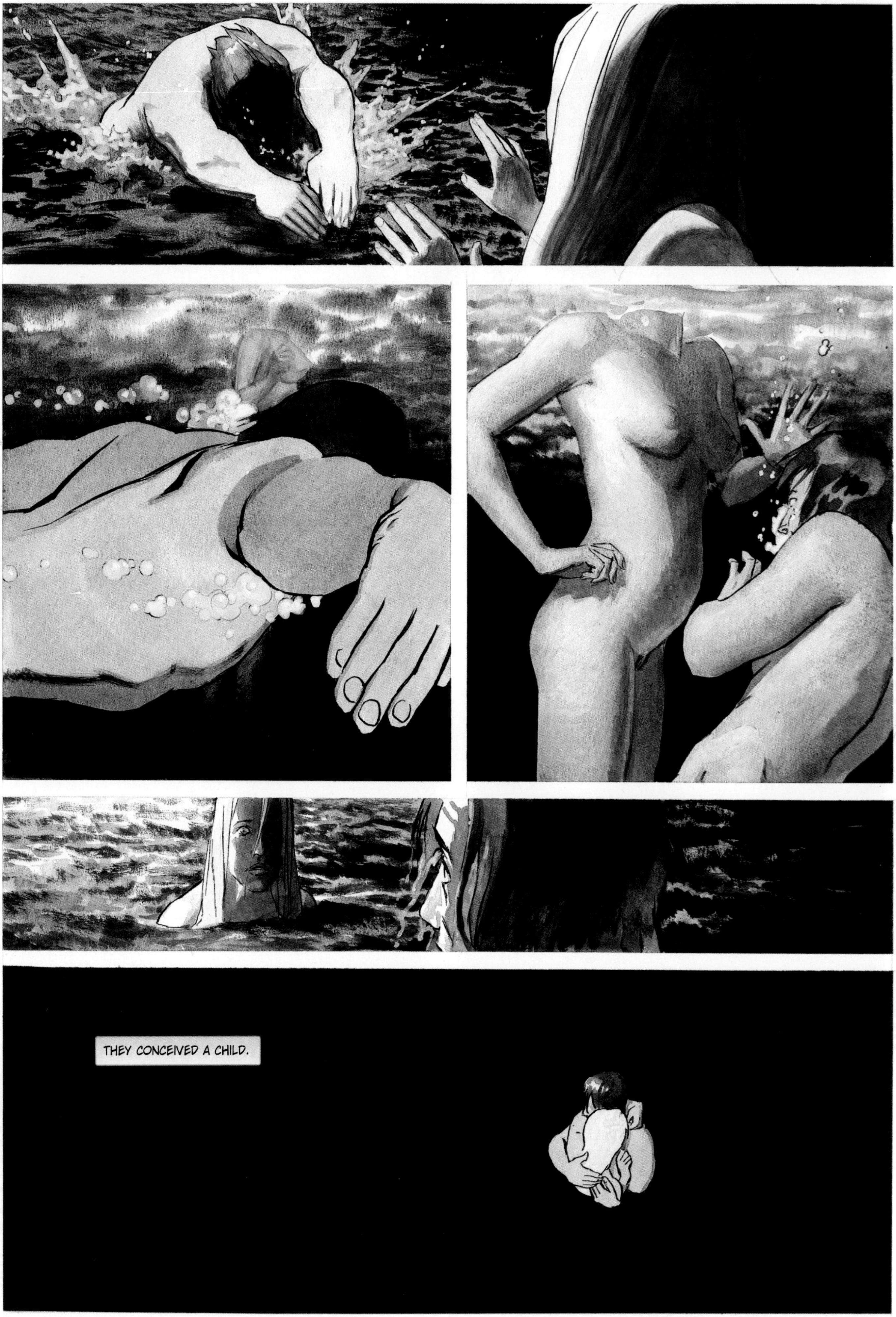
THEY CONCEIVED A CHILD.

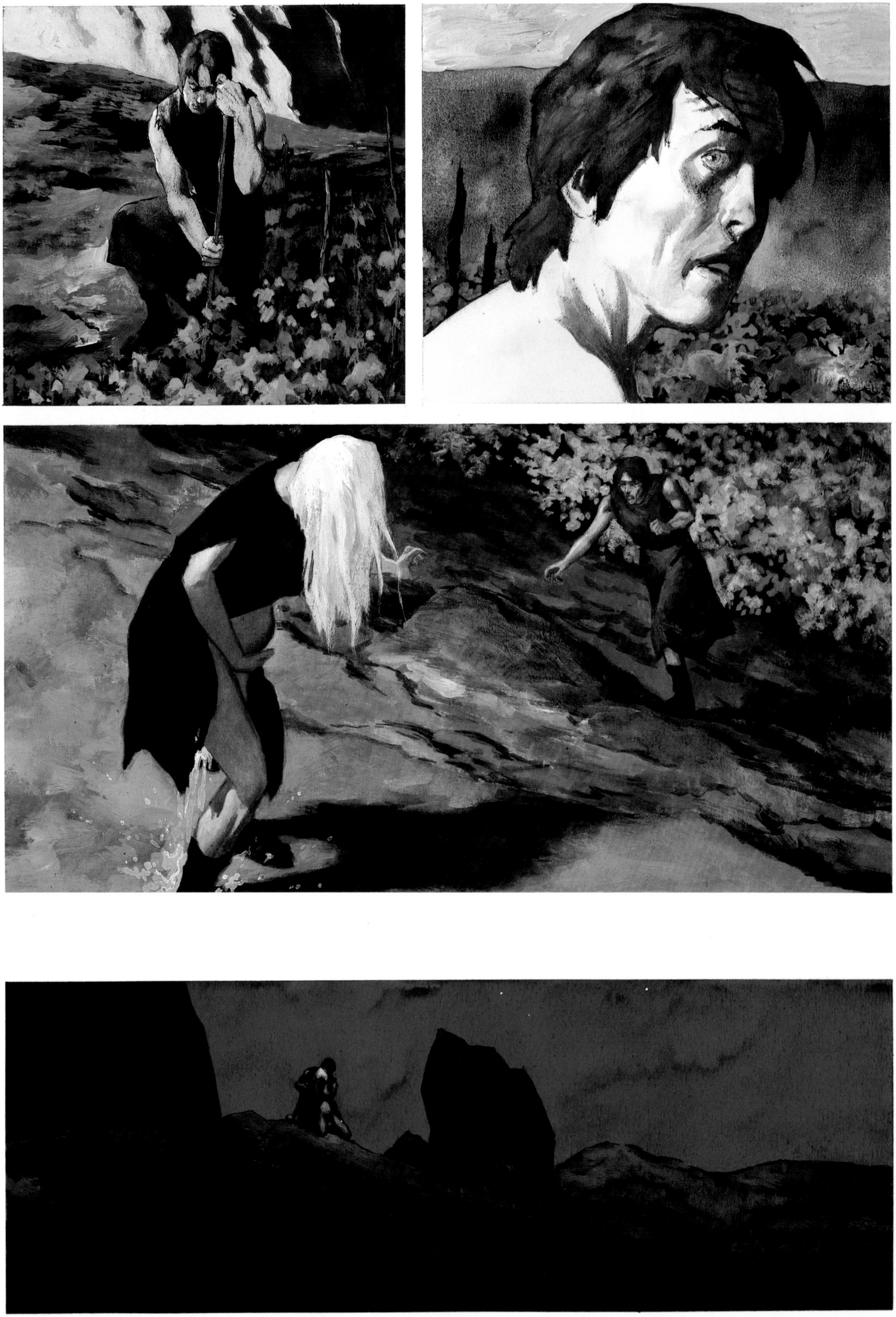

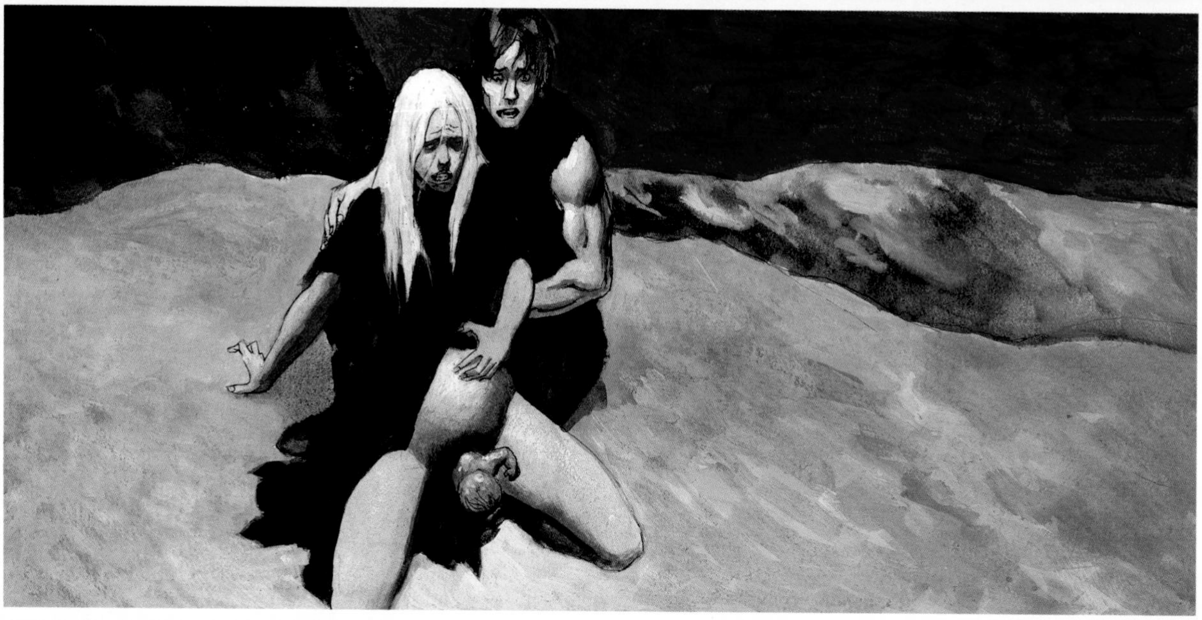

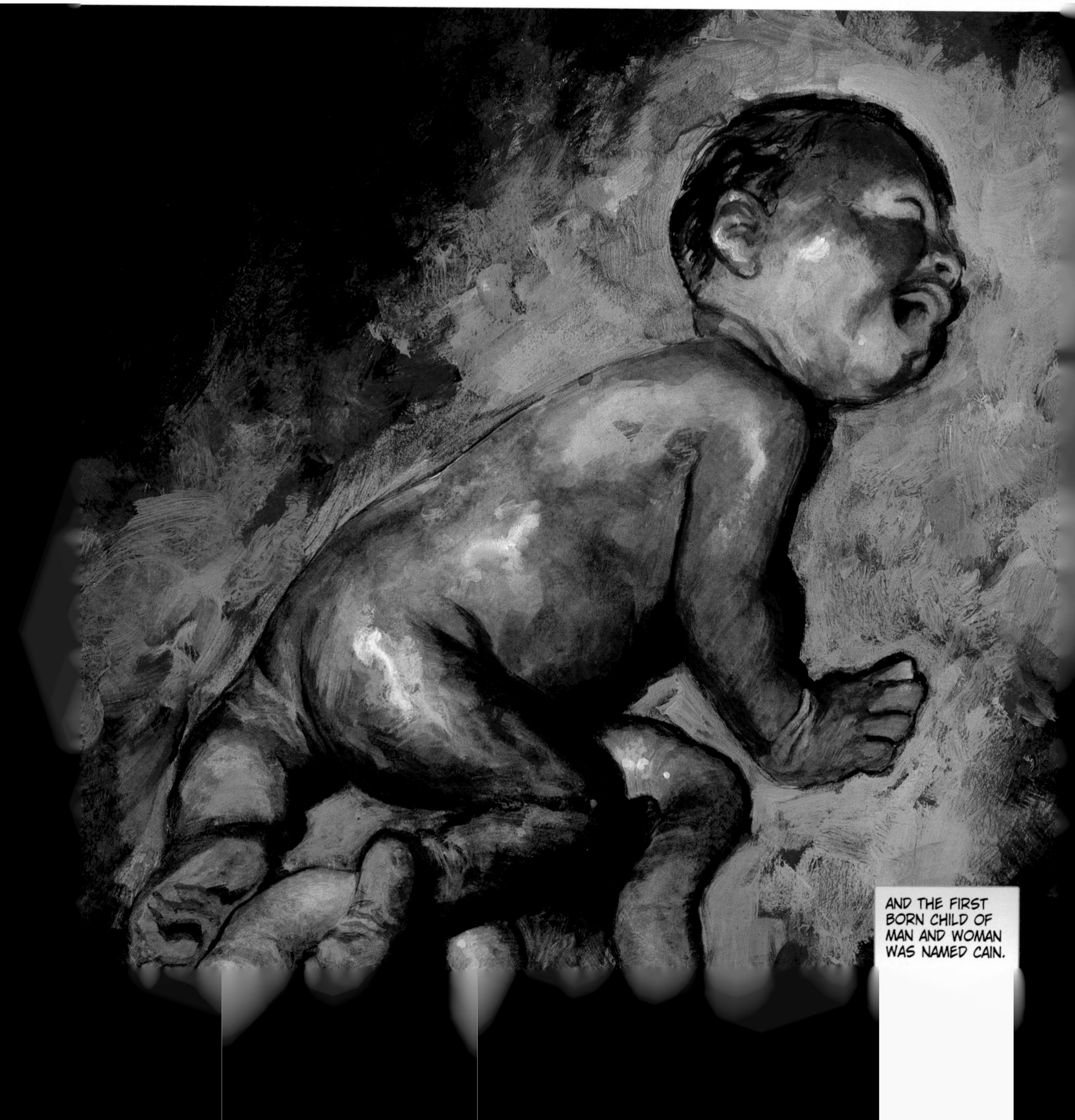
AND THE FIRST BORN CHILD OF MAN AND WOMAN WAS NAMED CAIN.

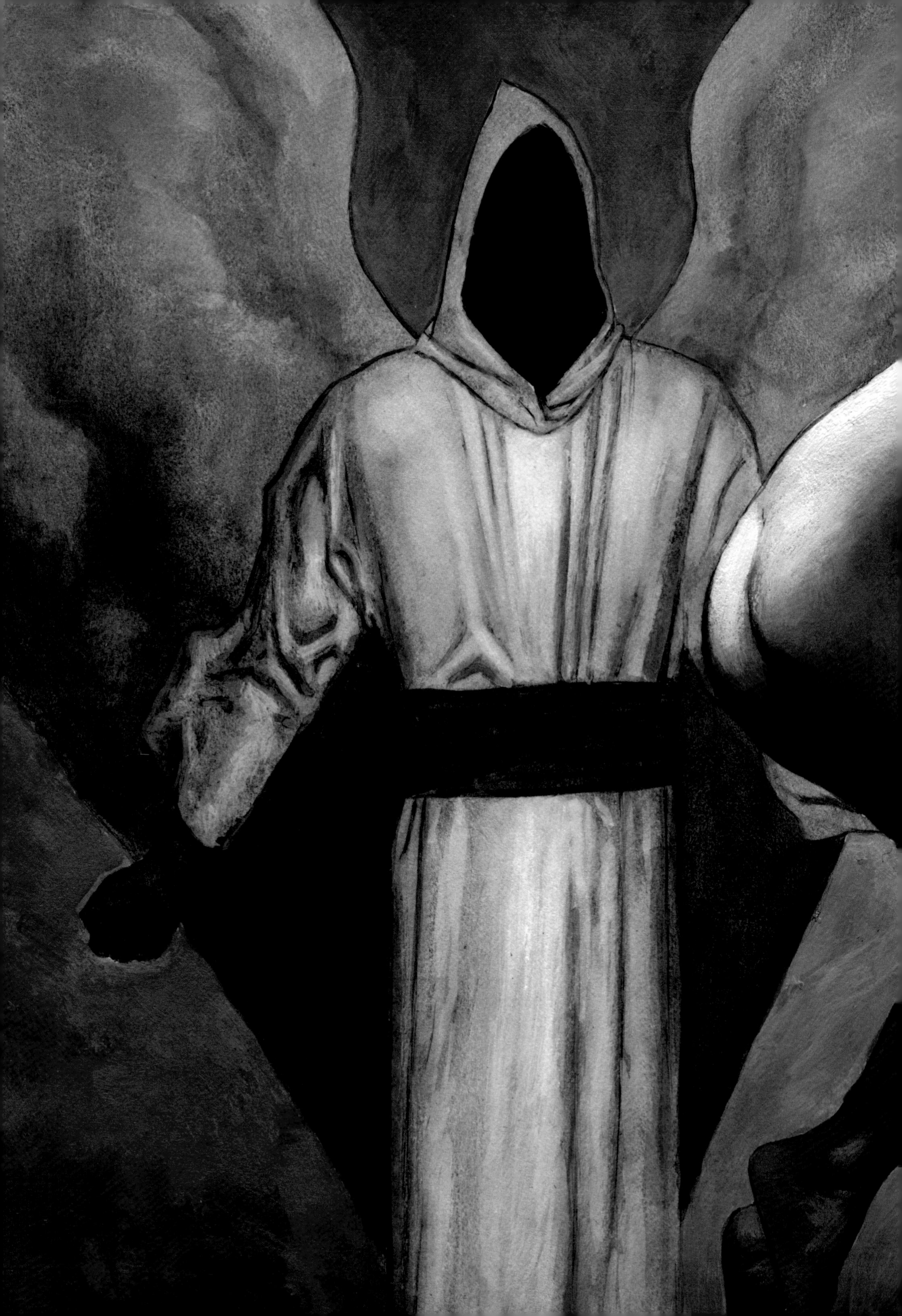

The New Testament

With the birth of Cain and the expulsion of Adam and Eve from Eden, Scott and myself took a break from the Old Testament to do a short story from the New Testament. The story we agreed would be great to start with was the story of the conception of Mary and how Joseph came to terms with the knowledge that his first born son would not be of his flesh, but of the Lord God's. This was supposed to be the first of many interwoven stories that we would tell from time to time from the New Testament that could later be viewed as a whole. *- DE*

Matthew

1:18 NOW THE BIRTH OF JESUS CHRIST WAS ON THIS WISE: WHEN AS HIS MOTHER MARY WAS ESPOUSED TO JOSEPH, BEFORE THEY CAME TOGETHER, SHE WAS FOUND WITH CHILD OF THE HOLY GHOST.

1:19 THEN JOSEPH HER HUSBAND, BEING A JUST MAN, AND NOT WILLING TO MAKE HER A PUBLICK EXAMPLE, WAS MINDED TO PUT HER AWAY PRIVILY.

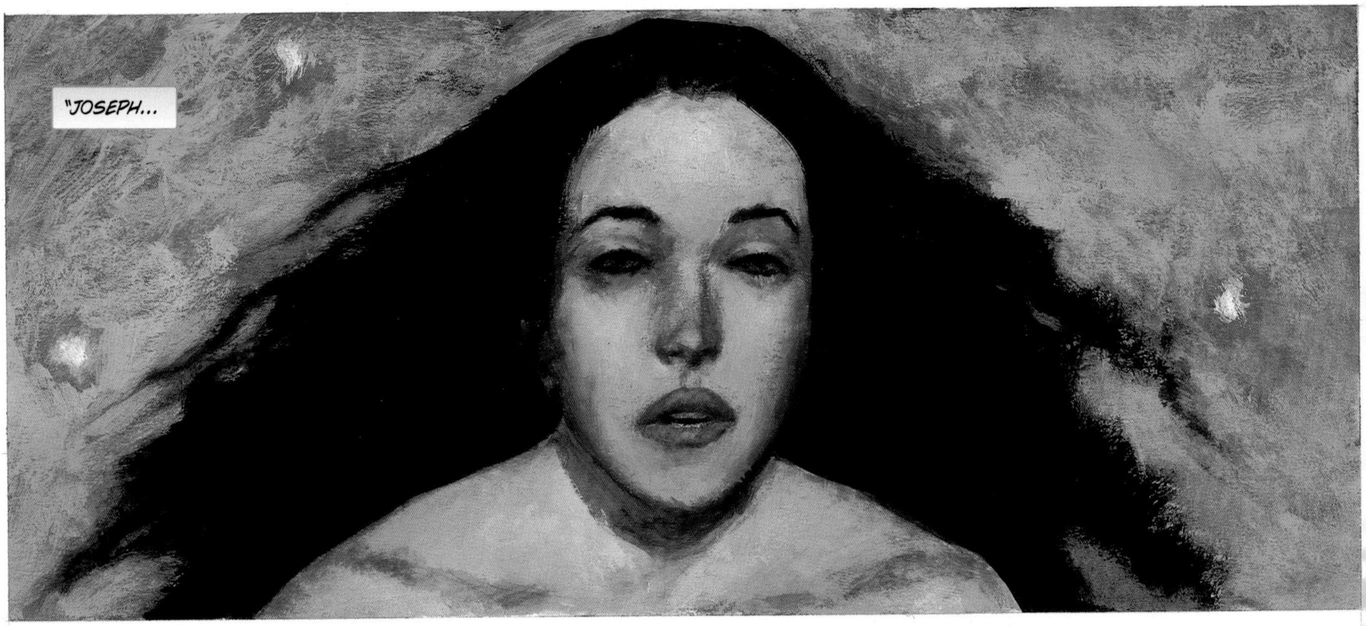
"JOSEPH...

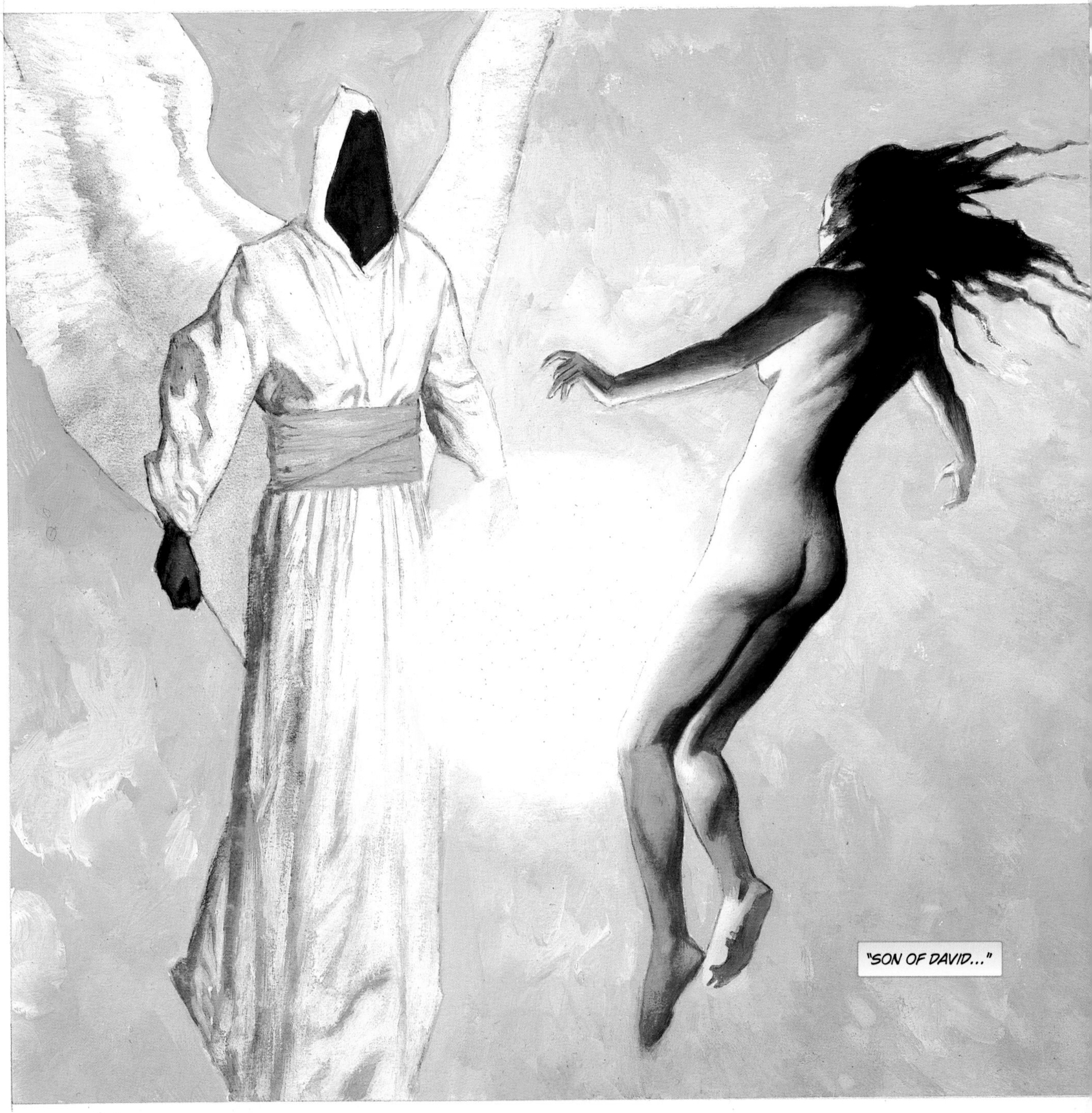
"SON OF DAVID..."

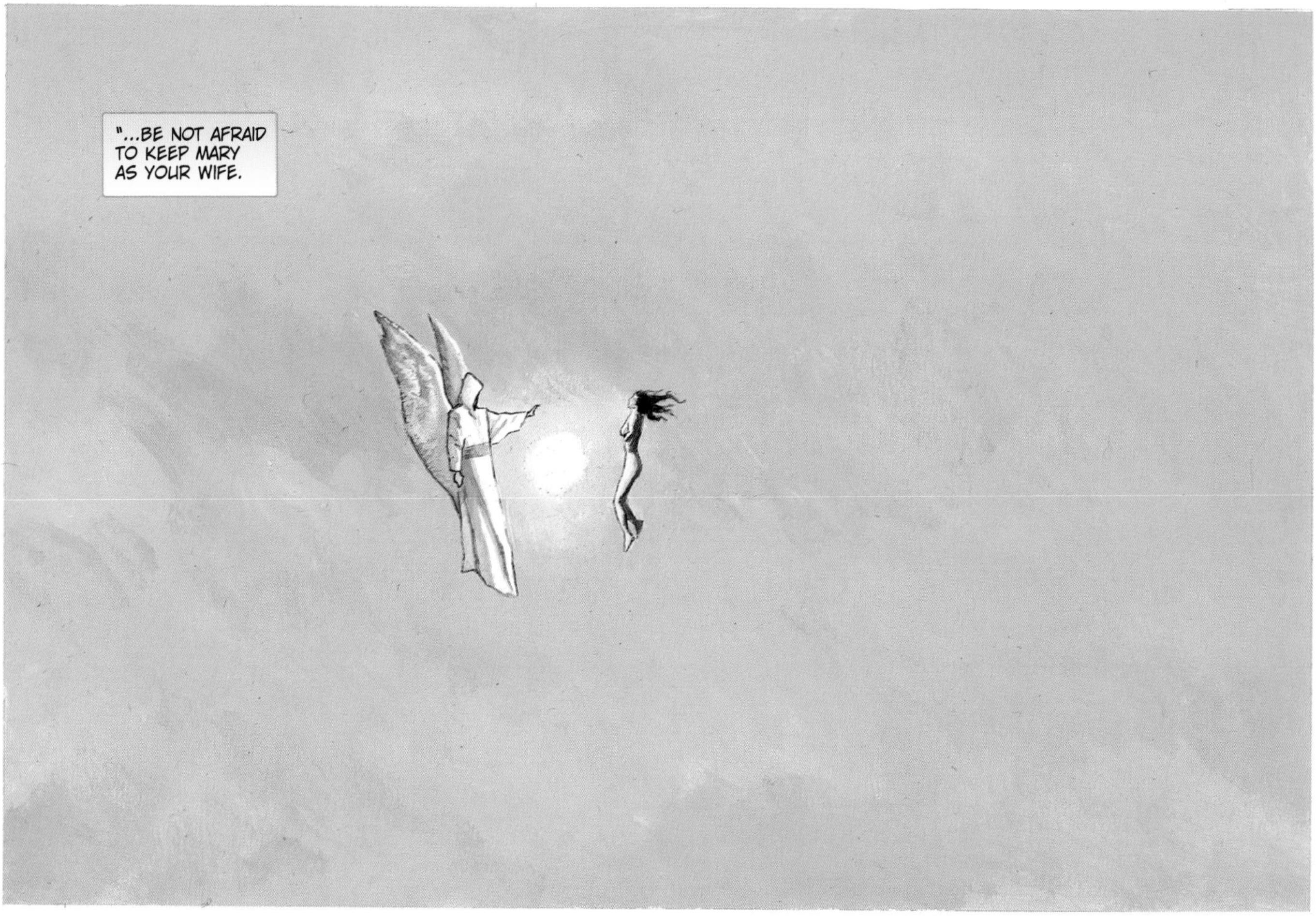
"...BE NOT AFRAID TO KEEP MARY AS YOUR WIFE.

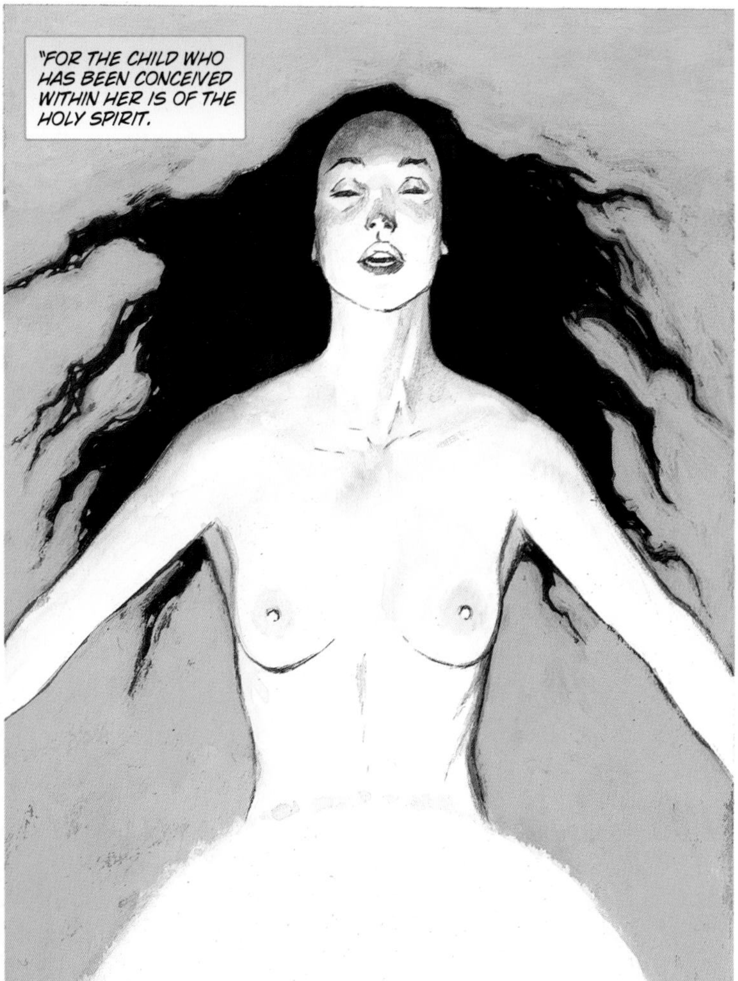
"FOR THE CHILD WHO HAS BEEN CONCEIVED WITHIN HER IS OF THE HOLY SPIRIT.

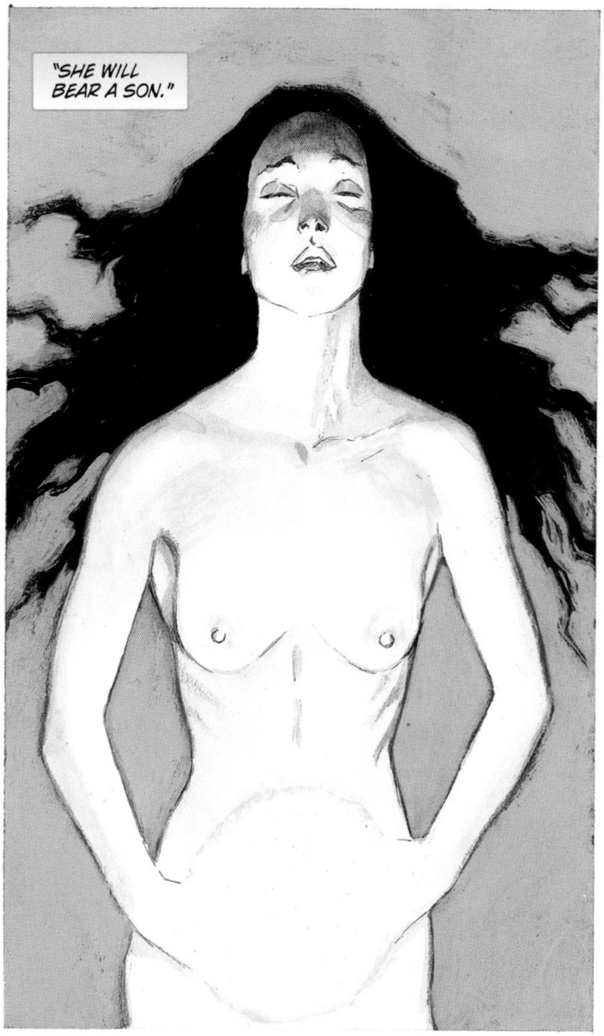
"SHE WILL BEAR A SON."

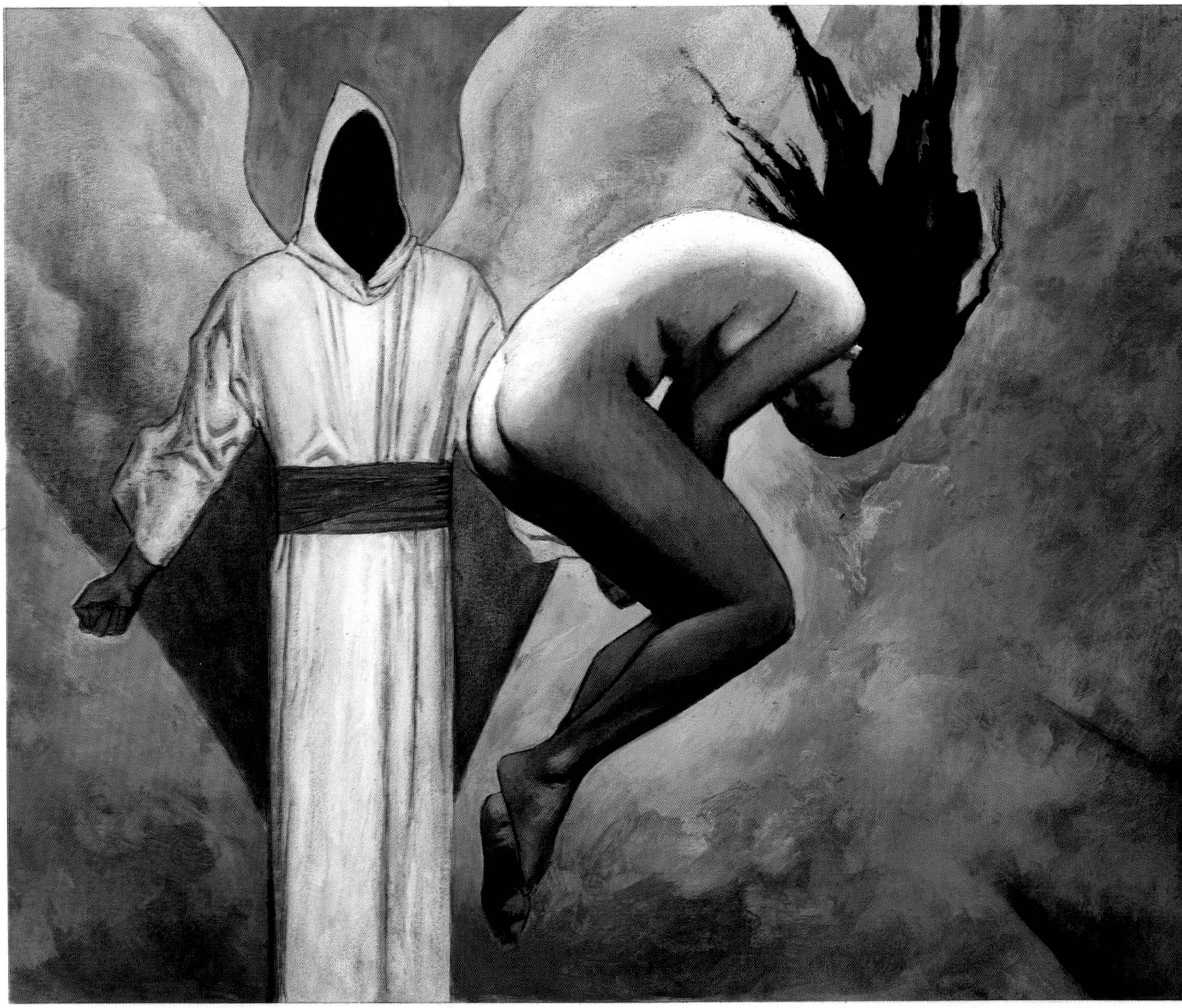

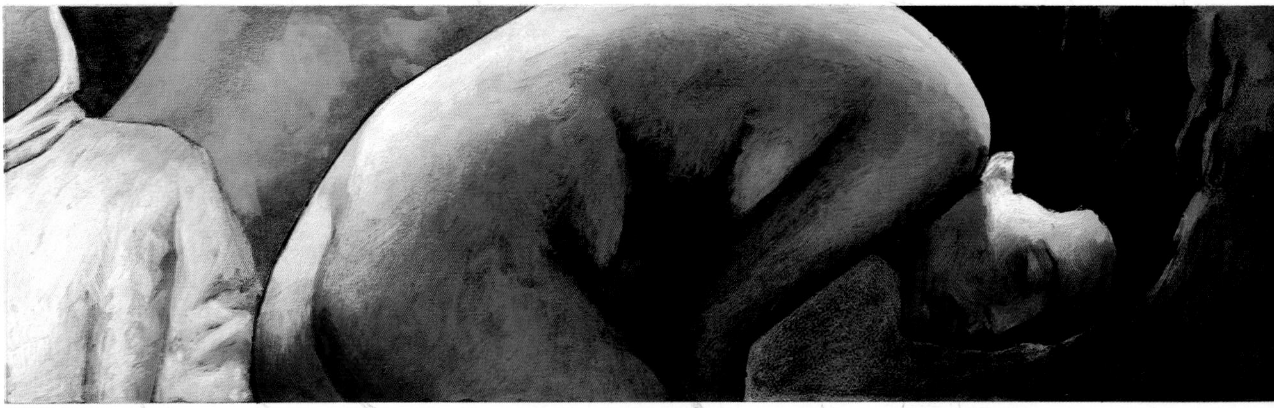

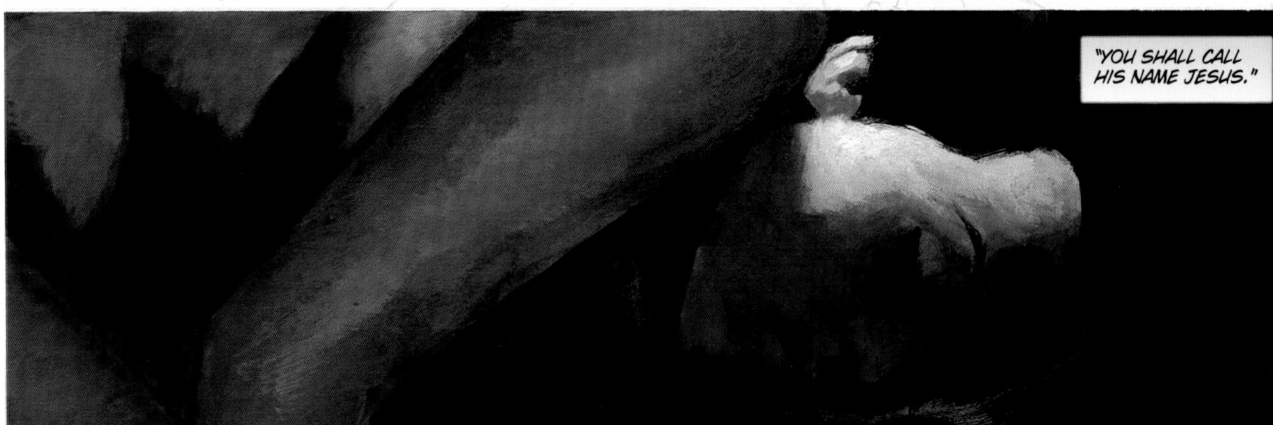
"YOU SHALL CALL HIS NAME JESUS."

"HE WILL SAVE HIS PEOPLE FROM THEIR SINS."

JOSEPH AWOKE FROM HIS SLEEP.

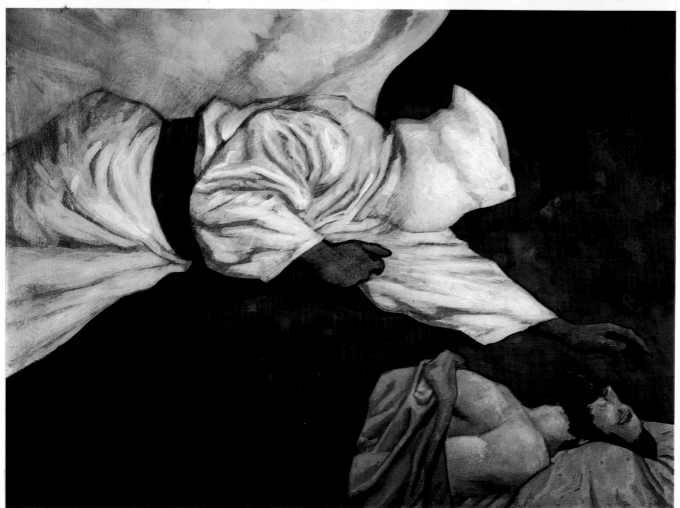

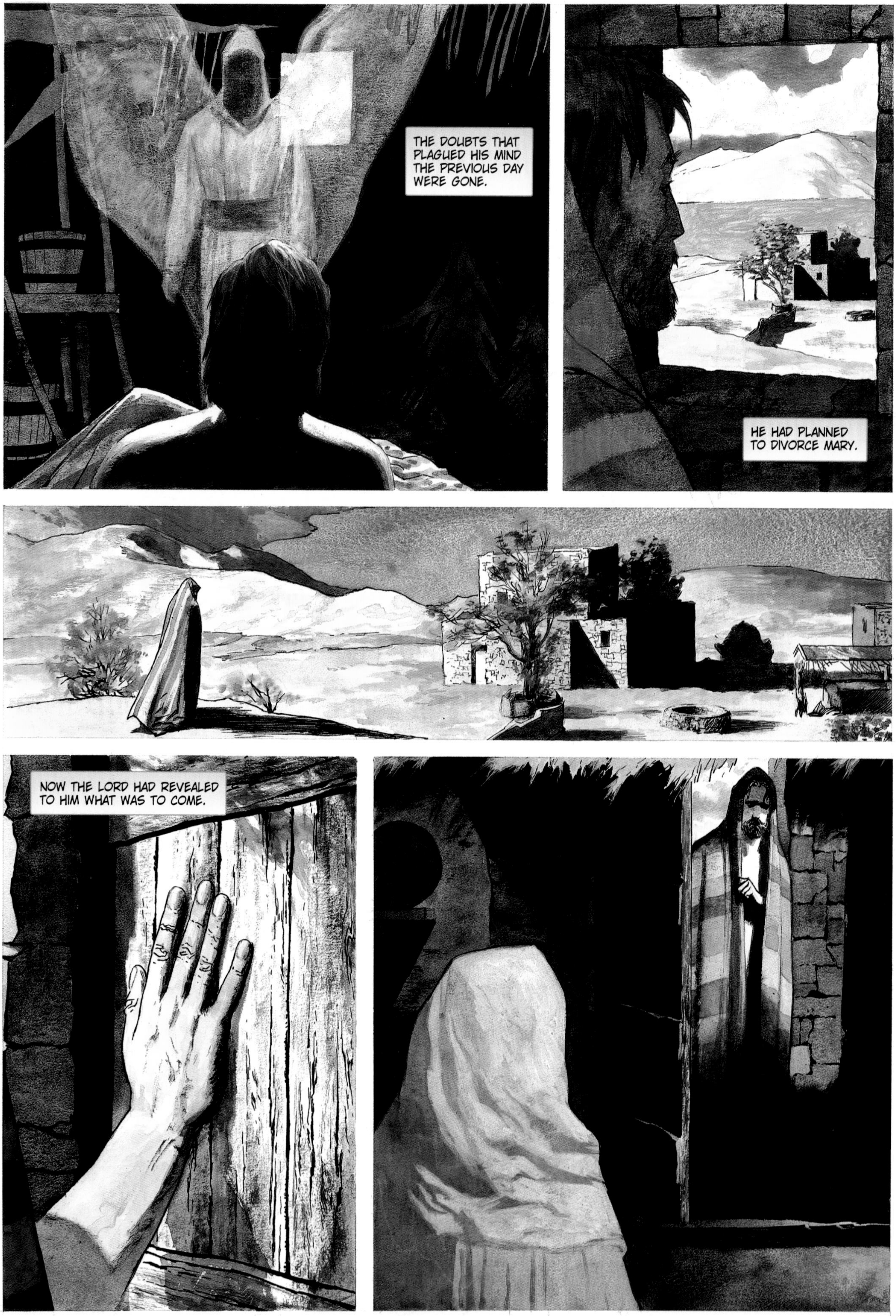
THE DOUBTS THAT PLAGUED HIS MIND THE PREVIOUS DAY WERE GONE.
HE HAD PLANNED TO DIVORCE MARY.
NOW THE LORD HAD REVEALED TO HIM WHAT WAS TO COME.

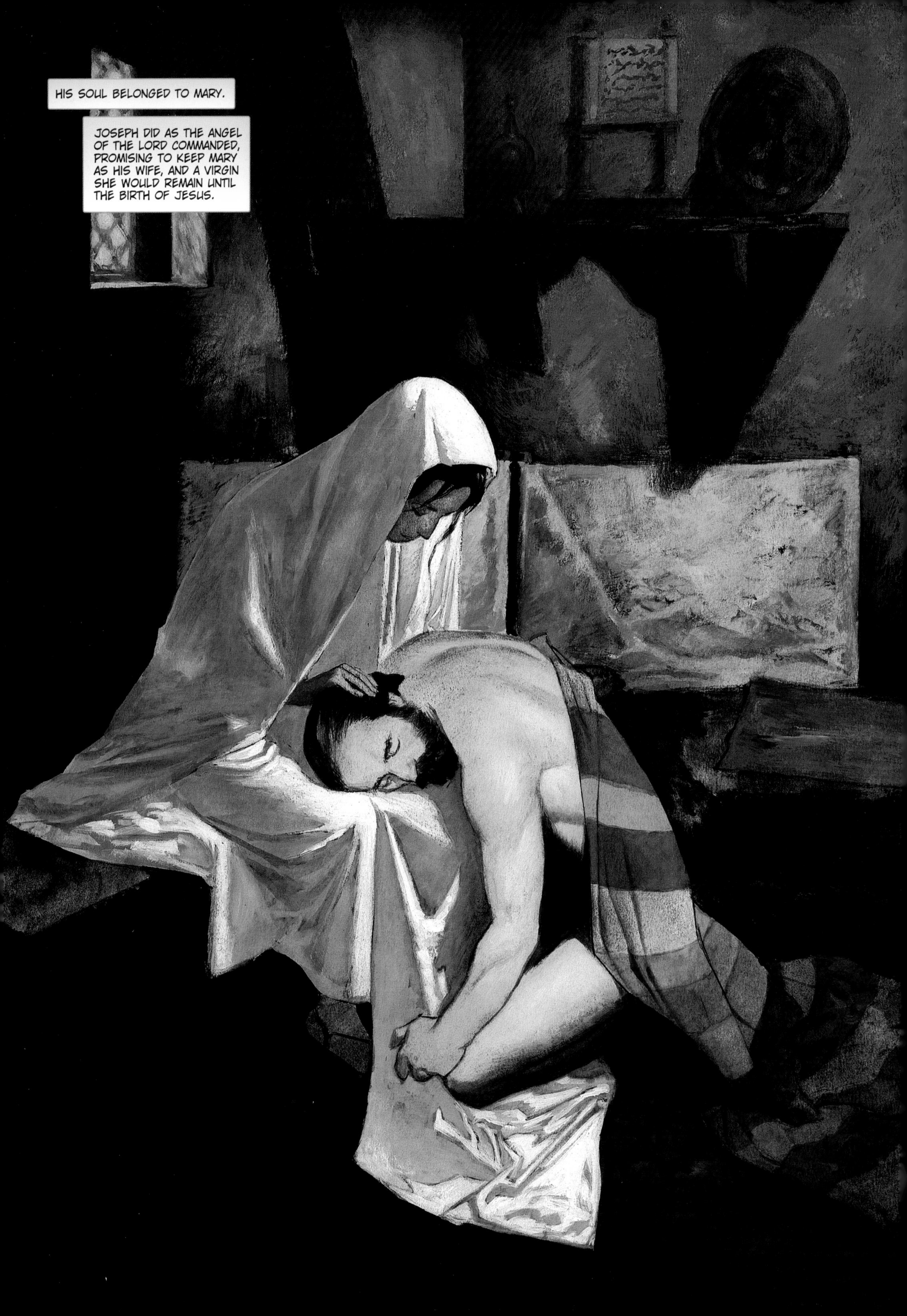
HIS SOUL BELONGED TO MARY.
JOSEPH DID AS THE ANGEL OF THE LORD COMMANDED, PROMISING TO KEEP MARY AS HIS WIFE, AND A VIRGIN SHE WOULD REMAIN UNTIL THE BIRTH OF JESUS.

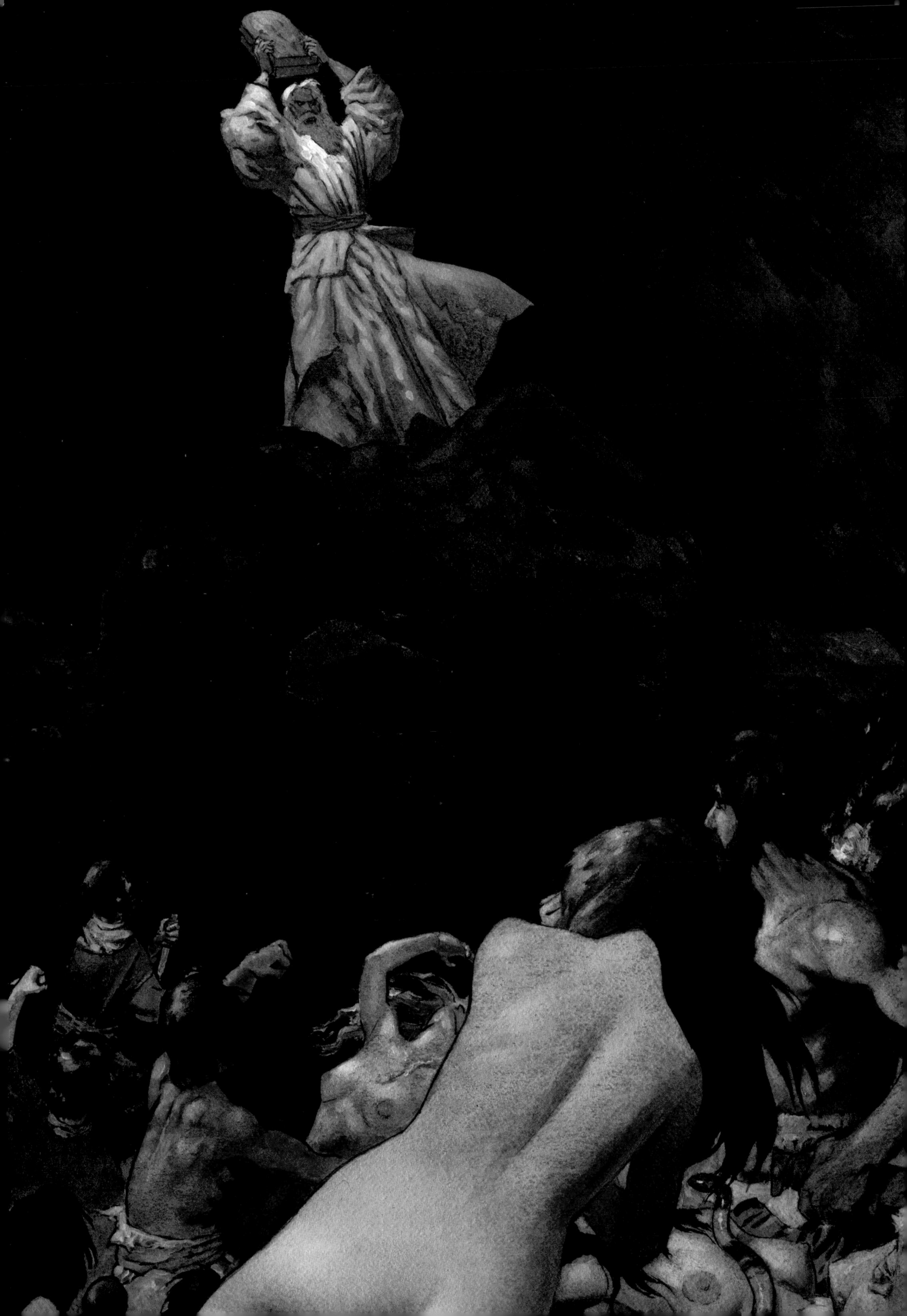

In selling the idea of doing such an enormous undertaking, Scott Hampton painted a few examples to show how the project would be visualized. The pieces were so good that it was decided that a full preview was to be run as a showcase. The following section is that preview.

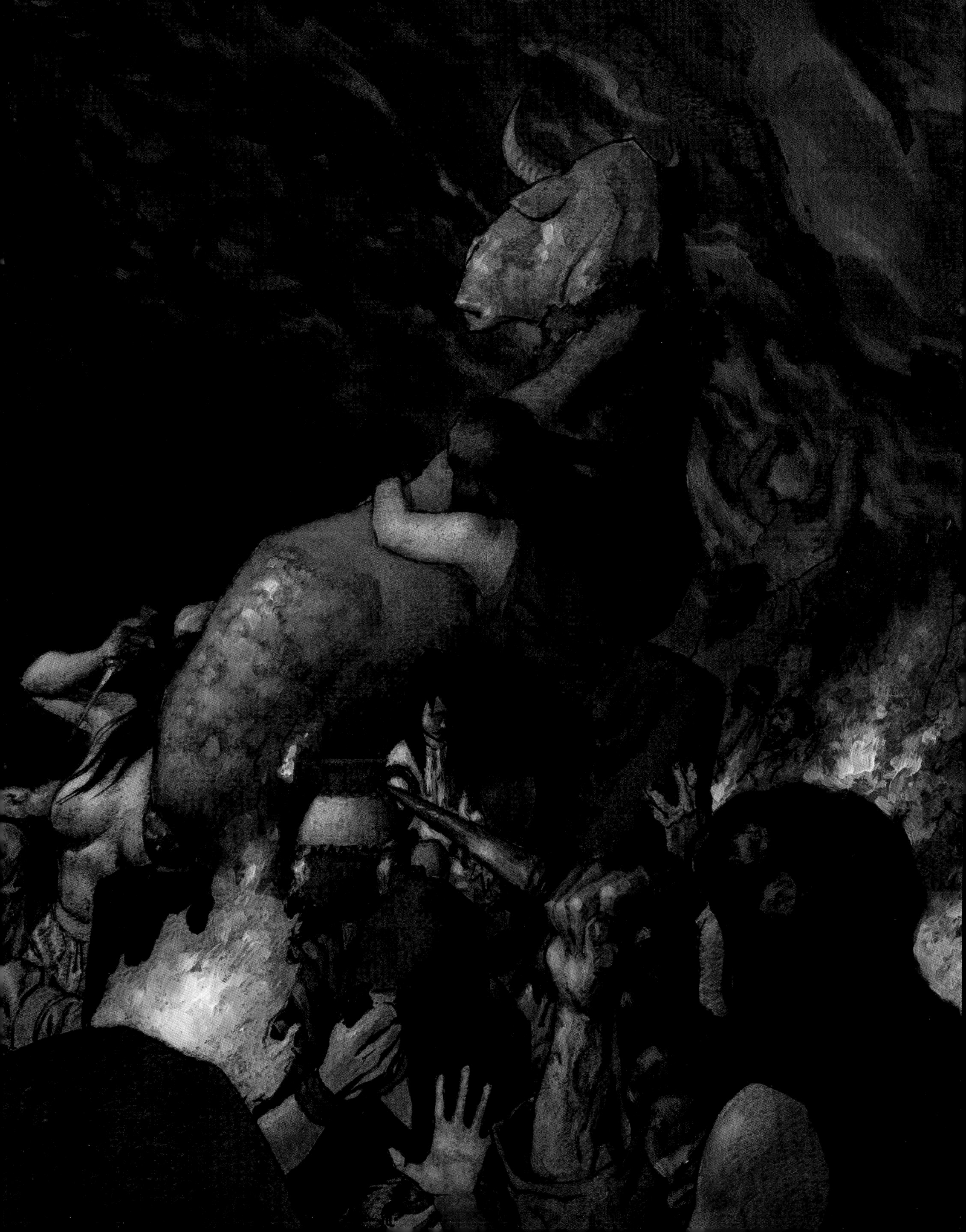

"IN THE BEGINNING..."

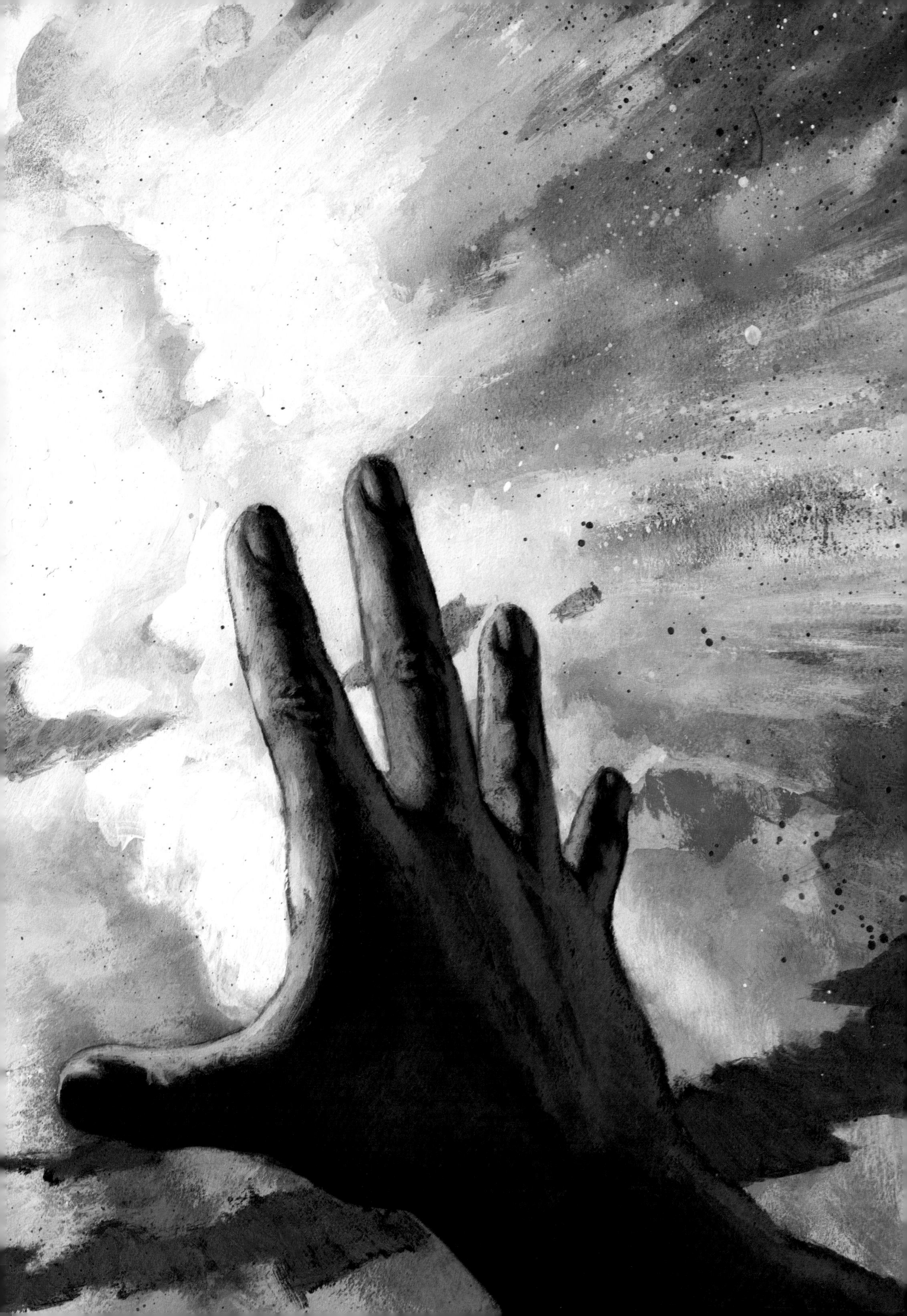

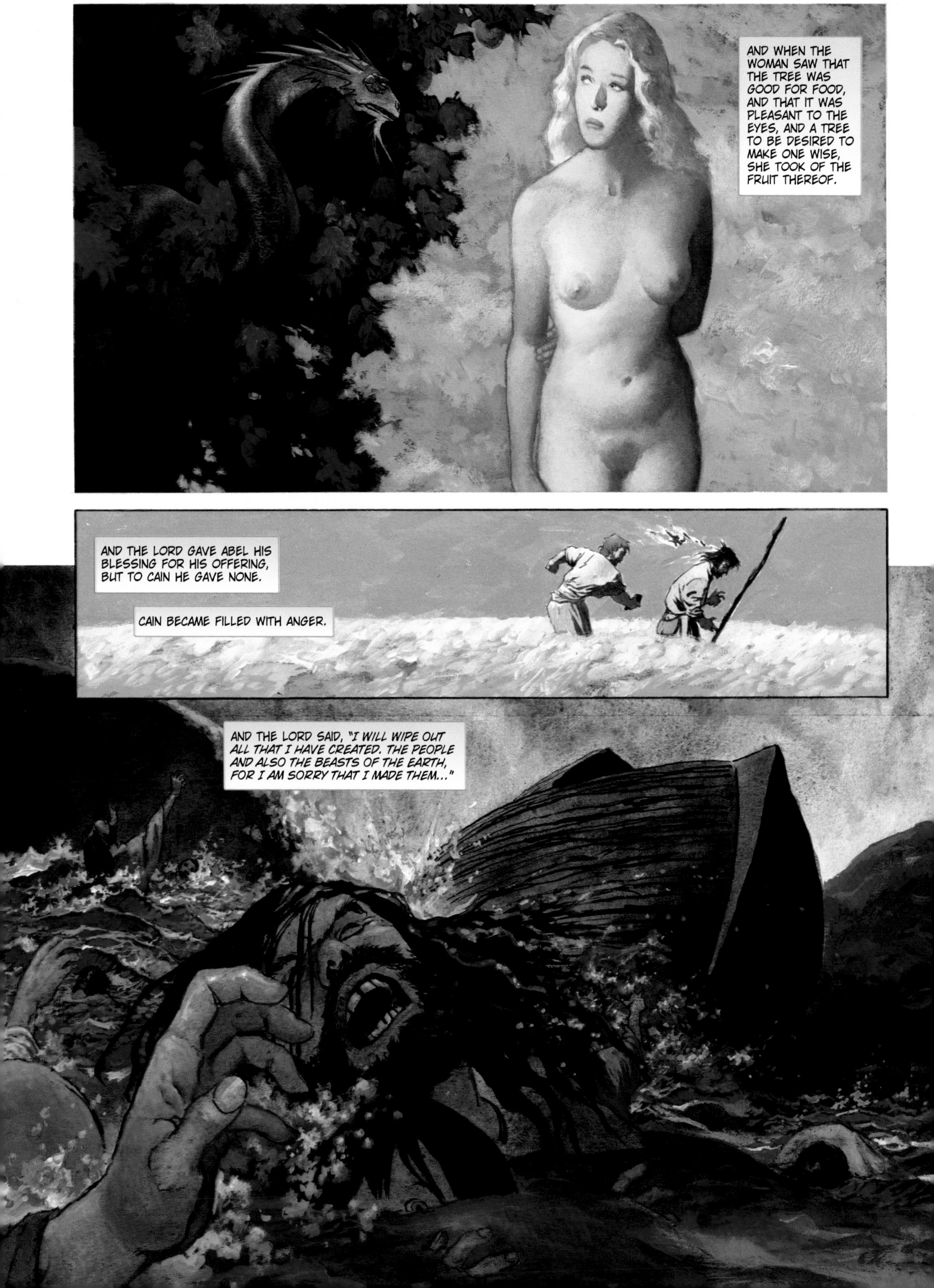
AND WHEN THE WOMAN SAW THAT THE TREE WAS GOOD FOR FOOD, AND THAT IT WAS PLEASANT TO THE EYES, AND A TREE TO BE DESIRED TO MAKE ONE WISE, SHE TOOK OF THE FRUIT THEREOF.
AND THE LORD GAVE ABEL HIS BLESSING FOR HIS OFFERING, BUT TO CAIN HE GAVE NONE.
CAIN BECAME FILLED WITH ANGER.
AND THE LORD SAID, *"I WILL WIPE OUT ALL THAT I HAVE CREATED. THE PEOPLE AND ALSO THE BEASTS OF THE EARTH, FOR I AM SORRY THAT I MADE THEM..."*

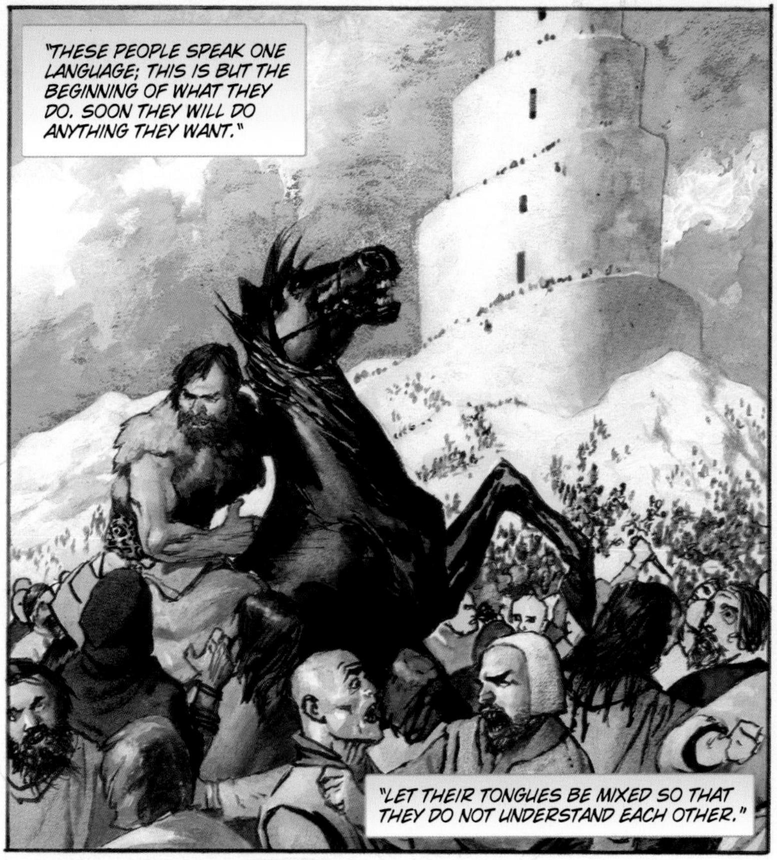
"THESE PEOPLE SPEAK ONE LANGUAGE; THIS IS BUT THE BEGINNING OF WHAT THEY DO. SOON THEY WILL DO ANYTHING THEY WANT."
"LET THEIR TONGUES BE MIXED SO THAT THEY DO NOT UNDERSTAND EACH OTHER."

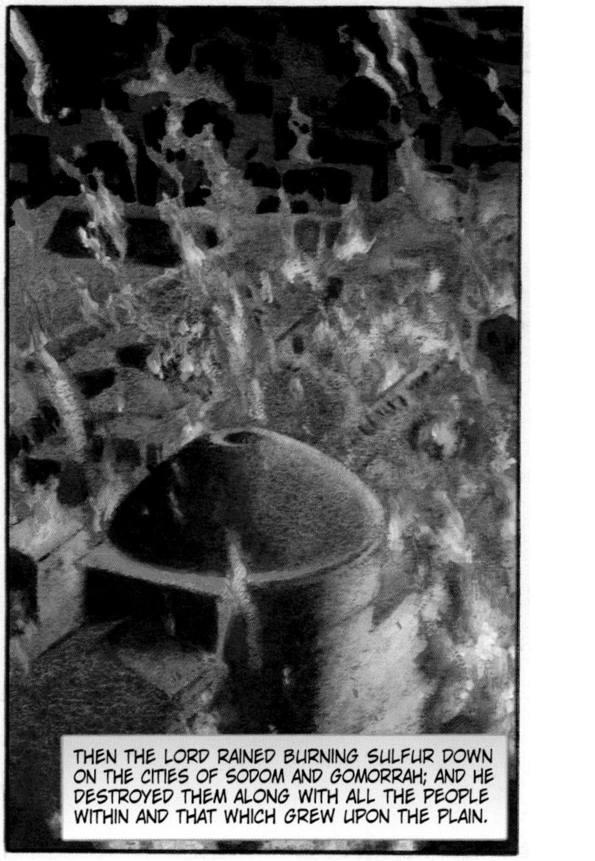
THEN THE LORD RAINED BURNING SULFUR DOWN ON THE CITIES OF SODOM AND GOMORRAH; AND HE DESTROYED THEM ALONG WITH ALL THE PEOPLE WITHIN AND THAT WHICH GREW UPON THE PLAIN.

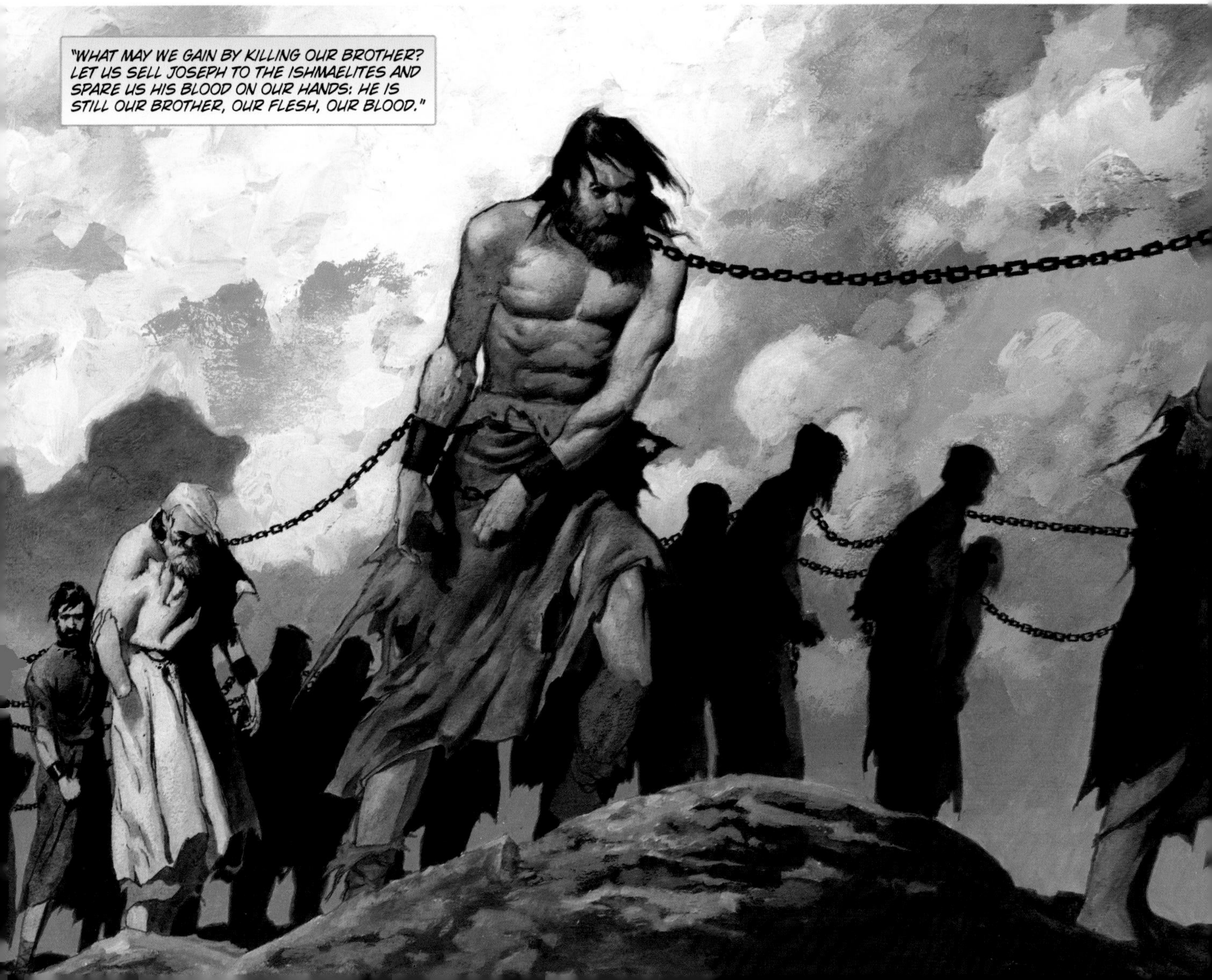
"WHAT MAY WE GAIN BY KILLING OUR BROTHER? LET US SELL JOSEPH TO THE ISHMAELITES AND SPARE US HIS BLOOD ON OUR HANDS: HE IS STILL OUR BROTHER, OUR FLESH, OUR BLOOD."

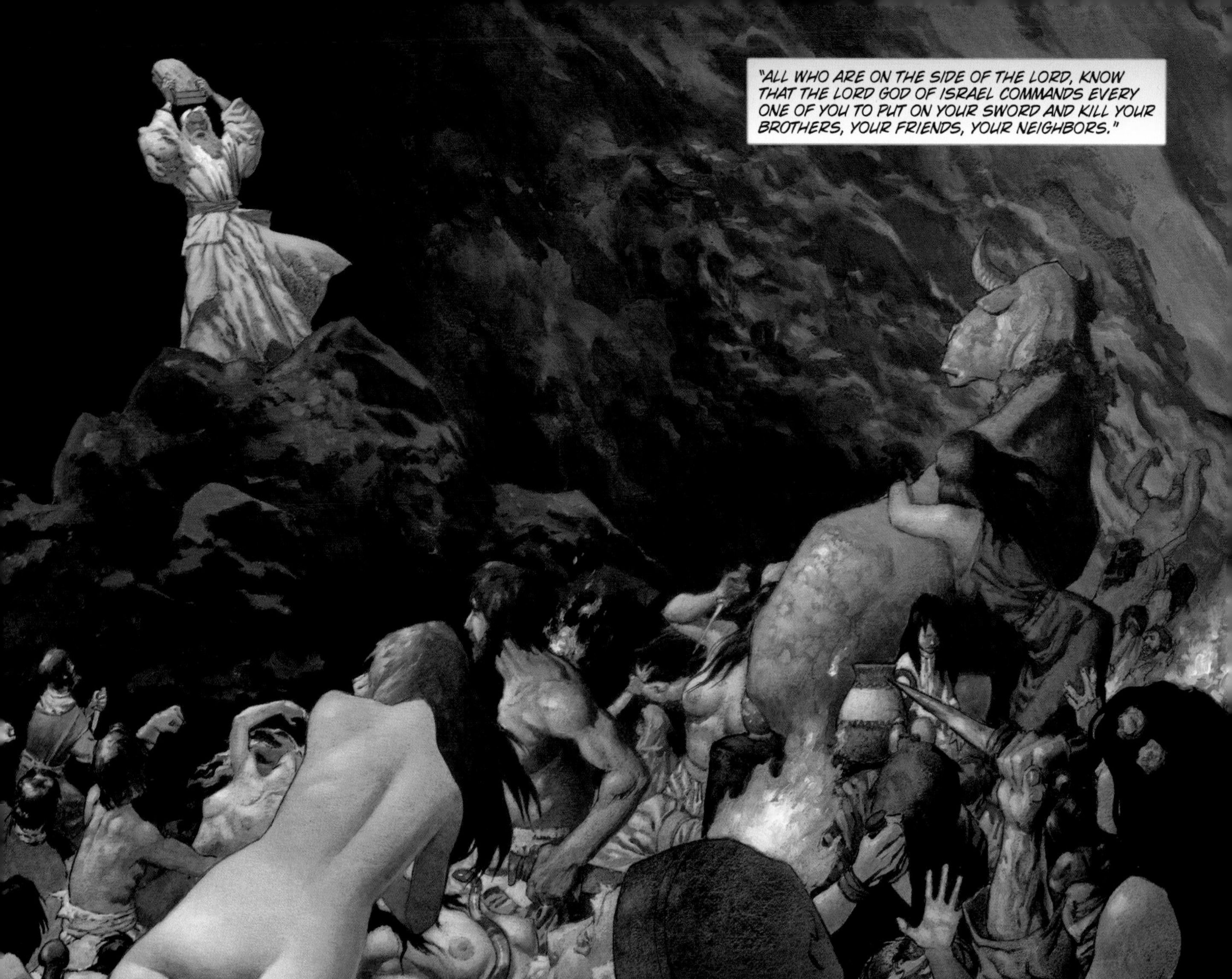
"ALL WHO ARE ON THE SIDE OF THE LORD, KNOW THAT THE LORD GOD OF ISRAEL COMMANDS EVERY ONE OF YOU TO PUT ON YOUR SWORD AND KILL YOUR BROTHERS, YOUR FRIENDS, YOUR NEIGHBORS."

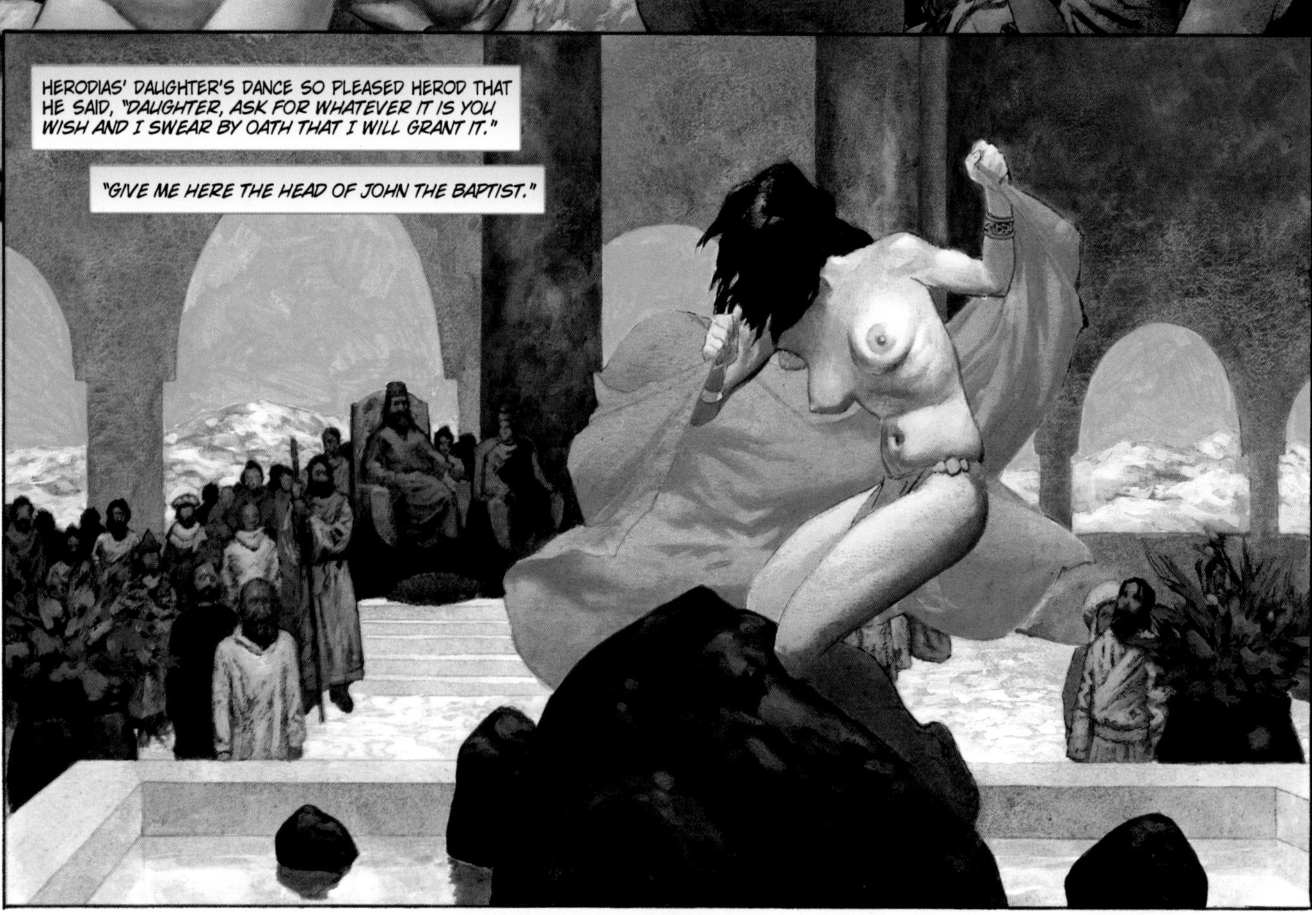
HERODIAS' DAUGHTER'S DANCE SO PLEASED HEROD THAT HE SAID, "DAUGHTER, ASK FOR WHATEVER IT IS YOU WISH AND I SWEAR BY OATH THAT I WILL GRANT IT."
"GIVE ME HERE THE HEAD OF JOHN THE BAPTIST."

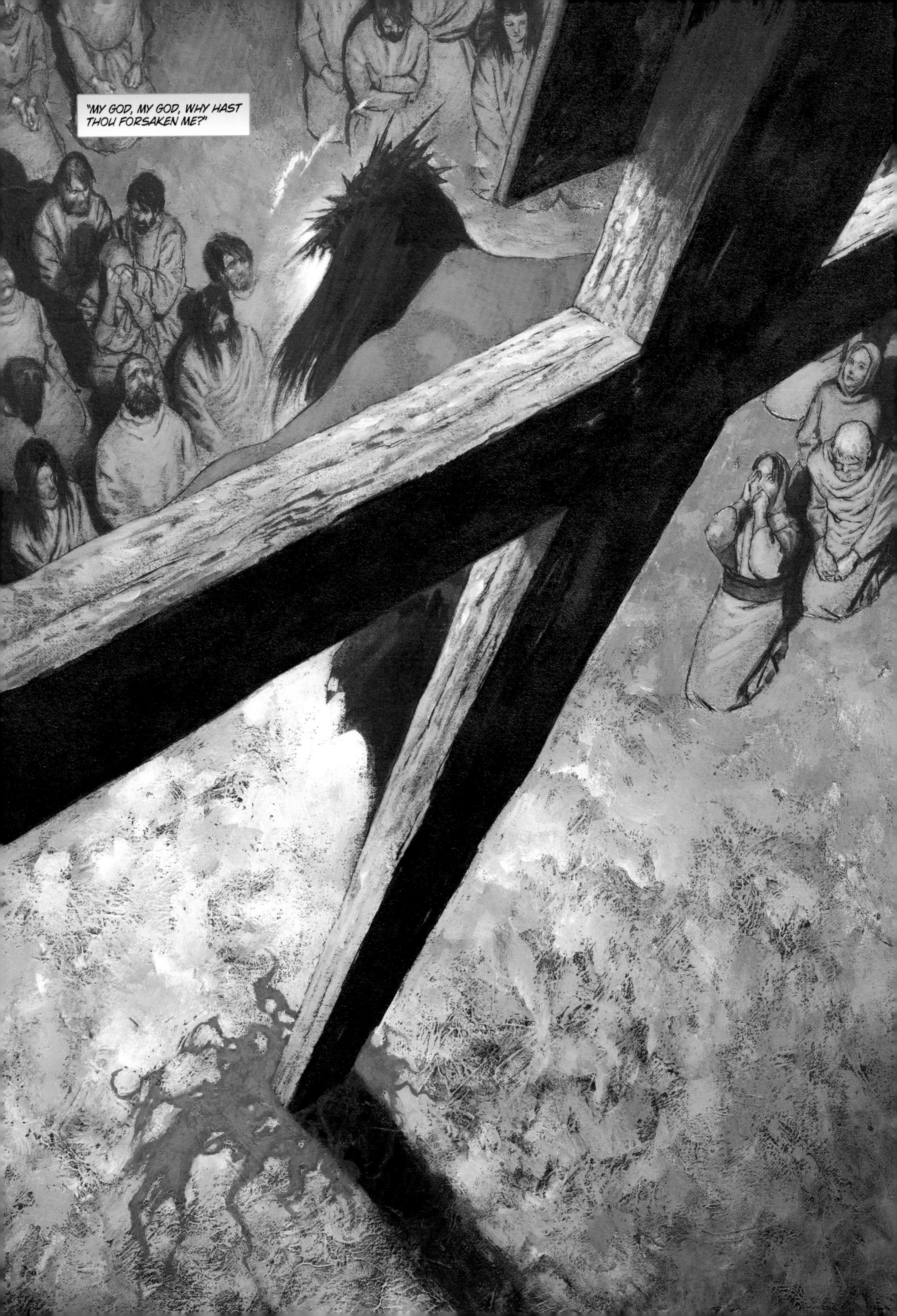
"MY GOD, MY GOD, WHY HAST THOU FORSAKEN ME?"

Scott came up with the idea of doing several one-sheets to further promote the work like a series of epic movies. "Exodus," "Daniel," and "The Song of Solomon" gave us the chance to show just a few of the many facets and themes that the Bible has to offer.

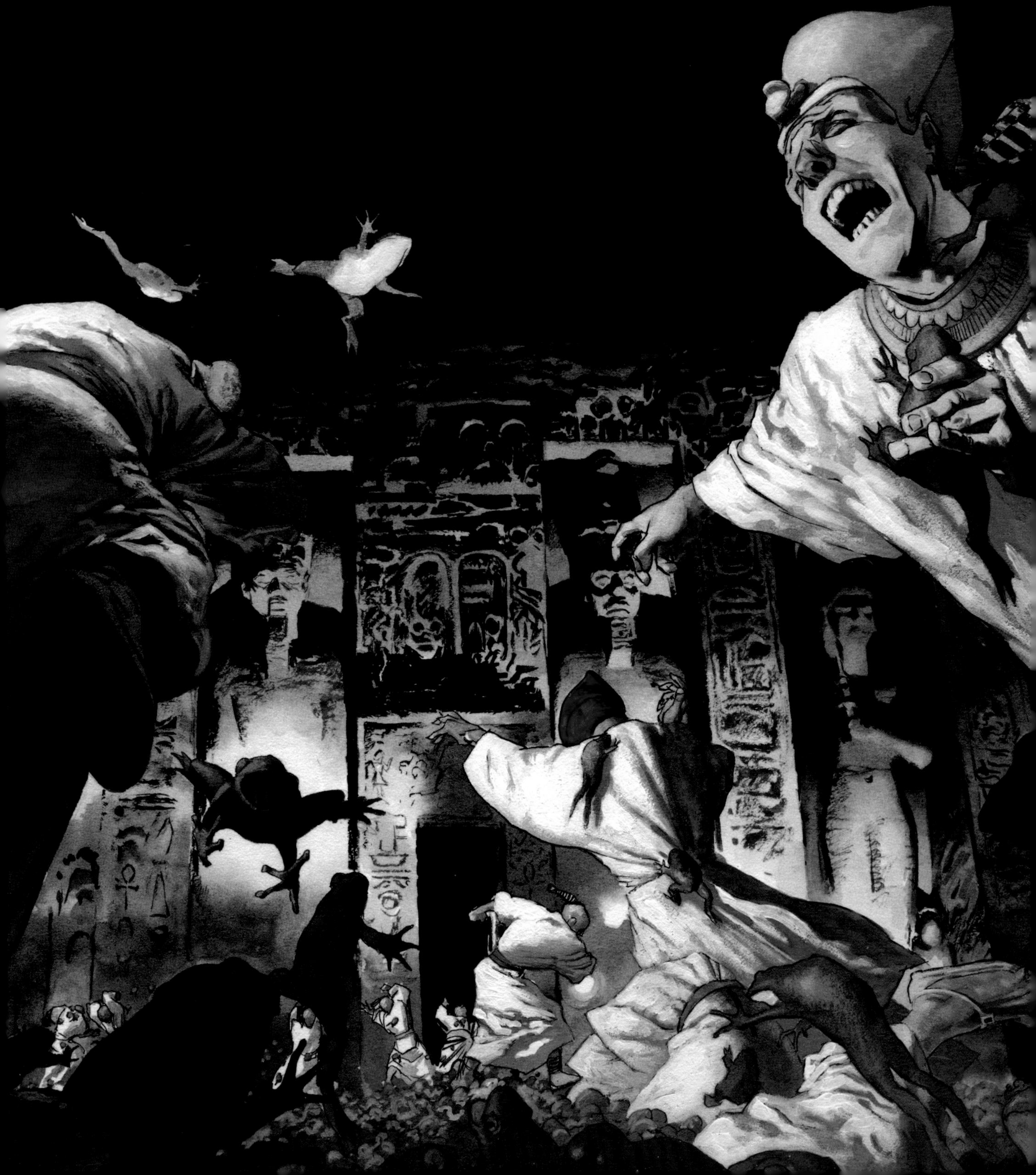

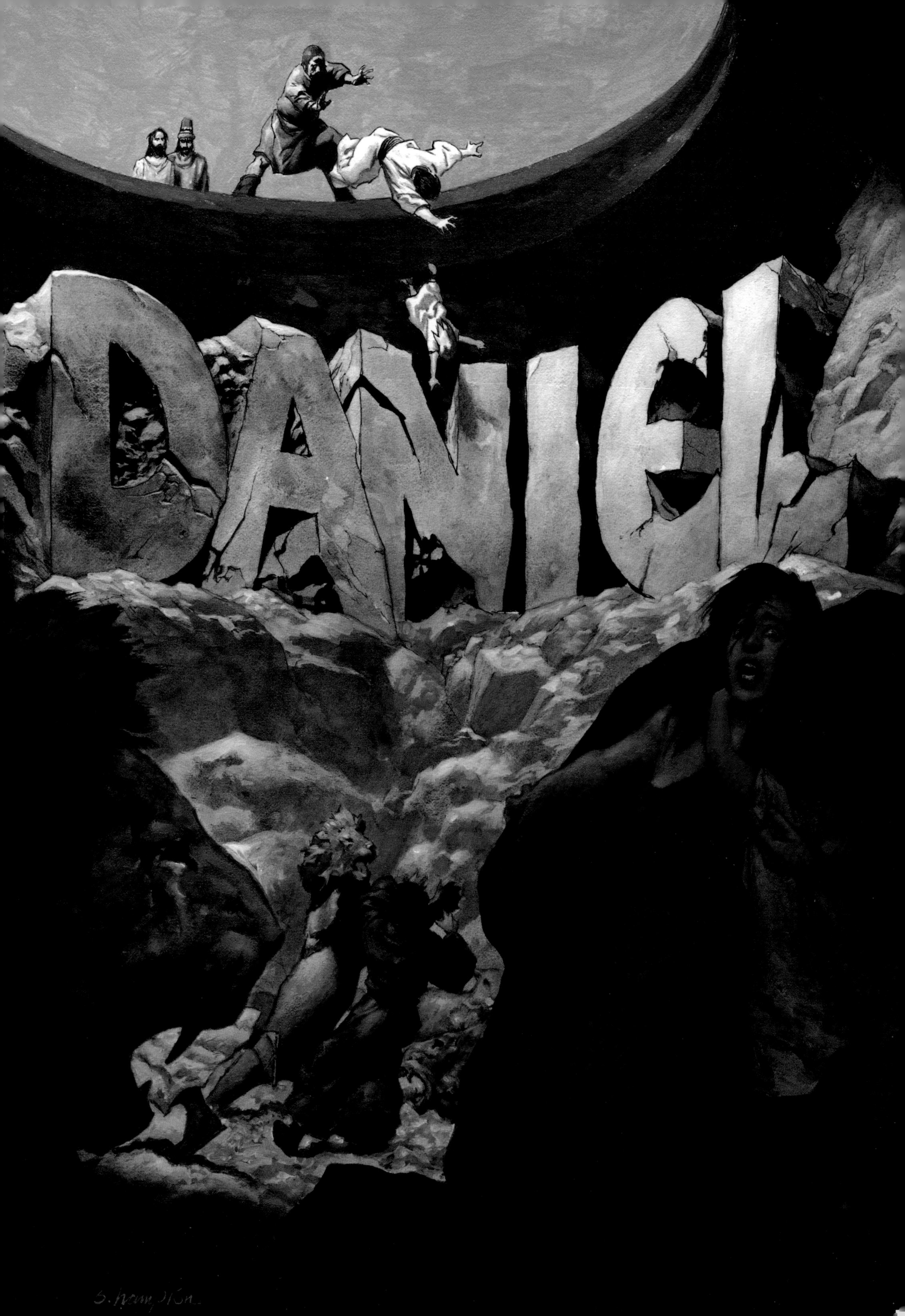
DANIEL
S. Hampton

Biographies and Acknowledgements

Scott Hampton

Scott Hampton has worked in the comics field for more than twenty years. He began his career with a three-page story in *Vampirella* and went on to produce a body of illustration and sequential storytelling that spans many magazines, publishers, and artistic media, from paintings for *Night Cries* and *The Books of Magic* to pen and ink work on "The Sleeping" for DC's *Batman: Legends of the Dark Knight*, which, along with *The Upturned Stone*, he also wrote. His most recent painted work is *The Life Eaters* for Wildstorm/DC.

First and foremost, I'd like to thank my editor/collaborator/good friend Dave Elliott for working so hard to see this project through its incarnations. Thanks to Bob Guccione, Jeff Mariotte, and Ted Adams for wanting to publish it. And thanks to readers new and old for... well, for reading.

Dave Elliot

January 13th, 1960: Due to adverse weather conditions Dave was born in the London bedroom of June and Geoffrey Elliott. He can't remember when he read his first comic; they have been with him all his life—probably why in the face of the adversity this industry can provide, he could never turn his back on it. Dave considers the high points of his career to be working with his fellow *A1* creator Garry Leach, his tenure as editor at *Deadline* magazine (created by Steve Dillon and Brett Ewins), and the enjoyment he had with the team who worked on *Penthouse Comix* with him (Merv, Eliot, Glen, Tim, John, Gary, Mark, and George). Dave is currently working with Garry on the relaunch of *A1* through their company Atomeka, teaching comic book classes to a new generation of artists, and has optioned his first screenplay.

The idea of doing a full adaptation of the Bible has long been a wish for me, so when the chance came I knew in my mind there was only one artist for this book: my friend Scott Hampton. I would also like to thank Bob Guccione , Jane Homlish, and Frank DeVino for enabling us to start this project in the first place, Ted Adams and Jeff Mariotte for wanting this to be part of such a distinguished line of books, and to Keith Giffen for being friend and fellow collaborator.

Keith Giffen

Keith Giffen was born in Queens, raised in Jersey, and has been involved in just about every major comic book character of the last thirty years. He is currently working with Colleen Doran on *Reign of the Zodiac*, the critically acclaimed epic science fiction series for DC Comics.